Steeling the Mind of America II

Steeling the Mind of America II

John Ankerberg • David Barton
Dale Berryhill • Tom Cloud
Anita Hoge • Charlotte Iserbyt
Alan Keyes • Berit Kjos
John Loeffler • Chuck Missler
Alan Sears • Genevette Sutton
Dwight Williams

Compiled & edited by Bill Perkins

New Leaf Press

First printing: February 1997

Copyright © 1996 by New Leaf Press. All rights reserved. Printed in the United States of America. No part of this book may be used or reproduced in any manner whatsoever without written permission of the publisher except in the case of brief quotations in articles and reviews. For information write: New Leaf Press, Inc., P.O. Box 726, Green Forest, AR 72638.

ISBN: 0-89221-334-5
Library of Congress: 96-69689

Dedicated to
America's Founding Fathers:

May we hold to their
incredible vision.

Contents

Foreword

The exchange of truthful information is one of the most critical assets we have as Christians. Today's world is driven by information and most of it is super-intended by a media force that is openly hostile to a Christian world view. In a front page story dated February 1, 1993, a *Washington Post* reporter referred to evangelical Christians as "poor, uneducated, and easy to command."

And who is in command? The media, which is liberal by its own admission, is helping to shape a very different world view. They openly slant articles to their perception of what is right. And what they believe is "right" or "politically correct" is not what most Christians believe Jesus would want us to embrace. Also, without many people realizing it, we risk losing our constitutional rights, our individual freedoms, and even our children.

Steeling the Mind is about getting the truth into the hands of rational thinking Christians. To "steel" your mind is to armor or brace your mind against deception. Ignorance is not bliss — it's dangerous. But armed with the truth, we can intelligently make those critical decisions that affect our families and businesses. To accomplish that, Steeling the Mind of America conferences were begun to bring together the best and brightest speakers who are highly knowledgeable in their respective fields. Each of the following transcribed speeches will give you great information and insight, but without the liberal slant. They cover a wide variety of topics. What you do with that information can make a difference. God is in control, He has a master plan, and the real privilege comes in being used as part of that plan. But reasoning people can be greatly influenced by the information they get, who they believe, and what they do with it. When God's people make major decisions based on the wrong information, the results can be far-reaching. Just ask Joshua and Caleb.

— Bill Perkins

1

America's Founding Fathers: Were They Christians?

David Barton

We as Americans are blessed because we have a strong religious heritage. I don't think there is any discussion or debate about that. We look at the artwork of the Pilgrims and the Puritans, and there's no question that we have a very strong religious heritage in America.

What I find interesting is the way we now portray our heritage in our public schools. I've recently been appointed in my home state to a committee of 15 individuals who oversee the writing of history textbooks for all the students in our state. As we go back and look over what was 50 years ago, and what we have today, it's radically different. Some textbooks today at least mention that the Pilgrims and Puritans were religious groups. But you will not find in the textbooks things like the Mayflower Compact. For 150 consecutive years after the ratification of the Constitution, you could find this document in any American history textbook because it's very important. It was the first government document created in this country. It is two paragraphs long, about 200 words, but we haven't been able to find this in a history textbook in nearly 50 years.

Why has it disappeared?

That's an easy question to answer. The Mayflower Compact says that those people came here to propagate the gospel of the Lord Jesus Christ. That was their goal and that's what they were going to pursue in America. The problem is that this government document has a lot of evangelical language in it. Most people today are willing to concede that religion is okay if you keep it in private. Keep it at home or keep it in church, but don't go in the public market with it. You don't want it at school, you don't want it in the courthouse, you don't want it in the public arena. Therefore, we pretty much ignore today those aspects of our heritage that are religious and which also show public religious expression. The Mayflower Compact is a good example.

We also have a lot of debate today over our holidays. There's no question that holidays like Thanksgiving and Christmas are religious holidays. There's also no question that they now end up in courts. So we don't have Thanksgiving anymore, we have "fall break" in our schools. We don't have Christmas; we have "winter break." We don't have Easter; we have "spring break." We've got all these things because we don't want to talk about our religious heritage. On top of that, most people don't even realize that for 150 years in America's history after the ratification of the Constitution, the Fourth of July was considered a religious holiday. Look at our government proclamations on that day. It was a day when we said, "People of America, we need to stop and thank God Almighty for what He has done in this nation, that He has raised this nation up to propagate the gospel across the world."

Even in previous generations, we fully expected our military and our political leaders to be highly religious. You've probably seen lots of pictures of George Washington kneeling in prayer. The reason you've seen so many of them is there is so much evidence for the validity of that image. There are many eyewitness testimonies of people like General Henry Knox, General John Marshall, and General Marquis de Lafayette. You've got the eyewitness testimony of all types of congressional leaders, such as Charles Thompson. You've got the testimony of his own children, his own family, his own ministers. There's so much out there.

Isn't it interesting that today, George Washington has become one of our leading "deist" founding fathers? "He didn't even believe in God; he wasn't religious." Why is that lie printed today? You'll find that has a great impact on public policy. You see, you wouldn't really want it to appear that someone with the credibility of George Washington might actually endorse public religious expression, so what we do is make him into a non-religious individual. This affects our policy very much. The portrayal of our history affects what we have right now as current public policy. There's no question that we have a strong religious heritage in our background, that it's not just a private religious heritage, it is a public religious heritage. But there's no question that our policies no longer reflect that today, just as our textbooks do not.

I don't say that lightly. We're very involved in the legal arena and we've been involved in several cases of the United States Supreme Court. I want to share with you a few recent federal court cases showing how we've kind of changed our policies to reflect what we show or don't show in our textbooks.

One federal court case is called *Warsaw v. Tehachapi*. It comes from a federal court in California. This federal court ruled that it violates our form of government, it violates the United States Constitution, for a cemetery to have a cross. Simply having a cross in the cemetery is way too much public religious expression. Let's not get this out in public where people can see it.

Then there's another one called *Brittany K. Settle v. Dickson County School Board*. This was settled in the United States Supreme Court in 1996. This case came out of Dickson County, Tennessee, where Brittany K. Settle, a sophomore in high school, was given the same assignment as everyone else in her English class. They were to write a research paper. The teacher said, "I don't care what you write about; just use four sources." Given that latitude to choose their topic, a lot of kids chose spiritual topics, albeit not Christian topics. One student wrote about reincarnation. One student wrote about the occult. One student wrote about spiritualism. But Brittany K. Settle decided she was going to write about the life and times of Jesus Christ. For choosing that topic, she was awarded a "zero." It was upheld all the way to the U.S. Supreme Court. "Write about anything else you want to, but writing about Jesus in the public school is too much religious expression."

Then there are cases like the one in Mississippi called *Ingebretsen v. Jackson Public School District.* Senator Roger Wicker of Mississippi, when he was a freshman United States congressman, said that the courts have given us so many goofy rulings that the kids in our state are confused. They don't even know if it's okay to pray if they want to pray or if student-initiated voluntary prayer is permissible. We need to clarify that for them. His conviction in this matter helped to gather support to pass a state law in Mississippi to clarify for teachers and superintendents, and all of the kids, that if a student wants to pray, *a student can pray!* Voluntary, student-initiated prayer is absolutely constitutional. Well, obviously someone didn't agree with that, because it did end up in court. On January 10, 1996, the Fifth Federal Circuit Court of Appeals handed down its decision, which said this is all wrong. Student-initiated voluntary prayer is not constitutional.

Their position was that a student couldn't pray, if he wanted to pray. They said, as a matter of fact, we will permit a student to pray in only one setting, and that is high school graduation. The courts said the reason for this is very simple. High school graduation is a once-in-a-lifetime event. Since prayer is also a once-in-a-lifetime event, it goes together real well with the high school graduation.

Another case, *Jane Doe v. Santa Fe Independent School District*, also dealt with the way that kids could pray at school. This court said graduation prayers were absolutely fine. They had no trouble with that — as long as you pray the right way. The court case reads, "This court will allow prayer if it's a typical, non-denominational prayer. The prayer can refer to God or the Almighty, but the prayer must not refer to Jesus. And make no mistake, this court is going to have a United

States marshal in attendance at graduation. If any student offends this court and mentions Jesus in a prayer, that student will be summarily arrested and will face six months incarceration. Anyone who violates these orders is going to wish that he or she had died as a child when this court gets through with it." What happened to free speech? Six months in jail for mentioning Jesus in a public prayer? Incredible!

Without exception, these cases are all built on the same foundation. The courts say we're doing this because our *history* demands it, it's simply America's heritage. What we're doing in this case is exactly what our founding fathers wanted when they gave us the first amendment to the Constitution. We're just following our *history*. Every time I hear that statement that "we're following our *history*," I'm reminded of a statement made by President Woodrow Wilson. President Wilson was himself a historian. This is what he declared: "A nation which does not remember what it was yesterday does not know what it is today, nor what it's trying to do. We're trying to do a futile thing if we don't know where we've come from or what we've been about."

This really is the difficulty we have today. We don't even know our own heritage, particularly in this religious arena. Fifty years ago, we were talking about people in our textbooks like Governor Morris, a man with a name and a face that unfortunately few people recognize today. He's a very important founding father: he was the final man to sign the Constitution of the United States and he was the most active member of the Constitutional Convention. In fact, he spoke on the floor of the convention 173 times. That was more than any other founder. Here is the most active founding father at the constitutional convention, the final founding father who signed the Constitution, and today nobody knows his name or his face. But I guarantee you will recognize his handiwork. Governor Morris is the man who physically wrote the Constitution of the United States. That's his handwriting you see when you read it. He is the penman of the Constitution. Doesn't it make just a little bit of sense that the guy who wrote the Constitution might understand the intent for the Constitution? But why is it nobody ever hears about Governor Morris today?

When it comes to faith in Jesus Christ, when it comes to public religious expression, or religious activities in general, Governor Morris, like so many other of those founding fathers, was absolutely politically incorrect. I read a Supreme Court case recently where one of the justices said that 200 years ago is a long time. We really can't be sure what these guys wanted 200 years ago. If you've never heard that "time clouds intent," you will. When you hear it, reject it. That's absolute nonsense.

Go down to the public library and start looking for the writings of George Washington. Count those volumes and you'll find 97 of the personal writings of George Washington. Now that's a man with an opinion on every subject under the sun. That's characteristic of the other founding fathers. Of the 250 founding fathers, you've got people like James Madison with 18 volumes of writings, John Quincy Adams with 23 volumes, John Adams with 33 volumes, Benjamin Franklin with 40 volumes, Hamilton with 60 volumes, and Jefferson with 60 volumes. These guys wrote it all down so that all generations in the future would be able to know exactly what they believed.

Governor Morris was no different. During 1790 and 1791, the two years following the 1789 ratification of the Constitution, Governor Morris authored two works on the Constitution. He said, "Religion is the only solid basis of good morals. Therefore, education should teach the precepts of religion and the duties of man toward God." That's nowhere close to the national policy we have today. But then again, what does he know? He just wrote the Constitution. This is the irony of not knowing our own heritage and not knowing what was in our background, not knowing what the intent was.

Another founding father I have a lot of fun with is James Wilson. You can always recognize him because of the glasses he wore. He was the next to the last man to sign the Constitution. His signature is right above Governor Morris'. James Wilson is the second most active member of the Constitutional Convention. He spoke on the floor of the convention 168 times. When George Washington became president, he put James

Wilson on the U.S. Supreme Court, so he was an original justice on the courts. In 1792 Wilson authored America's very first legal commentaries on the Constitution. Do you know what this founding father told us in those legal commentaries? "Human law must rest its authority ultimately upon the authority of that law which is divine." He starts out by saying that you cannot separate God's law from civil law. Those two things are inseparable. He says, "Far from being rivals or enemies, religion and law are twin sisters, they are friends, they are mutual assistants. Indeed, these two sciences run into each other."

That's a great description of where we are today, because today they do run into each other. It's like a head-on collision. You use something religious in the courtroom and you're in a lot of trouble, as evidenced by the case in the Supreme Court not long ago called *Commonwealth v. Chambers.* In that case, which came out of Pennsylvania, a man named Carl Chambers was convicted by a jury for taking an ax handle and brutally clubbing to death a 71-year-old woman to steal her Social Security check. Not only was he convicted by that jury, he was sentenced to death by that jury. And yet the court overturned his conviction because they pointed out that despite all the evidence and all the witnesses and all the testimony, something terrible had happened in the courtroom. They said that in a statement of less than five seconds, the prosecuting attorney had mentioned seven words out loud from the Bible. The courts said that we can't have that. So despite the evidence, despite the brutal nature of this crime, mention a Bible verse and they've got to reverse the sentence.

You see, today, law and religion are enemies. They don't get along. But back then, they were like two yoke of oxen pulling in the same direction, never to be separated.

Another founding father I have a lot of fun with because he speaks to a very contemporary issue is William Samuel Johnson. His signature is on the Constitution under the Connecticut signers. He was not only a signer of the Constitution, he was one of America's leading educators. He was the first-ever president of Columbia College in New York, which still exists today. As a leading founding father and prominent educator, he was very often asked to address public school graduations. Please don't think that public schools are something new in America. We've had public schools in America for over 300 years. At his time, they were over 100 years old, and so it was not unusual that he would address public school graduations.

It's interesting to see what he did at those graduations, because as I've already pointed out, we have a lot of trouble with what we can and can't do at graduations. A lot of that dates back to a Supreme Court case that occurred in 1992 called *Lee v. Weisman*. That case came from Providence, Rhode Island, a city that's had public schools for over 300 years. The school wanted to do what they've done every other year: have invocations and benedictions at graduation. That particular year, they went to Rabbi Leslie Gutterman and asked if the rabbi would deliver the invocations and benedictions that year. He agreed, so the school officials went to the rabbi to remind him of a few simple restrictions. They told him that this is a secular setting, a secular meeting, and we need for you to pray a secular prayer. How would you pray a secular prayer? What is a secular prayer? That's an amazing request.

But he knew what they wanted. They wanted a politically correct, non-offensive prayer that would offend no faith. So he tried his best to accommodate that. He came back with an admittedly bland prayer. As a matter of fact, it was so bland that when this case was challenged and taken to district court, there were actually discussions in the court over whether or not he had prayed. They weren't even sure it was a prayer when they got into court. It was that bland.

So during the graduation, he addressed these kids on their civic duties, responsibility, patriotism, justice, and all these great things. But he made the mistake of invoking the "g" word. He mentioned that three-letter "God" word one time, right at the very beginning. For mentioning that word, it went all the way to the U.S. Supreme Court. The hearing that year was November 5 at 10 a.m. One hour later, it was all over and done with. When the court rendered its decision the following June, by a 5-4 margin we lost the case. By a 5-4 margin the U.S. Supreme Court said that if a student were to hear the public acknowledgment of God, if a student were to hear God mentioned aloud in public, that would constitute not only religious but also psychological coercion against that student.

News of that ruling, of course, went across the nation, and schools started corralling what they did and made sure they didn't mention God at graduations. What resulted was a public perception in the minds of many in the public community that if it's unconstitutional to do this at graduation, that must mean those who gave us the Constitution didn't want this going on. *Too many people associate what is ruled by the court as the original tenet of the founders.*

I want to go back and show you what William Samuel Johnson did at his public school graduation. This is recorded in his writings. He said to the students, "You this day have received a public education, the purpose whereof has been to qualify you better to serve your Creator and your country." In other words, America paid for your education with tax dollars to teach them how to serve God and country, to teach them how to live by the precepts of God's work. He continued, "Your first great duties, if you are sensible, are those you owe to heaven, to your Creator, and Redeemer. Let these be ever-present to your minds and exemplified in your lives and conduct." And for the rest of his oration, he went through specific Bible verse after specific Bible verse.

Quoting from Acts 17:28, he said, "Remember that it is in God you live and move and have your being. Remember too, that you are the redeemed of the Lord, that you are bought with a price, even the inestimable price of the precious blood of the Son of God." He continued that way for verse after verse after verse.

I guess it's unfortunate that somebody didn't tell him that what he was doing was unconstitutional. I guess he just didn't realize that. This is the irony. If we did the exact same religious practices of those who gave us the document, today they would be struck down under that same document, supposedly by their authority.

How has this come to be? Particularly in the last three decades, we've really seen the changes in textbooks and in rhetoric, et cetera. We're told basically that America is a secular nation created on a secular document by a secular people who wrote that secular document and that's why it's to remain secular today. That's why we're not supposed to have this public religious expression. A great example of that is an article that ran in the *Los Angeles Times*. It ran across the nation and was picked up by a wire service. It was written by Steven Morris and is entitled "America's Un-Christian Beginnings." He basically said that the guys who founded this nation were atheists, agnostics, deists; they didn't even believe in God and the document they gave us reflected that — that's why we're a secular nation and not supposed to have this public religious expression today. Of course, that's simply not true. Even though the media continuously reports it as fact.

But that's what they are teaching throughout our universities. I speak at public universities across the nation. In the last three years, I've had students come to me on a regular basis, telling me that in their American history classes, they are being taught that not a single one of our founding fathers even believed in God. They are being taught that they were all atheists and agnostics and deists. Consider what that does for our public policy 15 years from now when these kids become our local, state, and federal leaders. There's no reason they shouldn't accept this; they're being taught it and they're being tested on it. Then 15 years later, these kids are in office and a question of religious expression comes before them. How do you think they'll rule? "What do you mean, can you have a nativity scene in public? The guys who gave us the Constitution didn't even believe in God, much less Jesus Christ. No way would they have wanted a nativity scene in public. . . . By the way, what in the world are we doing with 'In God We Trust' on the money? They never would have wanted that." And on it goes. This is how the perception of history affects public policy.

I will quickly acknowledge that neither Jefferson nor Franklin was a Christian. Jefferson would fight me on this because in his own writings on several occasions, he said, "I am a Christian, I am a true Christian. I am a true follower of Jesus." I disagree with him because, you see, by any orthodox definition, he doesn't fit. He thought that Jesus was a great prophet sent by God just like Moses or David or Samuel. And you'd better pay attention to the teachings of Jesus just like any other prophet. But was Jesus divine? Jefferson didn't believe that He was the Son of God or the Saviour of the world. So by orthodox definition, despite what Jefferson calls himself, I've got to say that today we would not qualify his definition as Christian.

So Jefferson and Franklin were not Christians. Beyond those two, try to prove that the men who gave us the Constitution were not Christians, much less that they were atheists or agnostics or deists, and you've got your work cut out for you.

One "atheist" founding father was Reverend Doctor John Witherspoon, minister. It sends a lot of people through the roof today to imagine a minister sitting in Congress. But that's the way it was back then. As a matter of fact, of the 56 individuals who signed the Declaration of Independence, 27 had seminary degrees. That's not bad for a bunch of atheists. That's like saying that half of the U.S. Congress today is made up of pastors. That would blow our minds. But that's the way it was back then. The Reverend Doctor Witherspoon is responsible for two American translations of the Bible. Charles Thompson was also responsible for an American translation of the Bible, Thompson's Bible.

Benjamin Rush was the founder of America's original Bible society. Francis Hopkinson was a church music director and choir leader, who authored the first purely American hymn book. He took the 150 Psalms and set them all to music so we could sing the Psalms like David sang the songs.

Thomas McKean was the chief justice of the Supreme Court of Pennsylvania and was also governor of Delaware. As chief justice, a number of cases, decisions, and sentences came before him. If an individual in his courtroom was sentenced to death by jury, he exercised a particular practice. You can find this in law libraries. In 1778 there was a great example, a case called *Republica v. John Roberts.* In that case, the jury found

John Roberts guilty of treason and the jury sentenced him to death for that treason. So Chief Justice McKean in his courtroom read the sentence. He said, "John Roberts, you have been indicted and . . . been convicted of high treason." The sentence for those convicted of high treason is execution.

Chief Justice McKean folded up the verdict, set it down on his bench, and said, "John Roberts, this sentence means that you have very few days left to you upon this earth. It behooves you, therefore, in this period of time, to make peace with your Maker. You need to find the remission of your sins through the shed blood of the Lord Jesus Christ. You need to call for someone who can lead you to that relationship with Jesus, whether it be a minister or a friend, or just the sacred Word of God. You are about to launch out into eternity and you're not prepared to meet God. So let's work on that right now." Now I have always found it hard to believe an atheist would deliver an altar call in the courtroom! But Chief Justice McKean did, in fact, deliver a heartfelt altar call.

Consider this line of thinking: People like myself are called the radical religious right. Quite frankly, I don't know that I've got the guts to deliver an altar call from behind the bench of a courtroom. If I'm the radical religious right and I don't have the courage to do that, what does that make them who had the courage to do that and who did it on a regular basis? This is public record. This is what is still in our law libraries. But again, we hear nothing of this side of our heritage or our history.

You have the same amount of fun when you get over to the 55 atheists at the Constitutional Convention. Abraham Baldwin is the founder of the University of Georgia, but he's America's youngest theologian. For seven years he was a chaplain in the American Revolution. At the age of 23 he received a Professorship of Divinity at Yale University. Charles Cotesworth Pinckney and John Langdon founded the American Bible Society, the same American Bible Society that still exists in America today, the same Bible society that over the last five years has given out millions of Bibles in Eastern Europe as the walls have come down. Rufus King was an original manager of the American Bible Society.

Then you have people like James McHenry, who was the founder of the Baltimore Bible Society, only today, we call it the Maryland Bible Society. These individuals, our founding fathers, founded 121 different Bible societies in America. These men were dedicated Christians.

There were also people like Roger Sherman, John Dickenson, Jacob Broom, who were all considered leading theologians of the day. They wrote large doctrinal treatises on the leading tenets of Christianity. Name after name, we can see in their own words, their own handwriting, their own declarations.

We don't have to begin with the founders and go forward. Let's go from the present backward. I've told you that the American Bible Society was started by these men. But let's look at other societies we have today that we enjoy, other activities and organizations that we as Christians participate in.

Sunday School

Where did Sunday School start in America? In 1791 the American Sunday School Union was formed by the signers of our documents. The first-ever president of the American Sunday School Union was Francis Scott Key, the man who authored the "Star Spangled Banner." For 52 consecutive years, he was president of the American Sunday School Union. His two great loves? America and getting kids into Sunday school to teach them about Jesus Christ. Who were the original officers of the American Sunday School Union? Chief Justice of the U.S. Supreme Court John Marshall, Supreme Court Justice Bushrod Washington, and revolutionary war hero and general Marquis de Lafayette. You just go down the list of the officers who presided over that organization over the years and it's incredible to see how many of our founders were there.

Tracts

Everybody's aware of evangelization, witnessing, and passing out tracts. The American Tract Society is one of the leading tract distribution companies in America today. It's not a new company. It was formed by our founding fathers. As a matter of fact, I have a number of the original tracts written by our signers of the Declaration, our signers of the Constitution, for the American Tract Society for the purpose of evangelization and witnessing. Passing out tracts in America is nothing new; our founding fathers started that.

I could go through society after society that we still have today, take you back to the roots, and show you the original founders of the societies were America's founding fathers. Consider the writings, for example, of people like Sam Adams, the father of the American Revolution and governor of Massachusetts. Read what he declared in one of his recorded writings: "I rely upon the merits of Jesus Christ for a pardon of my sins." You certainly can't call him an atheist! But this is the declaration you find all over their writings. In the same way, John Dickinson, the signer of the U.S. Constitution, declared, "Rendering thanks to my Creator, to Him I resign myself, humbly confiding in His goodness and His mercy through Jesus Christ for the events of eternity."

Then you get into people like Charles Carroll, a signer of the Declaration of Independence. Charles Carroll, the last of the 56 who signed the Declaration of Independence to pass away, declared in his writings: "On the mercy of my Redeemer I rely for salvation, and on His merits; not on the works I've done in obedience to His precepts." These are clear, evangelical declarations.

And John Jay, original Chief Justice of the U.S. Supreme Court, the governor of New York, was one of the three founders most responsible for us having the Constitution today. John Jay is also one of the original founders of the American Bible Society and the second president of the American Bible Society. He declared: "Unto Him who's the Author and Giver of all good, I render sincere and humble thanks for His manifold and unmerited blessings, and especially for our redemption and salvation by His beloved Son, blessed be His holy name."

All these men are called atheists, agnostics, and deists in our public schools today. We would know better if we would read their writings, which are available in public libraries. But when was the last time any of us have taken the time to sit down and read it — *or to even check out what our kids are being taught in their textbooks?*

Prayer Warriors

One of the best overall depictions of the religious nature of the founding fathers is a painting that was commissioned in 1848. It was based on the writings of the founding fathers concerning what they said happened on the morning of September 7, 1774. Go to the public library, get out the official records of Congress, and you'll find that September 7, 1774, is the original Continental Congress. It was a precursor to our current U.S. Congress. And as you read the official records, notice that they opened with prayer. As you continue reading, you'll notice it's not a dinky prayer. In fact, it's very serious. That's why so many of them wrote about prayer. Because, according to the historical records, the opening prayer in Congress lasted for *three hours.* May I point out that it's difficult to get atheists to pray for three hours! It's hard to get Christians to pray that long. But our "atheist" founding fathers prayed for three hours and many of them wrote about it.

People like Samuel Ward, Thomas Cushing, and Sam Adams wrote about prayer. Adams wrote a great letter about it. John Adams, in a letter to his wife Abigail, wrote about what happened. He told her that not only did they have prayer in Congress that morning, but also that they had a Bible study out of Psalm 35 and Psalm 36. Adams said, "God so spoke to Congress out of Psalm 35, [and it] built our faith," that because of that Scripture and that Bible study, they actually believed for the first time that they could defeat the British in the upcoming conflict. In this letter, he also said, "Abigail, I beg you, read my letter [which described the prayer], and read Psalm 35 to-gether. And then read them to your father [who was the minister at their church] and then have him read them to the church." He went on to say, "I want everyone to know what happened in Congress this morning with Psalm 35." We didn't even know they had a prayer, much less that they had a Bible study that they claimed had a major influence on their mentality and decisions.

Silas Dean, American diplomat, described that morning: "After this time of prayer, even the stern old Quakers had tears running down their cheeks." The Quakers were the least likely to cry.

These men are today described in our public schools as atheists, agnostics, and deists.

Out of 250 founding fathers, we do have about a dozen who were not Christians: Jefferson, Franklin, Joel Barlow, Henry Lee, Aaron Burr, Thomas Payne, Ethan Allen, Charles Lee, and Henry Dearborn, and two or three others. That's only 5 percent of the founding fathers. Five percent of the founding fathers not being Christian is a better ratio than what most churches have today, yet we're talking about the Congress of the United States in 1776.

But what happens is that articles like the one I mentioned earlier say, "The founders weren't Christians. . . ." And he goes through the few that aren't Christians and concludes that they're all non-Christians. Why not take the other 95 percent and say, "Your average founding father started the American Tract Society, the American Sunday School Union, the American Bible Society, the American Board of Commissioners for Foreign Missions, the Christian Constitutional Society, and much more."

Even in that famous portrait of the signers of the Declaration of Independence, by and large today, who do we recognize immediately of the 56 individuals? Jefferson and Franklin, the two non-religious ones. It's hard to find the others. Where's Richard Henry Lee? Where's Steven Hopkins? Where are all the other 54 who signed it, who we know nothing about? Today, all we hear much about are the non-religious signers. That's so dishonoring to our heritage.

Ben Franklin

Even if you don't believe what I've shown you historically, even if you don't think that our founding fathers were very religious, you would certainly have to consider Ben

Franklin. Everybody on any side of this debate agrees that Franklin is one of our least religious founding fathers. And I agree.

Franklin is an interesting individual. In pictures including him at the Constitutional Convention, he has a cane that is not for show. At that time he was 81 years old, by far America's elder statesman. The average life span in America at that time was 35 years. At 81 years of age, Franklin's body was falling to pieces. Today, in Franklin Court at Independence Hall in Philadelphia, Pennsylvania, you can see the wheelchair that he used to access the floor of the Convention. It took two men to haul him in and out every day because of his frail body. But his brain was all together. He was brilliant. This man was a true scientist. So many of his ideas are still part of our society today. As one of our most distinguished founders he is one of only six men who signed both the Constitution and the Declaration of Independence. Eleven years passed between the two historic signings, which means he was in all those Congresses when they had all that prayer.

Franklin delivered a speech on Thursday, June 28, 1787. The original is located at the public library in the writings of Ben Franklin and of James Madison. It's also included in the official records of the Convention.

> Gentlemen, in the beginning of the contest with Great Britain, when we were sensible of danger, we had daily prayer in this room for divine protection. Our prayers, sir, were heard, and they were graciously answered. All of us engaged in the struggle must have observed frequent instances of a superintended providence in our favor. And have we now forgotten this powerful friend? Or do we imagine that we no longer need His assistance? I have lived, sir, a long time. And the longer I live, the more convincing proof I see of this truth that God governs in the affairs of men.

That is fairly impressive considering that he was one of

the least religious founding fathers. He was admonishing others for not praying enough. And he quotes Scripture to prove his point. It is difficult for me to accept that our founding fathers didn't want public religious expression when even the least religious called for more of it. This is why, when we were a country who knew our historical roots, we had totally different national policies.

If you go back to the U.S. Supreme Court record and begin in 1789, you can look through the next 160 years — unalterable policy in America. A great case to read is the 1952 case, *Zoric v. Clauson.* (You can check out a copy of it in your local law library.) In that case, the U.S. Supreme Court questioned whether we should separate religious instruction from public education? Inconceivable. That would violate all of our history, all of our law, all of our tradition, all of our precedent. There is no way are we going to separate religious instruction from public education.

Isn't that amazing, that in 1952 the U.S. Supreme Court still thought it was utterly inconceivable to do that? And yet, just four decades later, we're giving out six-month jail sentences to kids who pray in the name of Jesus at school. We've come a long way in a short period of time. A lot of the change centered around ten years later, 1962. In this year we had a new Supreme Court, the Warren court, which was probably the most judicially active court we've ever had. It started a war against religious expression in the public. That year, in the case *Engel v. Vitale,* the court took the new approach that we shouldn't be praying in public, and prayers in school has got to stop.

So, for the last three decades, Americans have been faithfully taught that this is the chief reason the founding fathers gave us the First Amendment. The courts have been telling us that the founding fathers found school prayer reprehensible, that it was repugnant to them. The founders didn't want it and that's why they gave us the First Amendment. If the founding fathers were so opposed to prayers in school, then why in the world didn't they stop it? Why were school prayers constitutional for 170 consecutive years before the Warren court decided that we don't need this anymore?

Unfortunately, the Warren court didn't stop there. The very next year, in 1963, the court said that this thing about reading the Bible in schools . . . we can't let you do that anymore. The founding fathers would never have wanted the Bible read in schools. Obviously, they didn't read what the founding fathers wrote!

Our organization, WallBuilders, has been very blessed. We have been able to collect some 70,000 writings that pre-date 1812. We have thousands of the founders' original writings. One of the rarest works in our collection (or in any collection in America and the world) is the very first Bible printed in the English language in America. It was printed in 1782. Do you know who printed this Bible? The Congress of the United States.

Remember, in 1782 our founding fathers were in Congress. Why would they have printed a Bible? Well, it tells you right in the opening pages that this is a Bible "for the use of schools." Do you want to tell me the founding fathers didn't want the Bible in the schools? I have held in my hand the Bible they printed for the use of our schools. Twenty thousand were originally printed; 52 remain in the world today. This is absolute proof that the founders wanted the Bible in schools. Their records are clear on this Bible and what they intended. Yet the court says, "Oh, no. The founding fathers never would have wanted this."

It was the continuing series of cases in which the court popularized the phrase that we now hear so much. The courts say that the reason we're doing all this, you realize, is that the First Amendment mandates the separation of church and state. Certainly, as we read the First Amendment, it says very simply, "Congress shall make no law respecting an establishment of religion or prohibiting the free exercise thereof." I don't think I see that separation phrase they're talking about.

You see, what sends these guys through the roof is that not only is that phrase contained nowhere in the Constitution, but there's also another phrase contained in the Constitution that causes them a great deal of grief. The Constitution requires that everything said on the floor of the House and the Senate be recorded in public records for our public consumption. We, the public, can go to it at any time. There are 207 consecutive years of congressional records. We can read about any debate that's ever happened in Congress. Which means we can go back to when they framed the First Amendment. It's in the records of Congress from June 7 to September 25 of 1789. For months, these 90 founding fathers argued and debated on what should be included. Back and forth for months and months. Do you know what's amazing? During the months of discussion framing the First Amendment, not even one of our 90 founding fathers ever even mentioned the phrase "separation of church and state." It does seem that if that had been their intent for the First Amendment, somebody would have said something about it.

So what was their intent? We find that they had come to a consensus on August 15, 1789, when James Madison summed it up by saying, in effect, that what we wanted in America is what we couldn't have in Great Britain. You see, we didn't want a situation where the federal government made us all one denomination. We didn't want to all be Catholics, or Anglicans, or anything else. We wanted the ability to choose our own denomination.

That's why the First Amendment says, "Congress shall make no law respecting an establishment." We can't have an establishment of religion set up by Congress. We can't all be Anglicans or Catholics, or whatever the federal government wants — it's not their decision. That's the intent of the First Amendment. James Madison said it was to prevent the establishment of a single, national denomination. That's the founding fathers' concept of separation of church and state. It's not that hard to understand. But to say that means you can't have Bible readings in public or crosses in cemeteries is nonsense. Not even Franklin would have gone for that interpretation.

And you've got to admit, it's a pretty strange interpretation whereby the actual wording of the First Amendment that says, "Congress shall make no law" is now interpreted to mean the same thing as a rabbi mentioning God or a student mentioning Jesus in a prayer. Only an incorrect interpretation would contend that "Congress" means the same thing as a minister or a student and that making a law means the same thing as saying "God" or praying a prayer? Even if you know nothing of history, to read what we have in the Constitution today and to look in the interpretations, we are so far from what the founding fathers intended.

We've absolutely reached the point of the absurd. Three cases came to that court in one year on the same issue: Can kids see the Ten Commandments while they're at school? In my experience, if I want to find a copy of the Ten Commandments hanging somewhere, I don't go to a church. I have addressed hundreds of churches and have only found three that have the Ten Commandments on display. If I want to find a copy of the Ten Commandments, I head straight for a government building. I go to a courthouse or a legislature. I just go to the U.S. Supreme Court in Washington, DC. Engraved in stone in two separate locations are depictions of the Ten Commandments.

Why do the Ten Commandments hang in government buildings and not religious ones? Because even from a secular view of history, the Ten Commandments have formed the basis of civil law in the western world for thousands of years. That's where we get our civil prohibitions against murder, death, perjury . . . that's why they hang in our courthouses. We thought, *Surely, you're not going to tell us that these kids can't see what's hanging inside the U.S. Supreme Court.* But the Court says yes, they are. They worry that if the posted copies of the Ten Commandments were to have any effect at all, it would induce the school children to read them. And if students were to read the Ten Commandments, they would meditate on them. And if they were to meditate on them, they would respect and obey them. And that would be unconstitutional; we can't have students obeying religious teachings in schools.

What an amazing situation. Can you imagine what this

does? We have 46 million young people currently attending public schools. This is now national policy for those young people. "We can't let you see the Ten Commandments. You might obey them." Kids don't see them. They don't obey them. So why are we particularly surprised that now, according to the U.S. Department of Justice, violent crime has increased 694 percent since that point in time?

We go back to the logic of previous generations. Robert Winthrop, great statesman, speaker of the House of Representatives, explained it perhaps as clearly as anyone ever has. He said, "Men, in a word, must necessarily be controlled either by a power within them or a power without them. Either by the Word of God or by the strong arm of man. Either by the Bible or by the bayonet." Those are the only two ways to control human behavior. One is by internal restraints applied by the Word of God. And if somebody's not going to do it from the inside, you'd better learn to carry a baseball bat with you because you're going to have to beat it into them from the outside. It's either internal self-restraint or it's external coercion.

In America, what do we rely on today? The courts have told us the Bible is unconstitutional. So we rely on external force. Just last session of Congress alone, in our 50 state legislatures and our federal Congress, we introduced 170,000 new civil laws in America. We're passing laws at an incredible rate, trying to make people act right, think right, speak right, behave right, do right. We'll pass the laws until we're blue in the face. It's not going to make a flip of difference because if you can't handle the inside, you'll never handle the outside. That's what Jesus tells us in the Scripture. Jesus said that we must first clean up the inside before we can clean up the outside. That's what the founders understood. That's why the Bible was the textbook of our schools, given to us by the founding fathers, and published by the United States Congress.

It's amazing to see the changes we've gone through. I think that maybe Daniel Webster just really nailed this down solidly in the speech that he gave on the cornerstone of the

United States Capitol. He looked at the cornerstone and said that that rock was not the foundation of American civil government, this right here is [the Bible]." The cultivation of religious sentiment represses licentiousness. This inspires respect for law and order, this gives strength to the whole social fabric. The sum of his argument actually was very simple: "Whatever makes men good Christians makes them good citizens."

That's the truth. The police aren't having to arrest good Christians for drive-by shootings and armed robbery and gang violence. Good Christians make good citizens. That's what we knew and that's why we would never allow the separation of those basic principles from society. The whole key to a self-governing nation is self-governing individuals, and the key to individual self-government is in the Bible. That's what we knew and recognized for years and years.

You've seen where we were. You've seen where we are. The obvious question is, how do we get back to the sound principles that we had for generations in America? How do we get back even to the principles that the Supreme Court was recognizing in 1952?

The advice for that is given very well by one of our founding fathers named William Paterson, a signer of the Constitution from New Jersey who was also placed on the United States Supreme Court by George Washington. Paterson has the distinction of having served on the court for two decades after he had helped author the Constitution. In 1806, 1807, and 1808, he was still on the court. As a distinguished founding father, as a leading jurist in America, he was very often asked to address civic groups, legal groups and judicial groups.

Keep in mind that for two decades, America had already become a world leader and people were coming here from all over the world to see what made us great. Indeed, the records of that time show many foreign individuals coming here to find out why America had become a world power so rapidly.

Paterson knew it was our Constitution that was the foundational reason that we become a world leader so quickly.

He was gratified and humbled by that because he's one of the few men still alive who helped write it. But then he often warned of dangers. He knew that as great as this document is, this document will neither guarantee that America retains good government, nor will it guarantee that we have sound policies in America. As good as this document is, it does not guarantee the future of America. If at any time you ever couple bad leaders with this document, this document is worthless.

Let me show you how this works. Let's go back to that 1992 Supreme Court case, *Lee v. Weisman*, regarding invocations and benedictions at a public graduation. Our arguments in that case were very simple. We argued the historical arguments. We said, "Here are the signers of the U.S. Constitution who prayed graduation prayers at public school graduations. As a matter of fact, they didn't just pray prayers, here are some of the sermons that they delivered at public school graduations. As a matter of fact, it wasn't like they had trouble with religion in general, because here's the Bible they printed for the use of our schools." We went through the history. We still lost the case, 5-4. Justice Souter who voted against us, in his concurring opinion, acknowledged the arguments. He knew that the founding fathers participated in graduation prayers, that they condoned graduation prayers, they even advocated graduation prayers. But he felt that just proved the founding fathers didn't understand the Constitution.

How good is our Constitution in the hands of judges like that? Do we have any of the original religious liberty guarantees we had at the beginning of this country? No. Why? Because Justice Souter is not about to let God be mentioned in public. That's psychological coercion. He doesn't like that. He doesn't like public acknowledgment of God or those principles. Therefore, he interprets that document the same way. That's why Paterson said that if you put bad leaders with the Constitution, the Constitution is worthless. That's why he said the key to maintaining sound government in America is given us by God in a sacred writ.

Paterson quoted a single, simple, yet very profound Bible

verse. According to Paterson, this verse is the key to sound government in America. And according to the Bible, it's the key. The verse is Proverbs 29:2: "When the righteous rule, the people rejoice. When the wicked rule, the people groan." The key to sound government in any nation is not its Constitution, even though we have the best one in the world. It's the type of leaders you put with it. Good government is based on good leaders, not on good documents. We've got a great document, but it's not working for us now because we've got some really lousy leaders who surround it.

For the righteous to rule in America, there's only one way for them to get into leadership positions. According to John Jay, America is the first nation in the history of the world to belong to the people. In Exodus 18:21, the Scriptures call for choosing out leaders of tens, leaders of fifties, leaders of hundreds, and leaders of thousands. Choose your local, your county, your state, your federal leaders, but as John Jay pointed out, America is the first nation in the history of the world that got to do that. We got to choose everything from dogcatcher to U.S. president. Everyone else had parliaments which were by hereditary entry. Everyone else had monarchs or kings or dictators, but we, the people, got to choose this one. This is the government that belonged to us.

On the back of the Stamp Act Congress writings, Patrick Henry wrote out Proverbs 14:34, "Righteousness exalts a nation but sin is a reproach to any people." He said, "Reader, remember this. In a nice spirit, encourage virtue and practice it in thyself and promote it in others. The only key to America being sound are these principles right here."

Which puts it all back on us. You see, if America remains righteous, it is because we, the people, demand that it remain righteous. But if America ever goes wicked, it's because we, the people, let it go wicked and it will be we, the people — not our leaders — who will answer to God for the national wickedness, because the nation belongs to us. There is no title in the U.S. Constitution except, "We, the people." That's what they were so proud of — that this is a stewardship government.

Our difficulty is very simple. As Christians — as Christian Americans in 1988 — only one out of every four professing Christians even voted. One out of four is not going to put very many righteous people in office. But here comes the good news. When 1994 rolled around, we doubled Christian voter turnout. Two out of every four Christians voted in 1994.

In six years, we doubled Christian voter turnout. I'm going to suggest to you that that made just a slight difference in the outcome of the 1994 elections. Like maybe the 1994 voter revolution that we heard so much about: 73 new freshmen in Congress.

I spend a lot of time in DC. I go there about once a month to work on a variety of issues that you're not going to hear about. The media is going to tell you about the budget debates, Medicare debates, and the welfare reforms. You don't hear about the moral and religious things that are going on, but there's plenty going on. But I've got to admit, I've never had as much fun in Washington, DC, as I've had since the 1994 elections with this new freshman class, which is best characterized by its opponents. Do you know how they describe the freshman class in the media? "Bunch of Bible-thumpin' evangelicals." That's supposed to be an insult.

There's a lot of evidence to their influence. We have three Bible studies in Washington, DC, that have gone on for more than 50 years. They pre-date World War II and Eisenhower. But they're just for congressmen. I can't get in them; you can't get in them. During the first week of January 1995, when that new freshman class was sworn in, all three Bible studies blew their doors off because they couldn't cram all the congressmen in who were now going to Bible study on a regular basis. They've all had to move to a larger room at least once. One has had to move to a larger room twice.

And it's not just that. Freshman Congressmen Steve Largent from Oklahoma, a strong evangelical — former pro football star — decided that it's not enough that we get out there and fight for our families and our kids and moral values. He said, "We've got to do more than that. We've got to pray."

So he obtained a room there in the House and designated it as a room of prayer. Now, when a particularly vicious floor debate starts in the House, you'll hear a whisper run around on the floor. "Meet you in Room 270. Let's go pray." One congressmen said that recently he got that call. When he went in the room, he knelt down and he prayed. There were two or three other congressmen in there already praying. He prayed and prayed. When he looked up after about 10 minutes, there were almost a dozen congressmen in that room praying. He went back to praying. When he looked up at the end of 20 minutes, there were almost two dozen congressmen in that room. He went back to praying, and when he looked up at the end of an hour, there were more than 40 U.S. congressmen on their knees in that room praying for what was going on on the floor. I would consider that good news. But you won't hear much about that in the liberal press.

You also haven't heard about the revolutions that have been going on in the states. Take, for example, Oregon. So many Christians got involved in Oregon during the last elections, and there was such a dramatic change in the Oregon legislature, that for the first time in 40 years, according to their Senate leader, the state's legislature is opening with daily prayer. This kind of stuff is going on all over the nation. Do we need to stop and thank our congressmen for this? Certainly. The Scripture says, "Withhold not good from those to whom it's due." These guys get plastered in the media. They would love a letter of encouragement every once in a while.

But what we really need to recognize is that they were elected because we wanted something different. They're there because we, the people, said, "It's time to be salt and light and get back from this thing. I don't like the climate we've had there." We doubled our Christian voter turnout. Now 50 percent is a lot better than it was, but it is still pretty lousy when you look at the overall picture. We've got to get it well above that.

Recently, Dick Armey said that if we could get two more crops of evangelicals like we elected in 1994, we could have

Congress. We could do what we want to and get the right principles back in focus. But you see, whether that happens or not is not up to them, it's up to us. It's the kind of leaders that we choose. The kind of leaders that we put there. When the righteous rule — our choice — the people rejoice. When the wicked rule, the people groan. God has allowed the answer to be totally in our hands.

Now I've shown you where we were, where we are, and how we get back to the principles that we had back then. It's in our hands. If we want it to turn around, we can do it. We're moving in the right direction, but we can't stop. We've got to keep moving forward step by step. That's what Deuteronomy 7:22 and Exodus 23:29-30 tell us. God says, "I will give it to you little by little. But I will not give it to you all at once because it will overwhelm you." This is what we've seen in the last six to eight years. Little by little, we're starting to take this thing back. If you're counting on one election to turn America around, it will never happen. But if you'll get in there and stay there, and do what Galatians 6:9 says, that "If we weary not in well-doing, we will reap." We'll win if we'll get in there and stay to the finish.

That's what it's going to take, committed people getting in and realizing that it's time to get involved in education, in the media, in politics, in law, and in government. We've held ourselves back long enough. We are the salt, we are the preservatives. If we don't continue to get into these arenas, we may not have arenas to get into.

God bless.

For more information on David Barton call or write:
David Barton
Wallbuilders, Inc.
P.O. Box 397
Aledo, TX 76008
(817) 441-6044

2

The Corruption of America's Freedom

Ambassador Alan Keyes

The decay and corruption of our nation have gone further than most of us would ever have imagined possible. Thank God, more and more people are waking up to that fact . But I hope enough people will wake up in time.

I recently watched a nightly newscast where a 10 year old was being held for two counts of rape. I don't mention this to be shocking, because to tell you the truth, it's hard to shock people anymore. It's hard to be shocked when were hear that a 10 year old is being raped by a 14 year old, or a 16 year old is killing a 15 year old, or a 6 year old is leading assaults on a 4-month-old baby. We are starting to hear so much about these things that I think we're actually getting to the point where we believe, or start to feel, that this is normal. But this is not normal!

"Babies having babies." Remember? We worried about that. But that was just the beginning, because now the babies are killing the babies. But the really shocking truth does not lie in the babies killing the babies. The really shocking truth lies in the way in which we have allowed an environment to be created in which our young people are no longer feeling a prevailing wind in this nation, blowing them in the right direction. Instead, they walk as if through a fog. The bright stars that ought to be their guides, that ought to give them some sense of right and wrong and conscience, are blocked out. Our senses have become dulled. We just take bad news for granted.

If we open our mouths in protest, we are told that we don't have the right to talk about these things in public. What started out as the so-called "separation of church and state" has now been elevated into the "separation of public life from morality." And, unfortunately, some of our politicians are the best examples. But what we have to ask ourselves as human beings, as Christians, as Americans, is whether or not it is right for us to sit by and passively accept these ideas as good for us when we can already see the consequences that are being wrought by them.

Twenty years ago, when I was in college arguing about what would be the consequences of *Roe v. Wade*, we used to speculate on the things that would result. It was all speculation. But now, if you look at the world that has come about since the sixties, our worst speculations weren't bad enough to account for the reality that we face today. Our streets are filled with crime and violence and our schools filled with fear. And it's reaching into younger and younger generations of Americans. Not just distracting their attention, but destroying their lives, indeed, their very souls.

Why? When you start to deal with the issues that might somehow lead us to take these problems seriously, you're liable to be told this is not the business of public life. Oh, it's all right if you're in a pulpit. But have you noticed that if you confine your concern with moral things to Sunday morning or Sunday afternoon, the rest of the week starts to look pretty bleak? This is happening in America.

To any thinking person, this famous separation of church and state, separation of the public from the religious, is highly questionable. But I believe it's more than questionable. The logic used to justify this notion is so faulty that I don't understand how we could have allowed these things to gain a foothold in this nation. . . . I really don't.

Let's start at the beginning. What is America about? If you were to sum it up in one word, what would that word be? Freedom? Of course! Some time back, I was watching a television show on PBS. They were replaying the series "I'll Fly Away." In one scene, four black guys were gathered together planning their next sit-in. This scene was reminiscent of many scenes in American history, though many would like us to forget them. After these men had completed their planning and reached the point where they wanted to encourage themselves to have heart for the challenges they were going to face, what did they do? They prayed. And in this, they stood in a great, long tradition of American life, beginning with the founders themselves, who knew better than to try anything without turning first to the God who made them. After they prayed they joined their hands. The juxtaposition of these things was beautiful and appropriate. They then sang a bit of a spiritual song that was one of the anthems of the Civil Rights movement:

O freedom, O freedom, O freedom over me;
And before I'd be a slave,
I'd be buried in my grave,
And go home to my Lord and be free.

They were praying. Yet at the same time they were representing to me that "connection" Americans have always made between that which is considered to be most precious in our public lives: freedom and our reverence for God (which includes our dependence on Him).

As you look back at the history of the world have you ever considered that so many times, in so many places, a very few people were able to oppress and rule over great masses of people, depriving them of their freedoms? I have always wondered how that could have been possible. I think one reason it was possible has a little something to do with the phenomenon that you're reminded of if you watch an old western. They have the age-old scene where the sheriff, all by himself, stands off the mob that has come to lynch a prisoner.

The sheriff is upholding the law as he's standing his ground with the mob. There might be 50, 100, or 200 or more people that are angry wanting "justice." During those scenes, you always wonder, *Why don't they just rush the sheriff and get it over with?* If you analyze that situation, it's not as easy as it first appears. As the sheriff is standing there with his shotgun, he proclaims, "Yeah — you can try to get me, but I'll get one or two of you before you get me." That means there's always the question of who's going to go first.

Somewhere in the midst of that scene, it becomes apparent that nobody really wants to be the one who dies so that somebody else can be hanged. The cost appears to be more than the benefit. So eventually, everyone disperses and the scene closes. But that question of who's going to go first, who is willing to pay the price, even risk death, is what we are faced with today. We have allowed a few people to intimidate, rule over, and oppress masses of people. For us to have the courage to defend our beliefs, each one must weigh the cost and the benefit. Sometimes it's hard to find that courage to act when we consider the possibility that if we take the first step, we could be risking everything.

I know how so many Americans in the past have found their courage. They found it by remembering that if they take a stand, they're not standing alone! At the very beginning of this nation's life, our founding fathers understood the connection between justice and power. That's how they made it through all the challenges of launching our great nation. Why have we forgotten this?

Lessons from the Past

Consider our great Declaration of Independence, and its real significance. When our founding fathers wrote the Declaration, what were they doing? They were about to embark on a war. Unlike some people today, I think our founding fathers understood that you don't go to war lightly. War is not a game. When you go into war, especially the war they were going into, where they were going to risk their homes and their families against what was then acknowledged to be the greatest military power in the world, they had to feel pretty intimidated. England had already defeated great powers in Europe, already won wars in the United States. I suppose if there had been odds-makers in those days they would surely have commented on how crazy those lunatic revolutionaries were, to think that they could take on the British Empire.

So they didn't take the decision to go to war lightly, not only in terms of what they risked, but understanding that what they risked went beyond material things. You see, war is about risking your life and your goods, but it is also about taking the lives of others. What greater moral burden can there be than the knowledge that you have taken the lives of others for no good reason? So, they felt they had to justify the step in moral terms. That led to the famous words of the Declaration in which they stated the moral premises, the terms of justice.

What were the premises they stated? We all know these words, although I fear that our children don't know them as well as we do. Our children's children may not know them at all — much less understand their significance. And even when they hear the words, they may find that they have been strangely transmuted.

Our Declaration

"We hold these truths to be self-evident, that all men are . . . *created* . . . equal." I always like to pause on the word "created." It's a key word early in the most important document of our history. The word "created" reminds us of a very important fact — we are created. A lot of people want to emphasize the word "equal" — so they can whine about their rights. But you can't get to the word "equal" unless you first go through the word "created."

Next comes ". . . and are *endowed* by their Creator. . . ." This part is particularly embarrassing to the ACLU, who has been telling people for years, including kids in our schools, that their rights come from the Bill of Rights. They refer to ". . . my rights as granted to me by the Bill of Rights." But I think it is much more important to note that the first truth in the Declaration is that my rights are granted to me by God the Creator.

This means that when we stand up for those rights, we stand up not confident in our own strength, but confident in the strength and power of God. And as Christians we know that His right arm will strike for justice, and even should ours prove weak, His will prevails.

Imagine the strength that God has given Americans over the years. The strength to fight the Revolutionary War. The strength to fight slavery in the darkest days when it looked like it could never be turned around. The strength to stand up for workers' rights, women's rights, and children's rights. The strength to overcome all obstacles because we understood that our power comes from above. Americans have traditionally understand that in the struggle for right and justice, we do not rely only on a human strength.

If our rights come from the Creator God, then what happens to our rights if we reject God's existence, deny His authority, and look to other strengths to protect us? It's like a house without a foundation. God-less dependence will have clear, serious consequences for this country. We as a country cannot continue to offer an understanding of liberty, freedom, or rights that is based on the notion that we are the ultimate arbiter of our rights.

The "A" Word

In the course of my presidential campaign I refused to speak unless I was able to talk about the issue that I believe is of central importance to the moral challenge we face as a people — the issue of abortion. I was not allowed to speak at the Republican National Convention because I would not agree to leave that word behind. And I will continue to refuse to leave the issue of abortion behind because I believe that it poses one of the greatest threats to American character and America's future.

When the pro-choice people defend abortion, they say, "It's a woman's choice whether or not to take that life in the womb." Isn't that what they say? So, since it is wrong to take the life of a human being arbitrarily, that means we're putting the mother in the position of arbitrator of the child's humanity and rights. To borrow a phrase from the Dred Scott decision, the child in the womb has no rights which his mother has to respect. Therefore, it's the mother who decides whether the child is human or not human, whether the child has rights or no rights, whether, therefore, the child shall be treated as a human life. The mother decides whether babies are beautiful and must be nurtured and cared for . . . the mother decides whether to stop smoking and drinking to make sure it's healthy . . . and the mother decides whether it shall be treated as garbage, scraped out and flushed down the toilet. That's the mother's decision? I have a problem with this, because if that's her decision to make, that means that the mother, a human will, ultimately determines whether the child is human, whether it has rights, whether it lives or dies. And right there in our own creed (not a religious creed), it says that not a man nor a woman, not a court nor a judge, not a president nor Congress, and not a constitution nor the Bill of Rights, but God Almighty determines that we are human and have rights.

We must take seriously the language that was used. If our founding fathers used the word "creation," are they talking about anything we [parents] had to do with? The creation went on in God's time, not in ours. If all men are created equal, that fact and the rights that flow from creation are not in any way a consequence of our human will, of our human judgment, of our human determination. Our Declaration of Independence reminds all of us that the authority by which we claim to stand in dignity is an authority beyond our reach and beyond our will. It is an authority that implies a discipline upon our will. We must accept the responsibilities. We must protect our freedoms and insist on equality. But we must also to respect the fact that there is a boundary to what we can do, to what we can claim, to what we can rightfully profess to be.

Therefore, if someone argues for abortion rights, they're ignoring the foundational teaching of the Declaration of Independence. They're also saying, "You can be your own God. You create the children, you determine their humanity, you determine their rights. You are God Almighty." That statement is the heart of our challenge. For what we are doing is putting our own will above the throne of God and worshiping it as if we were the Creator. The Declaration of Independence, that document which is the foundation of this nation, especially warns us against that mistake. It reminds us that we must never accept the doctrines that replace God's will with our will when it comes to determining basic human life, basic human worth, basic human rights. That's what we're doing and the devastating consequences are easily seen.

Consequences of Abortion

I often went through this kind of reasoning during the course of my 1996 presidential campaign. I spent a great deal of time concentrating on the issue of abortion, because if you accept this God-less philosophy, there *are* consequences.

One consequence is that children cease to have any individual value, in and of themselves. If we respect their lives, it is only because it is a function of our needs, of our will, of our convenience. We decided it was convenient to allow them to exist. But children grow up to be adults, and the attitude that you extend to the children is actually one that you are extending to humanity. So instead of taking the view that human beings have an intrinsic kernel of dignity, a spark of God's will in them, we instead regard them only as a function of our needs.

What happens then? Well, if you happen to need an automobile and somebody else owns it, is that going to stand in your way? No, it's not. If you happen to need to make a profit and somebody else is going to suffer for it, is that going to stand in your way? No, it will not. Once we start to treat people as if they are instruments of our will, instead of creatures of God's will, then everything that we understand to be justice is destroyed. There is no difference any longer between right and wrong, good and bad, except what happens to look good to us today. And as it is said in Judges, every man becomes his own judge and does what is right in his own eyes. This is our time. And the consequences growing out of unrepentant abortion can be clearly seen.

In the biblical story of Israel's exodus from Egypt, Moses

approached Pharaoh time after time regarding the different plagues that God allowed upon Egypt. A phrase that keeps recurring is "and God hardened Pharaoh's heart." This was because Pharaoh thought he was God. And as you become prey to that delusion, your heart becomes harder and harder.

Mothers harden their hearts against their offspring, until, like Susan Smith, they're not convenient and are shoved off into a lake and killed. We as a nation were shocked by this terrible crime. But somebody has to explain to me how we can be a nation shocked at that terrible crime of two young children being put in the back seat of a car and drowned by their mother, and yet we are not shocked every time a woman walks into an abortion clinic to do what is, in principle, the same thing to her children. God hardened Pharaoh's heart and abortion is hardening America's heart.

It hardens the heart of fathers against their offspring. Not only have we allowed fathers to harden their hearts, but we demand them to do it. We tell them that that child in the womb is no concern of theirs. What is one of the most powerful instincts for a man in human life? It's the instinct to protect his children. It has been identified by civilizations throughout history to be one of those things that is the hallmark of decent male humanity — when his children are threatened, he will spring to their defense. And yet, in our society we are telling them that they must stand by while their children are destroyed in the womb and they can have nothing whatsoever to say about it. What kind of men are we? Unmanned in our very souls by a doctrine that has our children snatched from us before they even come into the world. This hardens men's hearts. After all, if it is not my child in the womb, how come it suddenly becomes my child in the world? What's the big difference? No big difference at all. So if you force me to abandon the child emotionally in the womb, how can you be surprised if I then turn my back on it once it appears in this world?

We are being told by all the experts that our children are at great risk. They're being abused and abandoned. More and more we're seeing children being raised without fathers because their fathers are begetting them and abandoning them. Many politicians talk about returning to personal responsibility. But how are we to achieve that in our families if we are forcing men to abandon their emotional relationship with their child in the womb? We can't have it both ways. We can't practice the abortion doctrine and on the other hand pretend that we want to re-establish responsibility which is the basis for family life! It will not happen.

Abortion, and what it represents, points to our most serious challenge. The attitude allowing abortion is the main source of moral corruption in our time. It's a corruption in our understanding of freedom itself. Freedom is the hallmark of our society. Our ancestors endured and died defending our freedom. Freedom — the blessings of which are promised to our posterity, and the cursing of which we see on our streets every day.

The Answer

If you look at our political discourse in America today, what is it that people seem to believe is our major challenge? The liberals really want us to believe that as we look around this country, as we see generation after generation sinking into the mire of promiscuity and drugs and violence and crime in the streets, and deteriorating education, that somehow or another the root of those problems is economics. If that were the case, how come we didn't have all these problems during the Great Depression? Why didn't families fall apart? Why did the crime rate actually fall? We need to look with great suspicion on these explanations because they are dealing with the surface problems, not the root of the problems.

From 1980 to 1992 the drug problem declined among America's youth. Then, starting in 1992 there was a sudden increase in drug use among our young people, and the numbers have continued to go up. I'm not going to dwell on what happened in 1992, but I will say this: During the course of the so-called Reagan years, a program identified with Nancy Reagan about the drug problem was called "Just Say No." Remember that? I sometimes wonder if everyone understood the real significance of that program. A lot of the usual suspects laughed because the idea that human beings might actually be able to control themselves in some area is considered laughable by many of those who fancy themselves to be sophisticated. I still have to wonder, though, about their reasoning, because these are the same people who think that we ought to recycle, save the whales, and so forth. They are also likely to be the same people who think we ought to stop smoking, eat less fat, and exercise. But I always say if you can't control your lust, then what makes people think you can control your anger? Therefore, you can no more control violence than you can control sexual passion. So how can the people who come to us and say "You can't control sexual passion" get all upset about violence? If you abandon the moral premise in one area, you abandon it in another area. Either we are, as human beings, capable of restraining and disciplining and controlling our passion and impulses, or we're not. So they laughed at the idea behind the drug program, that you could "just say no." But it worked because we are human beings, we *are* capable of moral conviction. It's one of the reasons that, no matter how mad you get at me, you probably won't kill me.

Nancy Reagan's Approach

"Just Say No" wasn't about calculating the health consequences of using drugs. Nor was it about figuring out that if you smoke too much, or use whatever drug is available, that your health will deteriorate. As a parent watching my children grow up, I'm amazed that anybody thought that telling kids "drugs are dangerous" would lead them to stop using them. That type of logic doesn't work for any of the other things we tell them are dangerous. In fact, in this day and age, telling many children something is dangerous makes it more appealing. In trying to prove that they have reached maturity, they end up doing things that are quite stupid.

What Nancy Reagan was doing with the "Just Say No" campaign was not to get them focused on the *consequences* of using drugs. Instead, it was to get them to understand that there are certain absolutes in this life. Some things are always right and some things are always wrong. If it is wrong, then don't do it, just say no. That's morality. Our challenge is to restore a sense of moral discipline, character, and capacity to our young people. If we don't understand that, we continue to lose the battle. And the losses will mount until we place the emphasis back on morality.

I know that there are people out there who will tell you that you've got to reform the behavior first and then the laws will follow. They haven't been around this planet for very long, apparently, because it's never worked that way in the past. Someone once said, "First men make laws, then the laws make men." That makes sense. If you have on your books an abortion doctrine that destroys the sense of moral limits, how can you acknowledge that there are moral limits? If you adopt an understanding of freedom that destroys the sense of moral capacity, how are you going to educate your children to believe that they have a moral capacity? It's not going to happen. Therefore, the laws and public policy we tolerate, can, on a large scale, undo the work that we're doing training up our children.

This, of course, doesn't mean that we give up on training up our children. God has commanded us to teach eternal truths, not temporal truths, to our children, family, and others He brings into our lives. We must never stop proclaiming truth because we'll never sustain this land of freedom if God is banished from our law and our public policy. We must proclaim respect for His will, and a sense of discipline resulting from that respect, because if we don't, who will?

We Are the Solution

So, when they tell you they're going to solve all your problems with a tax cut, I hope you're suspicious. I personally have never seen a tax cut I didn't like. But it's not because I am greedy for more money in my pocket. I actually think it has to do with respecting our moral capacity. If you take away all the material wherewithal for people to meet their responsibilities, how are they supposed to exercise their moral capacity? It can't be done. So there is a moral purpose behind tax cutting. But be suspicious when politicians come along in an election year and decide that they're going to increase the minimum wage and cut the taxes. You have one party bribing the poor, another party trying to bribe the working people, and other people trying to bribe the rich. Don't be fooled. The elected leaders of our nation may never understand what this country needs, but we do. It's not tax cuts, medical reform, or ending welfare, it's turning this nation back to God. For in the end, this nation is ours to make or break. Its character, its strength, its ultimate fate are forever linked to our dependence on Almighty God.

What are we going to do?

I think that's a key question for Christians today. I like to challenge people to take an active role in speaking out about the direction our country is headed. When I find a person who is a Christian, or even someone with religious conviction, I say, "Are you someone who is taking an active interest in the public life of this country? Of the schools? And of the community and of the state and of the nation?" If you're not involved, should you be?

If people of the faith don't challenge each other to speak out, how will this nation continue in grace? Our nation rests on the premise of God's authority and God's existence. Are we defending that premise? We must be the leaven in the loaf. We must be the salt. We are the people of God who are called by His name, who profess in their life to be believers. We believe that He is the only God, that His will must govern our nation and that salvation comes only through Him. We must be a light for all to see.

Can Christians Be Patriots?

That challenge should also include a special burden of patriotism for a God-centered country. Unfortunately, some people argue that being patriotic is contrary to Christ's teaching. They claim the Bible teaches that Jesus sanctioned this doctrine of the separation of church and state. They think that it is sinful to try to motivate Christians to become active in government. They quote Matthew 22:21 where Jesus said, "Render to Caesar the things that are Caesar's, and to God the things that are God's." This may sound like separation of church and state, but it's not. Let's look closer at that passage:

> Then the Pharisees went and counseled together how they might trap Him in what He said. And they sent their disciples to Him, along with the Herodians, saying, "Teacher, we know that You are truthful and teach the way of God in truth, and defer to no one; for You are not partial to any. Tell us therefore, what do You think? Is it lawful to give a poll-tax to Caesar, or not?" But Jesus perceived their malice, and said, "Why are you testing Me, you hypocrites? Show Me the coin [used] for the poll-tax." And they brought Him a denarius. And He said to them, "Whose likeness and inscription is this?" They said to Him, "Caesar's." Then He said to them, "Then render to Caesar the things that are Caesar's; and to God the things that are God's." And hearing [this] they marveled, and leaving Him, they went away (Matt. 22:15-22).

For a long time I was puzzled by this passage, because in Matthew 6 the Lord says:

> No one can serve two masters; for either he will hate the one and love the other, or he will hold to one and despise the other. You cannot serve God and mammon.

There seemed to be a problem because Jesus first says "No one can serve two masters;" and then later He says "Render to Caesar the things that are Caesar's and to God the things that are God's." I spent a long time grappling with this passage. Then one day the Lord blessed me with a little understanding of it. This is what I realized: Christ is the Word made flesh. That means that Christ's deeds are words and His words are deeds. So if you're reading through a passage and you don't understand the words, you've got to look at the actions that go along with them. What action goes along with these words? He says, "Show me a penny. Show me a denarius." And they show him the penny. He says, "Who's image is on here?" This is, in my opinion, the key to this passage. Christ gives it to us in that gesture, for what does He tell us? If you want to know what belongs to whom, ask whose image is stamped upon it?

If you go back to the very beginning of the verse, all the Pharisees were listening to Christ's words in context of the Old Testament. Their jaws dropped and they all went away marveling because of the answer He gave them. He answered their question with a question. He asked them whose image was stamped on the coin.

I found the answer in Genesis 1:27 where it says "So God created man in his own image, in the image of God created he him; male and female created he them." The Pharisees said the image of Caesar was on the coin. Well, whose image is on Caesar? Whose image is on you? Whose image is on me? Whose image is on everything? We are all stamped with the power and majesty of the Creator God! Christ was not saying that you should give a little to Caesar, give a little to God, and then go away, like the Pharisees, feeling good about what you did. Instead, Jesus was reminding the Pharisees that Caesar belongs to God. That you and I belong to God. That it all belongs to God. That they should give it all back to Him. That's what made them so mad.

So, as people of faith, are we going to follow Christ's words and example? Or, are we going to accommodate our detractors by believing that the separation of church and state means that we leave our faith in Jesus Christ at the church door when it comes time to be citizens? I hope we don't. For if we do, we are in fact rejecting the example, the essence, and the truth of our faith. Christ implores us that it is not just in the words but also in the deeds that we must be judged.

We *Can* Make a Difference

Can we affect this nation? I firmly believe that in the end it's only going to happen when our Lord and Saviour comes again to establish the true reign of justice. Our current attempts at justice are but a pale shadow. And yet in this life, we are here to be His witnesses and be used by God. What does it mean for us? Christ admonished us to tend the sick, visit those in prison, and clothe the naked. We are to also care for the body of Christ. There is a large part of the Body in America. For whatever reason, God has allowed it. This nation was born by His divine providence. It's sustained only by the fact that it was born in an acknowledgment that His will is the source of justice, that His power is the strength of right. We were founded as "One nation under God." Isn't this worth preserving?

The Real Problem

Politicians tell us that the answers to America's problems are in bigger budgets and the right fiscal policy. The budgets and policies may very well need to be amended. But in the end, the right budget and the right fiscal policy will become very clear if you are putting God as the number one priority. If you think through all the areas of crime, violence, education, etc., you begin to realize that the only thing that will give us long-term change is a restoration of the moral commitment on the basis of which this nation was founded.

Only one group of people in this nation have the heart and have the faith to rediscover that moral commitment and carry it once again, whatever the cost, into the arena of our public affairs. That group is you. If your light and fire of faith does not re-ignite the flame of decency in this nation, then nothing will. That is your challenge, that is your work. This nation's future is in your hands.

Never forget that regardless of the grim reality of the moral problems, economic problems, or whatever this nation faces, there is hope. We have to understand that when this nation began and fought for liberty, when we fought against slavery in the last century, when we went over the seas to fight against despotism and tyranny unheard of in the history of mankind, it also looked very grim. But for a people with faith, their hand in the hand of God, none of the obstacles proved to be too much to overcome. For there is nothing mightier than His will. We simply put our faith and trust in Him. That is how our founding fathers did it, that's how we must do if we are to succeed. Turning back to God will be the truth of America's salvation. It will be the rock of America's future.

Let's begin to build upon it.

For more information on Ambassador Keyes' Declaration Foundation call or write:

The Declaration Foundation
2580 White Bear Avenue, Suite 102
St. Paul, MN 55109
612-777-9086, Fax 612-773-8434
Website: http://www.declaration.net
Email: Declare@aol.com

3

New Age and the Last Days

John Ankerberg

In 1 Timothy 4:1 it says: "Now the Spirit speaketh expressly, that in the latter times...." That will be a key phrase throughout this discussion; in fact, almost every verse we will look at will express the thought that "this is going to happen in the latter times." Those of you who are serious students of the Bible know the latter times began after the death and resurrection of Jesus Christ. They extend to that time in the future when He will return to the earth. The apostles and the Lord himself refer to that period as "the latter time." This phrase can also apply specifically to the events that are going to happen immediately before Jesus comes back.

Continuing in 1 Timothy 4:1, "The Holy Spirit speaketh expressly, that in the latter times, some shall depart from the faith." Make note of the word "the" that proceeds the word "faith." In the Greek, we have what is referred to as an *article*, "the faith." The Bible says in the latter times, some are going to depart from the faith. "The faith" with an article in front of it indicates the content, the doctrine, the beliefs — that which makes up Christianity. Without these beliefs, without these doctrines, we would not have Christianity.

If we're talking about the bottom line of what we believe, we need to first understand what are the foundational beliefs in Christianity. They are:

> The Trinity: Father, Son, and Holy Spirit — One God, three personages.
> The inspiration and inerrancy of the Bible in the original languages.
> The virgin birth of Jesus.
> The deity of Jesus: He claimed to be, and in fact, was, and is, God.
> The bodily resurrection of Jesus Christ from the dead; He is now alive.
> The promise of the heavenly resurrection for all true believers.
> Man is born sinful and separated from God.

These are considered the foundational truths of what we believe as Christians. But the Holy Spirit says over and over in the Bible that as we get into the latter times, closer to the return of our Lord to the earth, some people will depart from these truths.

Let me illustrate. Do you believe that departure from the foundational truths of our faith is happening today? *Pulpit Helps*, a magazine that goes to 100,000 pastors, performed a survey in which 7,441 Protestant pastors were queried. The results:

> Percentage of pastors that did *not* believe in the physical resurrection of Jesus from the dead:
> Methodists 51%
> Presbyterians 35%
> Episcopalians 30%
> American Baptists 33%

This is despite the fact that the apostle Paul said in 1 Corinthians 15:14, "If Christ has not been raised, our preaching is useless and so is your faith." If Christ has not been raised, you are still in your sins, and all who die, even those in Christ, are lost. If there is no resurrection of Jesus from the dead in this life, Christians are to be pitied more than all men. Paul said this, yet all these ministers said they didn't believe that Jesus rose from the dead.

As believers, we all are looking forward to the time when Jesus Christ comes back to earth and takes the Christians away to heaven. This is referred to as the Rapture. We believe that Christ could come back any moment. First Thessalonians 1:10 said that the Thessalonians had been saved out of paganism. Paul, the author of Thessalonians, was commending them for saying they are waiting for God's Son to come back from heaven and save us from the wrath to come. The Greek word used here means they're "waiting up for," or in other words, every moment they're waiting. The imminence of Jesus' coming is in that verse. It's also in James and in 1 Thessalonians 4. They were expecting any moment for Christ to come back. This was, of course, 2,000 years ago.

The Bible teaches that Christ will return again to this earth. There is going to be a terrible seven-year time period called the "Tribulation." This is when the wrath of God is going to fall progressively on the earth. The nations are going to gather against Israel and the Lord himself will come back and defeat those armies. He will save Israel from destruction and will literally reign as King on this earth for 1,000 years.

We have many Scriptures dealing with the second coming of Jesus, but we don't know all of the facts about when He's coming. We have more facts recorded about Jesus' second coming than we do of the Rapture because there are no visible signs for the Rapture. We do know this: If there are signs that Christmas is coming, we know that Thanksgiving comes sooner. If we can see signs of Christ's second coming, then the Rapture must be closer.

When Will the Rapture Come?

The Bible says that prior to the Second Coming there will be a progression of evil that continues to increase, ending with one last major event. There is no secret about what the last event is: Armageddon. And when Armageddon occurs, the Lord comes back from heaven at that moment. We also know that the Rapture will have already occurred. So let's look at evil.

I've recently been studying the biblical outline of the

Lord's second coming in reference to the evil that will progress in the church. In 1 Timothy 4:1 it says, "In the latter times, the Spirit expressly says, some are going to depart from the content of the faith." We will come to a point at which we will have outright apostasy worldwide. We are certainly moving in that direction today.

Why do we have this apostasy, or departing from the faith? The next verse gives us the answer: ". . . giving heed to seducing spirits. . . ." Seducing means "to mislead purposefully; to get off the path." But what I want you to see is that it says seducing spirits are going to be the *cause* of some departing from the faith. Not only will there be seducing spirits, but there will be people who will leave the faith because they will believe in "doctrines of demons."

I remember a great German theologian who had dealt with the occult came to the seminary that I was attending. He warned, "Don't ever try to counsel people in the occult." Then he began to tell us all of the trouble that he had encountered because God had called him to serve in that area. Because of it, the spiritual warfare on his family and the things that happened to him were absolutely amazing. He persuaded me not to touch that area with a ten-foot pole! But when I started hosting a TV program, every other month or so I was dealing with leaders in the cults. These people would talk about their spirit guides giving them information.

The very first program I ever hosted was with a group called Eckankar. I asked for the Eck master to come on the program. I didn't know anything about Eck. I had simply read an advertisement in the paper and thought it would be an interesting television show. So I invited them to participate. The guy who was on that program is now the actual Eck master for the whole United States and the world. He was talking about the spirits being just as close to him and talking to him and being as visible to him as I was, sitting in the chair next to him. That was the very first program I did. At that time I hadn't noticed that verse.

The first time I noticed that verse was when Jose Silva

from Silva Mind Control wrote me a letter from Mexico. He said he wanted to come on the program. About 8 million people have gone through Silva Mind Control. On the third day of their course, they offer a money-back guarantee if they haven't taught you how to invite two spirit guides to come into your mind and body to give you information that you don't have. These guides will stay with you forever.

When we had Mr. Silva on the program, I said, "Look, you have taught everybody how to contact the spirits and get them into their life. Where did you get them? Who taught you?" He said, "I was born with them. I've always had them." All of a sudden, it clicked in my mind and made sense — his mother and father were into the occult! That's biblical. He had always had the spirits. That is what he was telling me on the television program, and all of a sudden I read this verse: "In the latter days, some shall depart from the faith." Why? Because of ". . . *seducing* spirits and doctrines of demons."

The Four Basic Lies from Satan

For all the people who are demon-possessed, spirit-possessed, or who have picked up a spirit guide, there are millions and millions more who haven't, but who believe the doctrines of demons. What's a doctrine, or a teaching, of a demon? In Genesis 3:1 (NIV) we find Satan's first lie. It reads: "Now the serpent was more crafty than any of the wild animals the Lord God had made. He said to the woman, 'Did God really say you must not eat from any of the trees in the garden?' " (NIV). The doctrine of demons is this: "God lied. He didn't really mean that, did He?" Satan's lie **#1** is that you can't trust God's Word.

The woman said to the serpent, "We may eat fruit from the trees in the garden, but God did say you must not eat fruit from the tree that is in the middle of the garden and you must not touch it, or you will die." Here's Satan's lie **#2** in verse 4: "The serpent said, 'You will not surely die.' " Does that sound familiar today? It's reincarnation.

I once had as a guest on the TV program, Dr. Elisabeth Kubler-Ross. She wrote the book on death and dying that all the kids had to read in college, the book about the four stages of death and dying, and about what you go through as you understand you're going to die. She's changed that course now to "Death, Dying, and Transition" because she now says she has had an out-of-body experience and now believes that everyone will be reincarnated. Shirley MacLaine describes reincarnation as, "It's like going onstage; you do it until you get it right. You don't have to worry about that; you will not surely die." More people believe that than you can imagine.

Keep going. "You will not surely die, the serpent said to the woman, for God knows that when you eat of it, your eyes will be opened." Here's lie **#3**: "... and you will be like God." Have you heard that one before? "You can be your own god." Remember Shirley MacLaine in the eighties movie, *Out on a Limb*? She was out in front of the ocean yelling, "I am God. ... I am God." They believe everybody can be god except Jesus.

The verse continues, "When the woman saw that the fruit of the tree was good, the perfect fruit, pleasing to the eye and also desirable for gaining wisdom. ..." Have you ever noticed how many groups have "steps" that they want to share with you? There is a ten-step program here, a certain methodology there. Most cults have a long list of the things you need to do and then you'll have enlightenment, this mystical experience, this out-of-body experience, or achieve what they believe is heaven. This is Satan's lie **#4**, "If you do certain things, you can go to heaven," or in other words, "salvation by works." Jesus' work on the cross is not a factor. These kinds of doctrines came right from Satan himself in Genesis 3 — right at the beginning of human history. They're still with us today and they're gaining more and more adherents.

I wrote this great big 500-page book on doctors. One of our top medical scientists today listens to spirits. Remember the earlier verse "in the latter days, some shall depart from the faith, giving heed to seducing spirits, and doctrines of devils." Andrisa Puharich has 50 medical patents on new technology in our country today. He said this: "I am personally convinced that superior beings from other spaces and other times have initiated a renewed dialogue with humanity. While I do not doubt their existence, I do not know what they look like, how they live, or even what their goals are with respect to human-kind."

Bernie Siegel is our top medical doctor at Yale University. He was curious about Elisabeth Kubler-Ross and her out-of-body experience. He is a straight skeptic and agnostic, doesn't believe in God, didn't think these things were true. But he said, "I'll give it a try." He put himself into a situation where he was opening himself up to the occult. He says this in his book *Love, Medicine, and Miracles*, "I approached this exercise with all the skepticism one expects from a mechanistic, skeptical doctor. I sat down, closed my eyes, and followed directions. I didn't believe it would work, but if it did, I expected to see Jesus or Moses. After all, who else would dare appear inside a surgeon's head? But instead, I met George, a bearded, long-haired young man wearing an immaculate, flowing gown and skull cap. It was an incredible awakening for me because I hadn't expected anything to happen. George was spontaneous, he was aware of my feelings and an excellent adviser."

After he had this mystical experience, he wondered if he should get out of medicine, so he checked with his spirit guide named George.

"I was still toying with the idea of a career change when I discussed it with George," he says. "He explained that I could do more by remaining a surgeon, by changing myself to help my patients mobilize their mental powers against disease. I could combine the support and guidance of a minister or a psychiatrist with the resources and expertise of a physician. I could practice 'clergery,' a term my wife coined. George says, 'You can go anywhere in the hospital; a clergyman or a therapist can't. But you are free to supplement medical treatment with love or death and dying counseling in a way that non-physicians are not able to do.' George has been an invaluable companion ever since his first appearance to me."[1]

That's our top doctor at Yale.

I first saw Norm Shealy from Harvard, a neurosurgeon, on "The Today Show" talking with show host Jane Pauley. Norman is also the founder of the Holistic Health Organization in this country. The television show was featuring this neurosurgeon and professor at Harvard as he was diagnosing a person. Shealy made a scientific, medical diagnosis, then he called a psychic a thousand miles away. The television screen then showed the psychic, who picked up the phone. Shealy said, "I have a patient sitting right in front of me and I have made my diagnosis. Now would you give me yours?" The viewers watched as the psychic went into a trance, a psychic scan of this person supposedly a thousand miles away. Then the psychic put down her information and told Norm Shealy, "This is what I think." He said, on television, "Unless I agree with what she says, I don't trust my diagnosis." Millions of viewers are seeing a credentialed physician trust a psychic over his own diagnosis.

Our top medical doctors and scientists today have punched into the mystical and are talking to the spirits. Are they a little bit skeptical about this thing? Have you ever heard a non-Christian person when you talk about your walk with the Lord? Don't they get a little bit skeptical? You'd better believe it. But their spirit guide demons make it hard not to believe. Andrisa Puharich said:

> Considering that I've had two years of intermittent experience of contact with them [the spirits], I am remarkably ignorant about these beings. On the other hand, I have complete faith in their wisdom and benevolent intentions [they always say they're loving] toward man and living things on earth. My lack of hard knowledge about them is a kind of deficiency but it does not erode my faith in their essential pursuit of the good, the truth, the beautiful, and the just.

He's saying, "I don't know anything about them, but I trust them." The Bible says, "In the latter times, some will depart from the faith, following seducing spirits and things taught by demons." It's easy to see in our medical community.

Let's go to another verse. This is 2 Timothy 3:1: "This know also, that in the last days, perilous times [terrible times; the Greek word actually means 'dangerous times'] shall come." Do you think we have dangerous times now? Do you feel safe leaving your car door unlocked or your house unlocked? Do you feel safe walking down the streets of New York after 6:00 p.m.? The next couple of verses tell me why the last days are going to be dangerous times because here are the characteristics of the people: "For men shall be lovers of their own selves, covetous, boasters, proud, blasphemers, disobedient to parents, unthankful, unholy, without natural affection, trucebreakers, false accusers, incontinent, fierce, despisers of those that are good." If you have those kinds of people in society, you're going to have a pretty rugged society. It's going to be dangerous out there.

In spite of those characteristics, people are going to have a "form of godliness." We're going to have form without content here. They're going to say the words but their lifestyle will not follow. I recently saw a Hollywood star dancing with a couple of women who were dressed with the equivalent of three band-aids. The star was singing, "I'm saved, I'm saved, Oh yes, I'm saved." One wondered what he was saved from.

Today, although about 70 percent of Americans claim to be Christians of one shape, form, or another; only 13 percent think the Ten Commandments have any moral validity for their lives. Seventy-four percent of Americans say that they would steal without compunction; 64 percent said that they would lie if there is an advantage to be had; 53 percent said that if they were given a chance, they would commit adultery in a heartbeat; 41 percent say that they intend to use recreational drugs; and 30 percent admit that they cheat on their taxes all the time. Eighty-six percent admit lying regularly to their parents; 75 percent admit that they have lied regularly to their friends; 73

percent say they have lied to their brothers or sisters; and 73 percent say they have lied to their lovers. We have an AIDS epidemic going on in this country, and if the question is asked, "Do you have AIDS?" seven out of ten will lie about the truth!

Only 11 percent of all these people say that if they were caught in any one of these things that they would be ashamed of what they had done. This is found in the book, *The Day America Told the Truth*. In that same book it's stated that 67 percent of Americans do not believe in moral absolutes; 70 percent do not believe that any truth is absolute, that it is enduring, and applicable to all people in all places at all times.[2] In other words, everybody does their own thing. There are no absolutes.

The Bible says they are going to have a form of godliness, but they will deny the power thereof. They won't have the reality. Today, the statistics say that day has arrived.

Second Timothy 4:3-4 says, "For the time will come when they [people] will not endure sound doctrine, but after their own lusts, their own desires, they shall heap up to themselves teachers, having itching ears; And they shall turn away their ears from the truth, and shall be turned unto fables." The Bible is saying that there will come a time when people won't want to hear sound doctrine. Instead, they're going to choose the church that preaches what they want to hear; not what they need to hear. There are some churches today that make a big point of going out and taking surveys, finding out what people like, what they want to hear, and then structuring their services around the surveys.

Sound Doctrine

About two years ago, 20 of my friends, some of our top evangelical leaders in this country — Pat Robertson, Chuck Colson, Bill Bright, J.I. Packer, some of our Southern Baptist denominational leaders, and some of our top college presidents — signed a document with 20 Roman Catholic leaders who were just as prestigious. I thought, *Great. I know these guys. These are friends and people I respect.* Up until now, we've had a 450-year split between the Protestants and the Catholics.

It was over how a person gets saved, how a person has his sins forgiven. The Bible is clear that salvation is by faith alone — nothing else needed, Jesus does it all. But the Catholic Church believes that salvation comes by faith, plus you also must do a little work. Martin Luther began the split by pointing out the incorrect doctrines of the Roman Catholics. The Roman Catholics held to their belief and said, "Anybody who believes in justification by faith alone is excommunicated; damned to hell." Each group believed that the other group was wrong.

When I read about these influential Protestant leaders signing this agreement, I thought, *I can't wait to read this agreement to see where those Catholic guys admitted after 450 years that they had been wrong.*

But it broke my heart to read this statement out of the document: "We together, Evangelicals and Catholics, confess our sins against the unity that Christ intends for all His disciples." They're saying we are admitting to the Lord that we have been wrong to have this split. It assumes that both Evangelicals and Catholics are first of all true disciples of Jesus, an assumption that was denied from the beginning of the split by both the Council of Trent and Martin Luther. Another statement reads: "There are different ways of being Christian." Try finding that in your Bible. "It is understandable that Christians who bear witness to the gospel try to persuade others that their community, Roman Catholic or Protestant, and their tradition are more fully in accord with the gospel." All I could think of was, are they saying that there are now degrees of correctness concerning the gospel? Can somebody be 10 percent correct, 50 percent correct, 75 percent correct? No, the Bible says either you believe it or you don't!

Another statement: "Those converted, whether understood as having received the new birth for the first time [faith in Christ] or as having experienced the reawakening of the new birth originally bestowed in the sacrament of baptism, must be given full freedom and respect as they discern and decide the community in which they will live their new life in Christ."

Are there two ways to get saved? No, but this document

leads you to believe that there are.

"As Christ is one, so the Christian mission is one," this document said, "and we are called and we are therefore resolved to explore patterns of working and witnessing together in order to advance the one mission of Christ." The problem here is that if we are to witness together, we have never agreed on what the message is. What are we are to witness together about? We disagree on both the message and the mission.

Another sentence says, "All who accept Christ as Lord and Saviour are brothers and sisters in Christ." Protestants and Catholics differ on how Christ saves a person. This was never established; it was simply glossed over as if the 450-year split had never occurred. I couldn't believe it. They later signed a statement that affirmed their belief in "justification by faith alone," but much damage was already done and their names are still on the original document.

Another biblical topic people today simply want to avoid is "hell." It is obviously a scary subject to many because the Bible is very clear about the heat, horror, and helplessness experienced by those who go there. There are hundreds of references to hell throughout both the Old and New testaments. I was asked to give an address at Trinity Evangelical Divinity School several years ago. The address was on, "What do evangelicals believe concerning hell?" So I researched all of the occult and cult figures in this country who are saying that there is no hell. There were 350 evangelical scholars from all over the country attending this meeting. As I was giving my address, there were so few people in the audience that it looked like I was speaking during the bathroom break. Many people were simply getting up and walking out. I wondered what was going on. Then I found out that if you read the Trinity Evangelical Divinity School affirmations, there is no statement that they believe that hell is where people go who reject Christ. Pastors around the country today place the salvation emphasis on "going to heaven" and tend to avoid talking about "burning in hell forever."

Second Timothy 4:3-4 says, "After their own lusts, shall they heap to themselves teachers, having itching ears." *Newsweek* magazine said in an article in September 1984, "People have developed a "pick and choose" Christianity in which individuals take what they want and they pass over what does not fit their spiritual goals. What many leave behind is a pervasive sense of sin."

There seems to be a progression of apostasy, a progression of leaving the faith, of following doctrines of demons and seducing spirits, and we're getting to a point that the Bible tells us will be the end of the line. Second Peter 2:1-3 says, "But there were false prophets also among the people, even as there shall be false teachers among you, who secretly shall bring in [damnable] heresies, even denying the Lord that bought them." Today a person may attend church and not realize that they are heading straight to hell when they die. If you go to certain churches and listen to what they preach, they are preaching damnable heresies. If you believe what they're preaching, it will damn your soul. You will go to hell. You might think they're right. You might like what they're preaching. But what they're preaching is a lie, and you'll go to hell if you don't discover the truth before you die.

What is a damnable heresy? ". . . even denying the Lord who bought them. . . ." In the August 23, 1996, edition of the *New York Times* it said, "Christians Split — Can Non-Believers Be Saved?" A pastor in the Reformed Church in Michigan, after serving there 25 years, said, *"I no longer believe that faith in Jesus is the sole way of salvation. Jews, Muslims, and others, he says, may be likely to enter heaven."* The Reformed Church, an American denomination of 200,000 members, was shocked.

But the controversy illuminates a far broader division.

Emerging among Christians is a debate over how to regard other faiths. Over the centuries, church teaching on salvation has been varied in nuance, but at their core is the conviction that only through Christ has God made salvation possible. In an often-cited biblical verse, John 14:6, Jesus declares, "I am the way, the truth, and the life. No one comes to the Father but through me," the essential teaching of the Christian faith. Mr. Rehm's critics say what is at stake in western Michigan is this teaching. "Theological pluralism like Mr. Rehm's," says Rosemary Keller, academic dean and professor of church history at Union Theological Seminary in New York, "is very much the effect of our global village." His view of salvation, which is similar to her own, she says, is gaining ground worldwide.

The *New York Times* is reporting that more and more Christians worldwide believe that Jesus is not the only way to heaven!

USA Today (August 23, 1996) featured a 15-page section about a fourth presidential candidate in the 1996 elections, a Ph.D. in Particle Physics from MIT. Here's what he wants to do for the farmers. "For the farmers to really be effective," he says, ". . . it's necessary for the individual farmer and society as a whole to develop consciousness and gain more support of natural law." When he says natural law he means that you get in touch with your true feelings in the universe — that's New Age teaching. The article states:

> The Natural Law Party therefore recommends educational programs to develop the consciousness of the farmer and thereby reduce stress, improve the farmer's health and well-being, and promote the skills to meet new management challenges. Such programs will enable farmers to spontaneously make better decisions and better use of the environment, and will bring them greater support of natural law in all their activities. Similarly, the reduction of stress in the collective consciousness of society, combined with the Natural Law Party's focus on education will influence consumer choice.

In the same article, the Natural Law Party also has some ideas for defense:

The end of the Cold War has come. We are now on the verge of a new era of global peace and harmony. Fundamental to the success of all these initiatives is the continued lessening of Cold War-era tensions throughout the world, and to quickly alleviate remaining global and regional tensions, the Natural Law Party would support the establishment of groups who practice transcendental meditation and TM city programs in key areas of the world. These programs have been uniquely effective in dissolving social stress and by preventing the outbreak of armed hostility and war.

If something breaks out in the Middle East, they don't want to send tanks; they want to send guys with TM to go over and do a little meditation.

In 2 Peter 3:3-4 it says, "Knowing this first, that there shall come in the last days scoffers, walking after their own lusts, and saying, 'Where is the promise of his coming? For since the fathers fell asleep, all things continue as they were from the beginning of the creation.' " In the latter days people will begin to scoff about the doctrine of the Second Coming.

Second Thessalonians 2:3-4 says, "Let no man deceive you by any means; for that day shall not come, except there come the falling away first [the apostasy], and that man of sin be revealed [the Antichrist], the son of perdition who opposes and exalts himself above all that is called God, or that is worshiped, so that he, as God, sitteth in the temple, showing himself that he is God." That's also touched on in Revelation 13:8: "All that dwell upon the earth shall worship him." The reference here is to the coming Antichrist or fake messiah. In seminary, I reasoned that would be a difficult task — all the world!? I knew we had skeptics in this country. I knew we had professors at Harvard who didn't believe in God at all. I knew there were many in Russia and China who didn't believe in God. I knew we had all those into Buddhism and Hinduism. But the Bible is saying that some day a man is going to show up and the whole world is going to worship him? It was hard for me to believe that could happen.

But today, Mormons and Jehovah's Witnesses are listening to spirits. The presidential nominee for this fourth party, the Natural Law Party, is saying, "Tune into your inner being and listen to the voice inside." You've got people now in China in Buddhism and Hinduism, who are having out-of-body experiences and the ascended masters are talking to them. People in Russia are listening to spirits. If you knew about all the things going on in the U.S. military it would blow your mind.

They might all put different titles on what they're talking about, and who they're talking to, but they're dealing with spirits from the dark side — Satan's side. Remember Rajneesh up in Oregon? Pat Matrisciana, who's a fearless filmmaker, went into that little pagoda up there and filmed Rajneesh coming in and sitting down in a chair. Immediately the 10,000 people in the temple went into out-of-body experiences. They all attributed it to the god-man Rajneesh. The spirits were giving them a mind-trip, an out-of-body experience, and making them think this was God.

One of my friends, Tal Brooke, was on an LSD drug trip and he contacted a spirit. The spirit sent him to India. He came in contact with Sai Baba. The first thing Sai Baba did was say, "Here," and Sai Baba gave him food and a ruby. He also watched when Sai Baba gave a diamond to the president of India. Brooke has watched millions of Indians have out-of-body experiences at these meetings. The Indians believe it is because Sai Baba has special powers, but the Bible says it is because he communicates with spirits. I think some day Sai Baba is going to come to America. Do you think that our university students and our high school students will fall for him? If Sai Baba came up to the college crowd and asked, "Would you believe me?" and one guy said, "No; I don't believe in you," Sai Baba would say, "I'll give you this diamond if you'll believe in me." Do you think that our kids would fall for that? The pragmatic American kids? "If you can do it, I'll believe in it."

The Bible says some day a man will come up quickly on

the world scene, make peace, and the whole world will follow and worship him. He will eventually go into a rebuilt Jewish temple saying, "I am God," and insist that the world worship him as God. The Bible says he's going to do great miracles and false wonders.

Thirty years ago, this seemed improbable. The first time I did a television program on the New Age, I thought, *This is weird; I don't know why I'm doing this program.* Today New Age thinking is accepted. Some years ago Shirley MacLaine made a highly publicized proclamation from the top of a mountain. She said, "I am God," at the top of her lungs. That was the beginning, and now people are getting used to hearing that phrase. The Bible says there is going to be a man who is going to say the same thing, but this time the world is going to believe him. The problem is that the Bible says all that follow him may experience temporary relief from the world's problems, but ultimately will go to hell forever. Not a smart choice.

We are living in a time period where the same expressions used in the biblical outline of the days preceding the second coming of Jesus are part of our vocabulary. We can also understand it. We even have people who are already practicing it. The evidence is all around us. And remember, these are things that are prophesied to happen during the middle of the Tribulation years, over three years *after* Jesus comes silently for His Church!

How close is the Rapture? Any moment. Are you ready?

For more information on John Ankerberg call or write:
The John Ankerberg Show
P.O. Box 8977
Chattanooga, TN 37414-0977
(423) 892-7722

[1]Bernie S. Siegel, *Love, Medicine, and Miracles* (New York, NY: Perennial Library, Harper Collins, 1990).
[2]James Patterson and Peter Kim, *The Day America Told the Truth* (New York, NY: Prentice Hall Press, 1991).

4

Prophetic Thunder

Chuck Missler

Often a presentation like this is titled "The Signs of the Times," but by the time we're through, I think you'll discover it may even be more appropriate to call it "The Times of the Signs." To lay a foundation, keep in mind that these 66 books that we glibly call the Bible were penned by 40 different authors over thousands of years, and yet we discover that this is an integrated message from outside our time domain. That's really a rather preposterous idea. And yet it's the idea that underlies our whole understanding of prophecy.

Time as a Dimension

Let's look at a misconception that most of us grew up with. Most of us assume that this dimension that we call time is linear and absolute. When we were in school, the teacher would draw a time line across the blackboard. There would be a point that would be the beginning of something — the founding of a nation or the birth of a person — and on the right of the line there would be the end of that nation or that life.

From that experience, when we encounter the concept of eternity most of us jump to the impression that what we're talking about is a line that starts at infinity on the left and continues to infinity on the right. We visualize eternity as simply having lots of time. That turns out to be a misconception, because you and I should take advantage of the discoveries of modern physics in which we've now discovered that time itself is a physical property, that you and I exist in more than three dimensions. Thanks to Dr. Einstein, we've got the fourth dimension, the dimension of time. Particle physicists today have discovered that we live in at least 10 dimensions and that time itself is a physical property.

I am emphasizing this because time itself changes, or varies, with mass, acceleration, or gravity. To give you some examples of that: If I had an atomic clock and I raised it one meter, it would speed up by one part in 10 to the 16th. If I raise it 100 meters, it would speed up by one part in 10 to the 14th. That's not the fault of the clock; time itself changes due to mass, acceleration, and gravity. Another example: In 1971 the United States Naval Observatory put an atomic clock on an airplane around the world eastward and it lost .06 microseconds compared to one at rest at the observatory. They put one on an airplane going around the world westward and it gained .27 microseconds. Not a lot, but exactly what Einstein's theory of relativity predicted: time changed by mass, acceleration, or gravity.

The other example you often encounter if you study this in particle physics is the hypothetical example of two astronauts. They are both born at the same instant. We're going to send one to the nearest star, Alpha Centauri. We'll send him there and back. If we apply a 4X transformation here, it turns out that Alpha Centauri is four and a half light years away. If we send him there at half the speed of light, it will take him nine years to get there and nine years to return. When he returns, he will be two years and nine months younger than his twin brother. Time, for him, has changed. Time changes with mass, acceleration, or gravity. We can apply these same equations if he went at 99 percent of the speed of light, he would arrive there in four and a half years. But during that time, 318 years would expire on the earth. Time is a variable.

Is God subject to gravity? Hardly. God is not someone who has lots of time. He is someone who is outside the dimension of time altogether. That's what Isaiah meant when he said that "he is the one that inhabiteth eternity." That's also the mechanism that God uses to authenticate His message to us. Since God has the ability to create us in the first place, does He have the ability to get a message to us? Of course. The challenge is, how does He authenticate His message? How does He let us know that this message is really from Him and not a contrivance or a fraud? Isaiah declares this in saying "the end from the beginning and from ancient times the things that are not yet done." In other words, He authenticates His message by proving that its origin is from outside time. He does that by writing history in advance so that we might know that it's really from Him. The whole idea that God has given us, in advance, the things that happen through history is what we call "prophecy." Yet it's a demonstration, a tangible demonstration, that He really is who He said He is.

I'm going to highlight some of the main themes that you will discover in the Bible if you are a diligent student of God's Word. These are all themes that have to do with "end-time" events where God is going to finalize His dealings with mankind.

Babylon

The first theme is Babylon. This has been a big controversy among Bible scholars for centuries. Most of us who have studied the city of Babylon know that it has its origins in the Book of Genesis. It ultimately rose to power and then fell to the Persians in 539 B.C. It's unfortunate that many of your biblical helps will confuse the fall of Babylon with the destruction of Babylon. In Isaiah 13 and 14 and also in Jeremiah 50 and 51 you find these often confusing prophecies that detail the *destruction* of Babylon. Many very good Bible sources teach that it happened in 539 B.C. But that causes a problem. If you take the Bible seriously, reading Isaiah 13 and 14 and Jeremiah 50 and 51 together at one sitting, you'll discover that Babylon is destroyed like Sodom and Gomorrah. Genesis 19 tells us that Sodom and Gomorrah were destroyed by fire from the sky. It also details in those passages that after that destruction, Babylon will never again be re-inhabited. In fact, Jeremiah emphasizes that the building materials won't even be reused.

So this led to a controversy among Bible scholars, some arguing that those prophecies need to be allegorized, that it already was fulfilled in 539 B.C. Others say, no, if you take it strictly as written, it has not happened yet. That leads to a theory that Babylon, the ancient city literally on the banks of the Euphrates, the pride of the Chaldeans, as Jeremiah calls it, is to re-emerge on the planet Earth as a major world center. Not many people, even today, among Bible teachers, hold that view.

On the other hand, many Bible scholars lean the other way. Part of the reason they do is because when you get to the Book of Revelation, chapters 17 and 18, you encounter this strange thing called Mystery Babylon. Most of you will have no trouble encountering materials which highlight the allegorical implications of the term "Mystery Babylon" as referring to Rome, Italy, and even specifically to the Vatican. Alexander Hislop has a classic work called *The Two Babylons*, which details that view. Also, a book that I consider a must-read for any serious Christian studying Bible prophecy is Dave Hunt's book titled *A Woman Rides the Beast*. He does an outstanding job at reconciling the passages in the Book of Revelation and the past and current activities of the Vatican.

The alternative view is whether Babylon will emerge literally on the banks of the Euphrates and both views are widely debated. I believe these two views can be reconciled from Zechariah 5:5-11. Here Zechariah encounters a vision of a woman who is called "wickedness" and is put into an ephah (a large commercial measure) and sealed with a lead weight. Two women with a stork carry this ephah to the plain of Shinar. This occurs seven times in the Old Testament, always referring to Babylon. I believe that woman is the same woman as in Revelation 17 and 18, and I believe that it implies a return — Babylon being returned to its origin to receive her judgment.

Saddam Hussein has spent 25 years and more than $1

billion rebuilding the ancient city of Babylon. He rebuilt the palace of Nebuchadnezzar and used it for affairs of state as early as 1987. He has minted coins that have Nebuchadnezzar and himself stamped on them, trying to position himself as Nebuchadnezzar the Fifth, the only one of that ethnic background that ever conquered Israel.

The reconstruction of the city of Babylon includes many of the old temples, and even a guest house. The Euphrates has moved a little bit since those days, but Hussein has hired the best archaeologists available to confirm the foundations of Nebuchadnezzar's palace. This means it includes the very room that had that famous handwriting on the wall from Daniel 5.

The newly constructed Babylon was not a military target during the Persian Gulf War. CNN's coverage centered on Baghdad. But if you look at the military intelligence charts of Desert Storm you'll notice that 62 miles to the southeast along the Euphrates River are numerous large buildings. They were not military targets.

Now what's New Babylon's destiny? Are they just a few ceremonial buildings? There is no real evidence that this is going to be anything more than a tourist oddity. But if we understand our Bible, I believe that Babylon will reemerge as a major power center on the planet Earth in order to fulfill the prophecies of Jeremiah and Isaiah.

Israel

You can't talk prophecy and signs of the Bible without talking about Israel — national Israel. Israel's pre-written history is well-documented in many, many books. One of the interesting books in which to study the history of Israel is Benjamin Netanyahu's book, *A Place Among the Nations*. It was written in 1993, by the one who is now prime minister of the state of Israel.

When we study the history of what we refer to sometimes as the "Holy Land," we want to be sensitive to distinguish between the history of Israel and the history of the church. The nation Israel has 73 references in the New Testament. But Paul spends three chapters in his definitive statement of Christianity that we call the Book of Romans, chapters 9, 10, and 11, hammering away at the fact that God has a prophetic destiny for Israel. Revelation 6 through 19 details the interesting events that occur during a period of time called the seventieth week of Daniel.

It's easy to accept the fact that the people of Israel have been re-gathered in their homeland exactly as was prophesied in the Book of Ezekiel and other passages. In fact, Isaiah 11:11 points out that God says, "When I regather them the second time, they'll never again be uprooted." The first re-gathering was after the Babylonian captivity, the second re-gathering started in the late 19th century and was climaxed by the formation of the state of Israel in 1948.

Another issue is that Israel has regained the Old City of Jerusalem. In Zechariah 12:2-3, God, through Zechariah, makes an interesting statement: "Behold, I will make Jerusalem a cup of trembling unto all the people round about." He continues in the next verse, "And in that day, I will make Jerusalem a burdensome stone for all people. All that burden themselves with it shall be torn in pieces though all the people of the earth be gathered together against it." On the one hand, that passage is specifically referring to a military engagement in the future. It also deals with the struggle of Jerusalem. The phrase that Zechariah uses is "a cup of trembling to all nations of the earth." Frankly, that's ridiculous.

This city has no natural resources, no harbor, no river, no reason to be significant except, of course, for religious reasons . . . and to whom? A very small minority of Jewish people. Not all of them, a very small minority. It wasn't significant to Islam for the 1,000 years they controlled it until they discovered it was important to the Jews. Then it became very important to Islam.

It's interesting to discover that the late lights are burning in every major capitol of every nation on the planet Earth. The staff people are struggling to figure out what position to take with respect to the issues concerning Jerusalem. So already, we begin to see the positioning of this prophecy.

This leads to another comment, of course. The fallacy of the so-called "peace process" that fills our media. The primary tragedy of that peace process is that it's built on a false premise. It's based on the premise that you can appease the Muslim interests by reducing the borders of Israel. But in reality, the mandates, speeches, and overt declarations by the leadership of the Muslim community has made it clear that they will not rest until Jerusalem is driven into the sea. All other issues are but milestones to that end. So our present predicament of planet Earth is that we have allowed the Muslim expectations to be raised to a point that can never be resolved.

From the private briefings I've had at NATO's headquarters in Brussels and elsewhere, I know that the expectation is virtually a certainty that there will be a confrontation in the Middle East — and this time with nuclear weapons. In NATO's terms, "it's not 'if,' but 'when.' " Next time there is a major conflict in the Middle East, realize that both sides will be in possession of nuclear weapons. The tragedy of the so-called peace process is that it has moved us closer to a war.

The Rebuilding of the Jewish Temple

But as we explore Israel and Jerusalem and we start looking for some major milestones, we cannot miss the issue of rebuilding the temple. How do we know the temple is going to be rebuilt? Because Jesus, Paul, and John all make reference to it, Jesus in Matthew 24:15, Paul in 2 Thessalonians 2:4 and following, and John in Revelation 11:1-2. The rebuilding of the temple is something that, for the last 1,900 years, people have been watching for as a prophetic sign.

The preparations to rebuild that temple have already begun. There are currently 200 young Levites in training in Israel. Israeli scientists are researching sacrificial issues in earnest. They are searching the world for the right marine snails to yield the levitical blue and the royal purple. They have ground-penetrating radar and thermographic fly-bys over the Temple Mount to try to locate the exact spot the last temple was built. There is only one spot the temple can be built — where Abraham offered Isaac.

Unfortunately, they have to do all this indirectly. Israel captured the Temple Mount area during the Six Day War. But Moshe Dyan, ten days later, handed the administration of the Temple Mount to the high Muslim council of Jordan as his land-for-peace gesture. So Muslims now control the Temple Mount. They will not let archaeology occur and when something is discovered, they try to cement it over. It's an unfortunate situation. The issue over the tunnel extension is not one of safety or structural support, it's archaeological.

An interesting alternative of where the new Jewish temple could be built is currently being researched. The traditional view is that the temple previously stood where the Muslim Temple (the Dome of the Rock) now stands. But recent scientific evidence seems to support Tuvia Sagiv's theory that the Jewish temple originally stood to the south of the Dome of the Rock by about 100 meters. He backs up his theory with infrared photos and seemingly indisputable archaeological facts. This has biblical scholars buzzing over the possibility that the new Jewish temple could actually be built without moving the Muslim Dome of the Rock. In other words, construction could begin immediately, under the right circumstances. There are hundreds of conjectures as to how the political circumstance will allow them to rebuild.

The Israel Temple Institute is very busily building the implements to be used in the new temple, regardless of where it's to be built. Sixty-three of the 103 necessary implements have already been built. When you visit Jerusalem on any responsible tour of the Holy Land, you'll get a chance to see those implements that are completed, like the headdress of the high priest, the breastplate, and so forth. It's very exciting to watch preparations underway to revert back to the sacrificing of animals in a rebuilt Jewish temple.

The Future Russian Invasion of Israel

There's another major milestone that I personally believe is right on the horizon. That's the invasion described in Ezekiel 38 and 39 by Magog and his allies into Israel. I hold the view that Ezekiel 38 and 39 could happen at any time. The more you know about the passage and the more you're up-to-date on the current intelligence picture in the Middle East, the more it would seem that it could happen, literally, at any time.

When you first read these passages it's apparent you must identify Magog. In fact, many people wonder why the Bible even deals with all those strange names, especially early in the Book of Genesis. The reason is because you and I force it to. We keep changing the names of cities and countries. The Bible generally deals with peoples by names of their ancestors. In Genesis 10, we have the descendants of Noah and his three sons, Ham, Shem, and Japheth. One of the sons of Japheth was Magog and his descendants, fortunately, are well-identified. In Ezekiel 38, it speaks of them, as the Bible usually does, by their ancient tribal names. So one of the things that we do need to pin down is who, really, is Magog.

Fortunately, a contemporary of Ezekiel, a guy by the name of Hesiod, a Greek didactic poet in the eighth century, identifies the descendants of Magog as the Scythians. Heroditus, in the fifth century, wrote a great deal about the history of the Scythians. The Greeks were very interested in them for many good reasons. They terrorized the southern reaches of Russia from the Ukraine all the way to the Great Wall of China from the 10th through the 3rd century B.C. In my book, *The Magog Invasion*, I have more than 405 footnotes nailing down the fact that the area we now call Russia is referred to as "Magog" in the Bible. There really isn't room for debate on this any more. Ancient writers even refer to the Great Wall of China as the ramparts of Gog and Magog. We also have the benefit of recent discoveries by the Soviet archaeologists, who have a great interest, of course, in their ancestry. They've found bodies, tombs, and things frozen in Siberia linking them to Magog. Since they're still frozen, there is an enormous amount of information they can gain from the research.

Nuclear Warfare

Ezekiel 38 and 39 are passages well-known to Bible students for two reasons. First, because it is the occasion in which God himself intervenes to quell this ill-fated invasion by

Magog and its allies. The passage is also well-known by many because it appears to anticipate the use of nuclear weapons. As a student of military history and also as a student of the Bible, I've obviously taken a great interest in biblical battles. And in all the biblical battles, nowhere does the Holy Spirit generally bother to deal with anything other than the conclusion of the battle — then the narrative moves on. In only one case does the Holy Spirit bother to spend any time on the cleanup of the battlefield after the engagement. In this case, He spends virtually all of chapter 39. Since there is nothing trivial in the Scripture, He had a purpose in doing so. We discover that cleanup of the leftover weapons provides all the required fuel for the nation Israel for seven years. That's kind of interesting. The ancient commentators felt that must have been symbolic — what on earth could burn for seven years? We smile at that today because we know nuclear weapons can indeed burn for seven years.

We also find that Israel hires professionals. In the King James idiom, "they sever out men of continual employment" to clean up the battle, and whatever they find, they bury east of the Dead Sea. That means they must bury it "downwind." In fact, in chapter 39, verse 15, Ezekiel points out that a traveler who finds a bone that the professionals have missed doesn't dare touch it. Instead he marks the location and lets the professionals come and deal with it. This is very contemporary language for all of you who have been briefed on nuclear biological chemical warfare procedures. We also find contemporary language in Ezekiel although he wrote it 2,550 years ago.

Before I leave the subject of seven years, as you probably know, there are more than 10,000 nuclear warheads that are not accountable in the former Soviet inventories. Many of these are finding their way to the black market and are on their way to the Middle East. Now, if you're Saddam Hussein, Assad, or Khadafi and you purchase one of these nuclear weapons, you inherit a problem, because a nuclear weapon has a limited shelf-life. That shocks many people because it means you either use it or lose it.

The natural question is, what is the shelf-life of a production Soviet warhead? We're dealing here with an implosion-type device in which you shape charges to compress the core materials into something a little larger than a grapefruit. It turns out that the impurities of the materials control one of the major factors in determining the shelf-life. It has now been published that the shelf-life of a production Soviet warhead is seven years. They reprocess them on a six-year turnover. I thought that was kind of interesting. Of course it doesn't surprise us that Ezekiel figured that out.

From the passage, we know that the leader of Magog is one called in the Scripture "Gog." The Russian leaders are always changing so it's hard to get a clear picture for very long. But it's safe to say that there are several men who have the potential of being "Gog." Even those who watch the Kremlin with great expertise are kept guessing as to who has control of the nuclear button. In NATO, they admit they have no idea what the procedures are to prevent a nuclear accident, or worse, some kind of opportunism by a johnny-come-lately.

Many potential leaders of Russia believe dictators are good, and point to Peter the Great and Stalin as men who really made Russia strong. They believe they should go back to a strong nationalistic Russia. If something on that order comes about, only three religions will be acceptable in Russia: Eastern Orthodox, the Russian Orthodox church; Islam; and Buddhism. True Christianity is out of the question and the evangelical door will close immediately.

Russia's Strategic Dilemma

Russia has an economy that is heavily dependent on the external export of raw materials and arms. They have a military five times the size of the United States. To re-emerge as a world power they must build a new power base. But if they look west, they see a German-dominated European Union, their traditional enemies. If they look east, they find China and Japan getting together. China, growing as it is as a major military power, is also their inevitable adversary. Russia has an undefendable land border between them, and China's most powerful strategic weapon is the 5 million per year surplus population that's crossing that border. Russia has no viable way to deal with this. There's a tension building there. Consequently, from Russia's point of view, they have only one option available to them, and that's to the south. The intelligence analysts for many years have been predicting this and, indeed, it is happening. They are embracing radical Muslim nations.

The United States Senate approved the Strategic Arms Reduction Treaty, part 2 (the START II Agreement). What that did, knowingly, deliberately, is hand over to Moscow the world nuclear supremacy. It also reduced the United States targets by a factor of 2:1 that they would have to hit in a first strike. And Yeltsin has announced that their strategy is a first-strike strategy. Most observers have always believed that they had a first-strike strategy, but they have always denied it.

Realize that START II deals only with land-based missiles and it doesn't count the missiles in the Ukraine. So while we are reducing our military commitments, especially in the strategic area, Russia is currently producing 75 new strategic missiles, 8 new strategic submarines, and 20 new strategic bombers, including a new Stealth bomber. But the press keeps reporting that they are broke.

Russia seems to be aggressively preparing for nuclear war. They have extended the private subway under Moscow another 25 kilometers. They're in the process of finishing a major command post that we know from our reconnaissance satellites to be about the size of the Washington Beltway. We have no idea what's really going on in Russia because they've stonewalled us. To make matters worse, the United States government has recently released $10.2 billion in Russian aid. Guess where they're spending it!

Their obsolete strategic missiles are being retired and they are being replaced by new, modern, solid-state, three-stage, triple M types. While we're filling our silos with concrete under the supervision of the Minister of Defense of Russia, they are *modernizing* 90 of their 176 silos! And, they are continuing to rehearse nuclear hits on the United States with their subs and their weapons. They are also continuing training procedures, the last one having been held recently.

But as you research these things, one thing that you might overlook is the submarine picture. Remember, the START II Agreement deals only with land-based missiles. Let's take a look at the submarine picture. The primary deterrent of the United States is the Ohio Class Trident Ballistic Missile Submarine. The counterpart for Russia is the Typhoon Submarine. The Trident is 560 feet long, displaces 18,700 tons. The Typhoon is only 1 foot longer, but it displaces 25,500 tons and the clue to that is that there's only a 42-foot beam on the Trident. The Typhoon has double titanium hulls; it's designed for combat and survivability, and has a 78-foot beam. It also has closed-circuit television. It's been designed to break through the Arctic, fire its missiles, and then dive back down under the ice. The Russians simply have a much more rugged vessel than we do.

The Typhoon is larger than the largest British cruiser of World War II, just to give you a perspective of it. Admiral Jeremy Borda, Chief of Naval Operations, testified to Congress first of all the shocking discovery that the new Russian submarines are now silent. For many decades, we've faced a relatively noisy adversary. Our entire naval investment in anti-submarine warfare is into passive sonar, because we've had a fairly noisy adversary. Russia, on the other hand, had the opposite problem; they've faced a fairly silent adversary. Now they have redesigned their submarines to be more quiet than ours. Admiral Hyman Rickover made the statement to Congress that "making our Navy silent is a bigger and more critical strategic problem than making it nuclear." So the fact that the Russian submarines are silent is very significant.

Also, the Typhoon class that we've talked about is not their latest. Their next generation is even more advanced using both standard torpedo tubes with about 30 weapons on board, but also adding eight vertical tubes for cruise missiles. They have advanced satellite capabilities. We now know that they have technology that allows them to track our Trident submarines in real time. In less than just a few minutes, they can pin them down to a 50-foot accuracy wherever they are. That comes by some very advanced laser satellite technology that is now operational with the Russians.

Admiral Borda made this assessment to the United States Congress. Then a strange thing happened: A few weeks later, he committed suicide. There seems to be a lot of suicides in our national picture lately.

Something else that you might find indicative of Russian capabilities is their new small torpedo. It's a 200-knot underwater torpedo, or actually an underwater missile. It moves by some kind of technology that we don't fully understand yet. It's been theorized that it involves super-cavitating bubbles from a double skin with perforations enabling them to enshroud themselves with super-cavitated bubbles breaking down the hydrogen barriers. But, however it works, the incredible torpedo is operational today. It has a nuclear warhead, it's fired from their standard torpedo tubes, and we have no countermeasures available. And if that isn't enough, we know there is a 300-knot version under development. Imagine yourself being a submarine commander and trying to evade a 200-knot, heat-seeking, nuclear torpedo. That's a little scary.

Magog's Allies

The lead ally in Ezekiel 38 is Persia. In 1932, Persia changed its name to Iran. It's the strong man of the Middle East. Rafsanjani has purchased at least seven of the nuclear warheads on the black market. I had the privilege of having dinner with the guy who checked the bank accounts in Luxembourg that were used in the transaction. But Rafsanjani doesn't solely have to lean on those nuclear warheads. He has spent more than $14 *billion* on his air force alone. You may recall that 115 combat aircraft fled Iraq during the Persian Gulf War. Today they are still in Iran. Rafsanjani has purchased spare parts for them as well as another 110 of the most advanced Soviet aircraft available.

Here's something most people don't know, but it's common knowledge within the intelligence community: Rafsanjani has signed a military assistance treaty with Russia. Yeltsin has committed to back him in his military intrigues. That's right out of Ezekiel 38:5. Russia is currently installing nuclear plants in Iran, several of them, despite the United States protestations. The CIA tells me there are over 7,000 former Soviet engineers and scientists developing Iran's nuclear capability. They're now even practicing full-scale strategic military training maneuvers. They're involving over 150,000 ground troops. The code name for it, in Arabic, means "the Road to Jerusalem." You see, their goals are in no way masked.

This leads us, then, to something else that you really need to understand if you're going to understand the Middle East. That is Rafsanjani, what he calls his "grand design." His dream is to unite the Muslims from the 200 million in Indonesia all the way to Senegal, Muritania, and Africa. You're talking an Islamic crescent with more than 1.2 billion followers who are not only anti-Israel, they are anti-Christian and anti-West.

The rise of Islam is the biggest challenge to the West, and Christianity in particular, in the world today. This is another one of these places that you don't want to be hoodwinked by the pabulum served up in the mainstream media. Most people have no concept of what Islam is really all about. They have no idea of the origins of Islam. For instance, do you realize that Islam did not begin with Mohammed? When Abraham was called out of Ur of the Chaldees up in pre-Islamic Asia, Arabia, they worshipped the moon god, Al-ila. The worship of Al-ila involved 360 idols. What Mohammed did, when he came along, is make it monotheistic.

By the way, don't confuse the word "allah" in Arabic with the name for God. The allah of the Koran bears little resemblance to the God of the Old Testament. Many people think they are labels for the same thing. No. Allah is clearly presented in the Koran as arbitrary, fanciful, capricious. Read that "untrustworthy." The God of the Old Testament is One who makes and keeps His promises. The more you understand both, the more you realize that they are opposites. Not to mention the fact that Islam has a cultic origin and is openly hostile to the West.

Islam divides the universe into two parts: the domain of the faithful, and those with whom they are at war with until Judgment Day. They have, thus, an irrevocable commitment to conquer the West. Now that they have nuclear weapons as well as the oil revenues, their agenda can no longer be ignored, or it's ignored at our own peril.

That leads to a corollary topic called terrorism. Iran funds 30 schools in the Sudan that are training professionals to operate in the United States and Europe. More than 13 Muslim groups are out to prove that the PLO doesn't speak for them. They are funded by Syria, and most heavily, Iran.

The rise of terrorism in the United States is expected to increase. Watch for it. Avi Lipkin is an officer with the Israeli Defense Force (IDF) and works with the Institute for Western Defense in Jerusalem, the think tank for the IDF. More than a year ago he began traveling around the United States trying to convince anyone who would listen that there are surface-to-air missiles missing from inventories. The IDF information is that some of those missing missiles are here in the United States, controlled by terrorists. He claims their strategy is to bring down 747's on takeoff. There was an incident in New York that we're all very familiar with: TWA Flight 800 to Paris. It's been widely reported in the European press that more than 100 witnesses in boats and on the nearby shoreline, confirm that they saw Flight 800 get hit with a missile. What many Americans also don't know is that there was another flight scheduled to leave in the 8:00 p.m. time slot, but was on gate hold for 30 minutes due to a late-arriving passenger. The implication would seem that they may have hit the wrong plane. The flight that was held up was a TWA flight, fully loaded with 435 people, headed non-stop to Tel Aviv, Israel. Flight 800 to Paris was only half full.

Is that what happened? Let's hope not. But, whether true or not, it should not surprise us to see a rise of terrorism in the United States.

Russia's Allies in the Invasion

Turkey has spent 70 years abandoning their alphabet,

their religion, their entire culture to be a member of Western Europe. They finally discovered, after an agonizing time trying to develop a relationship with the new European Union, that the entry door is closed. So they are shifting back to the only option available: the Muslim world. In Turkey's last election they elected, for the first time in more than 70 years, a Muslim in charge as president.

Cush settled south of the second cataract of the Nile and is idiomatic for black Africa. That's why it's translated to Ethiopia in English bibles. "Put" in Hebrew refers to the people of North Africa, a different ethnic group altogether. Because they settled west of Egypt, that's typically labeled Libya in English Bibles.

But what's most interesting about the list in Ezekiel 38:5 are the allies that are *not* mentioned: Egypt and Saudi Arabia. Saudi Arabia does show up later, but they're on the sidelines, very nervous. And if you understand Saudi Arabia's fear of Iran, you can understand that. Rafsanjani has as his strategy the invasion, somewhere along the way, of Saudi Arabia, because he needs to gain control of Mecca and Medina to accomplish his grand design.

We have Africa included with Cush and Put, but the biblical term for Egypt is conspicuous in its absence of mention. It's strangely not mentioned, nor is Babylon or the Antichrist. Later, in Daniel 11, Egypt is the instigator of what later becomes the whole Armageddon scenario.

For a number of technical reasons I firmly believe this Russian invasion of Israel described Ezekiel 38 and 39 will happen prior to the 70th week of Daniel. Maybe before the Rapture, maybe after the Rapture, but definitely before the "covenant," or peace treaty, is confirmed which begins the 70th week of Daniel. There is nothing that would forbid Ezekiel 38 and 39 from happening today.

Daniel's Prophecies

Now the Bible generally talks about history through the lens of Israel. But there are two interesting exceptions and I think it will be very illuminating for us to compare them. They are found in Daniel 2 and 7. In Daniel 2, Nebuchadnezzar has his famous dream that Daniel ultimately is called upon to interpret. All the future empires of the world are envisioned in his dream as a poly-metallic image of a man. It had a head of gold, arms and chest of silver, belly and thighs of brass, and legs of iron. And the feet were made up of iron mixed with clay. This image turns out to be an easy-to-understand prophecy of the succeeding empires of the world, from Babylon in the days of Daniel, to Persia, to Greece, and then to Rome.

Babylon was conquered by the Persians, just as Daniel 8 details for us. And Persia was, indeed, conquered by the Greeks, as is also detailed in Daniel's prophecies. The Romans conquered the Greeks. Therefore we have the four empires — Babylon, Persia, Greece, and Rome — perfectly detailed. But who is prophesied to conquer Rome? No one. Instead, Daniel 2 depicts Rome as breaking up into pieces, that in the latter days will come back together to reform a reunited version of that original empire. And that's exactly what happened throughout history. About A.D. 476, Rome broke into pieces. And each of the pieces has made at least one bid for world dominion. The Dutch had their day; Spain had its day under the Spanish Armada; France tried to conquer the world several times; Germany did twice, under Bismarck and Hitler. We see each piece of that original empire have its bid, but never quite get to full dominion as would be suggested by the passages. At some point in the future, the old Roman Empire will again become a world power.

Daniel 2 occurred when Daniel was a very young man and Nebuchadnezzar was a young king. But Daniel 7 occurred late in Daniel's life. He was standing by a river and saw in a vision a series of strange creatures come out of the sea. Even though the idioms in chapters 2 and 7 are quite different, they portray the same sequence of empires. In Daniel 2, a man's dream is being interpreted and we see the empires envisioned as man sees them — bright, shiny metals. In Daniel 7 we see the empires as God sees them, as a series of voracious beasts, but nevertheless representing the same empires.

In Daniel 7 we also get a glimpse of that forth empire. It was described as a beast so terrible he couldn't even draw an analogy to the animal world. Most scholars who have studied these passages recognize the parallelism between Daniel 2 and 7 and the fact that we have this strange second phase of that fourth empire. That's what gives rise to the scholastic term, "the revived Roman Empire."

If you closely examine this future European super-state, the first thing you realize is that in 1993 the signing of the Maastrich Treaty made the Treaty of Rome obsolete. This new treaty provides for a centralized, single European super-state with a common foreign policy, a common military, and a common currency. Europe, as most people know, is struggling as a potential power, but still moving toward these common goals. If anything were to happen that changed the United States from dominating the world, a unified Europe is the logical choice to fill the vacuum. The United States has a population of about 265 million. Europe represents about 400 million. And it's industrialized. It's economic potential is larger than that of the United States by a significant factor if they get their act together.

So we've discussed major prophetic themes like the re-emergence of the city of Babylon, the nation Israel, the struggle for Jerusalem, and the rebuilding of the Jewish temple. We've looked closely at Magog (Russia), and its allies, and its preparation to invade Israel. I've touched on the rise of Islam and the emergence of the European super-state and movement toward a one world global society, both politically, economically, and certainly religiously. Every one of these themes are taking shape before our very eyes. If you're familiar with the 70 weeks prophecy of Daniel, then you know that the clock has been stopped at 69 weeks. When the clock starts again, the incredible Church Age that we live in will be over and the earth has only seven years before the Lord returns to reign as King from Israel for 1,000 years.

We are being plunged into a period of time — that period of time, about which the Bible says more than it says about any other period of time in human history, including the time that Jesus walked the shores of Galilee or climbed the mountains of Judea. The ultimate issue, of course, has nothing to do with Babylon or Europe or Magog. The real issue is, "Is the Bible really true?" and "Was Christ who He said He was?" If so, do you know Him personally? If you don't, or are not sure if you do, you're risking spending eternity in flames and horrible agony.

I have found that there are three things God can't do. First, He can't lie. Second, He can't learn, because He already knows it. That means if He can't learn, He can't be disappointed in you. Think about it. You might be disappointed when next week you fall flat on your face. God's not surprised. He knew it in advance. That's why He had to die. The third thing He can't do is force you to love Him. The staggering gift that you've received is your free will. In order to love Him, He's got to give you the choice not to love Him. That's a frightening gift.

There are also four things that God doesn't know. First, He doesn't know a sin that He doesn't hate. He doesn't know a sinner He doesn't love. He doesn't know an alternate path to His throne — it's only through His Son. And the fourth thing that God doesn't know is a better time to receive His Son than right now. Don't wait a second longer!

For more information on Chuck Missler or to order a free 12 month subscription to his newsletter, call or write:

Chuck Missler
Koinonia House
P.O. Box D
Coeur d'Alene, ID 83814
1-800-546-8731
email (update@khouse.org)
website: www.khouse.org

5

The Incredible Battle for Religious Freedom in America

Alan Sears

It is an incredible battle for religious freedom in America today. The Lord has been giving us some astonishing victories. Victories hard-fought and through much prayer. Some of the victories are almost unbelievable. In fact, if I didn't have personal, firsthand knowledge of these cases, I would find it hard to believe the results. And, of course, we have had some stinging defeats.

I'm going to share some actual court cases that are examples of what's going on in America in the Christian arena. Some will get you excited, some will make you angry. Regardless, they are all true.

As an example, a major university in this country recently discriminated against Christians in a very overt and obvious way. When asked about that discrimination, the official explained, "Christianity, unlike Islam, is not politically correct." Now that's not surprising, but the official went on to say something like this: "Christianity is just not a part of the (American) culture. So when we discriminate against you as Christians, we're justified in doing so because these other groups are part of the (American) culture and you're not. So therefore, we can do anything we want to you." Fortunately, they're not saying that anymore, because the Supreme Court has decided differently. But the view of that institution's representatives towards Christianity says volumes about the current mind set of America.

In this chapter we will look into mandatory taxpayer subsidies for the lifestyle and sexual appetites of those who want to redefine the family. These are attempts to make you, as taxpayers, subsidize their activity on the municipal government level. The homosexual lobby, with the blessings of our government, wants to redefine what the family is so that it includes same-sex partners, multiple partners, etc. We're going to look into the fight by Christian parents to keep their children from biblically outlined abominations, such as the case of a Christian mother who is involved in a very difficult fight to keep her two boys from a man who was once her husband. He has undergone surgery and now calls himself a woman. He lives with two other men who have gone through the same surgery, and he wants his children to move in and address him as Aunt Susan.

We'll look into the state Supreme Court that ordered private groups to include opposing viewpoints in their private activities at their own expense. In other words, if somebody with an opposing viewpoint wanted to come to an event like the Steeling the Mind conference in Vail (an audience who paid to hear certain conservative viewpoints), the court ruled that a person was entitled to stand on the platform and say whatever he or she wanted to say, and the Steeling conference organizers must pay for this alternative view. You, of course, would get the privilege of paying for that speech.

I'm going to tell you about a Christian woman. This lady is an immigrant from the old country in the purest sense. Some of you may be first-generation Americans. This dear lady just understands simple things. She's a little bit of a scholar of the Bible — there are certain things in there that she believes to be right and certain things that she believes to be wrong. She has an apartment she wants to rent, and she's been told by a government agency that she has to permit fornication or sodomy on her own property. We're going to talk about her fight and the threat that she faces ultimately. If we don't win the fight on her behalf, then she will go to jail because, I assure you, this lady will not bow to a court order in any other direction.

We'll include some of the so-called equal access cases, the front-line of evangelism today. They've put the very ability to engage in evangelism in jeopardy. I'll tell you about the nurse who's under threat of losing her job, seniority, and benefits if she will not help her employer hospital engage in second-trimester abortions. That's six months, folks — three months away from delivery — and they're telling this dear lady "Your conscience or your job."

But before we get to these incredible cases, and before we get to some of the extraordinary victories the Lord's been giving us through the efforts of many of the Christian lawyers out there through the work of the Alliance Defense Fund and other groups, you need to understand how some legal principals may conflict with some Christian teaching.

First, Jesus Christ said in John 14:6, "I am the way, the truth, and the life; no one comes to the Father, but through Me."

And then He went on to say in John 14:15, "If you love me, keep my commandments." Is there anything in what He said that was a suggestion? No. Was it a proposal? No. He said, "*If* you love me, you *will* keep my commandments." And, "I am the way." This is an important concept for the things we're going to be examining.

Lawyers always like to title, and have a file for, everything. Matthew 28 is called by many the Great Commission. I call it the "Mission Statement for the Corporation." That was the mission statement of the church of Jesus Christ. And in Matthew 28, what did He tell us? "Go ye therefore and *teach* all nations, baptizing them in the name of the Father and of the Son and of the Holy Spirit, teaching them to observe all things whatsoever I have commanded you." Now again, those words are not compromises. Those are not suggestions. He said,

"Teach them to observe every single thing that I taught you."
And He tells us in Malachi 3:6, "For I, the Lord, do not
change." And in Hebrews 13:8, "Jesus Christ [is] the same
yesterday and today, [yes] and forever."

These verses are very important because with these
words and concepts began the conflict of the ages as well as the
legal concept and the legal conflict of our present age. That
conflict results in what we're calling the Incredible Battle for
Religious Freedom in America.

I speak from a lawyer's viewpoint, and I'm going to
explain this legal battle. Unfortunately, it's an area which most
Christians really don't want any part. Who, in their right mind,
wants to be a party to lawsuits? Or to have everything they own
threatened to be taken away? No. You don't want a part of it.
And most of the people in the cases we'll discuss didn't want
any part of it, either. But if you read John 14, or Matthew 28,
and you trusted it as truth, there may be a conflict ahead in your
life. Even if you didn't want or expect it. And it all goes back
to Christ's command to His followers.

What if you were faced with compromising your beliefs
or losing your property or wife or children? As you will see, it's
not always a simple and easy decision — even though Christ's
commands are non-negotiable.

Let's look at another concept. We believe as Christians
that there are certain things that are right and certain things that
are wrong. This is considered basic doctrine for all Christians.
Most Christians believe that the law, the rules, the program,
what's sin, and what's not sin, does not change. But wait till
you get to the courts. This theology creates a world view that
has major conflicts with other world views. And it conflicts
tremendously with many of the things going on in the legal
system and many of those involved in the world of the law.

You see, there are many judges, lawyers, and people in
public life who write laws who believe that the Constitution
and law is "changing." They believe that it's a living, breathing
thing, and that it will change itself to fit the times.

A perfect example of this was a decision from the Florida

Supreme Court in June of 1995. Consider this summary of the case: "In a 4-3 opinion, the Florida Supreme Court struck down the law that made it a crime for children to have sex with each other." This law had been around for quite a while. Now read what the justice on the Supreme Court of Florida said about that law when they struck it down, because this is a good example of the prevailing world view. "The 1892 law is a painfully shortsighted relic of a bygone era that was willing to punish non-marital sexual acts." The judge was basically saying, "God forbid that there was ever such a view in this country."

It was a 4-3 decision. Even though there were three justices on that court who were somewhat shocked and outraged that this law would be overturned, the world view that's illustrated by the language of that decision is one that's going to affect us a great deal, — not just today, but into the future. What that court (and world view) is telling us, is that with the passage of time, changes should take place in the most basic law. And those changes should take place whether or not the legislature — that's the elected body that is supposed to write laws for the citizens — wants to change it or not! It doesn't matter whether or not the voters, the people, the public, want to change that law or not, either. They will change it for you.

This is considered "forward thinking." I've noticed that striking down the old is always called "moving forward." I wonder where they get that idea. Christians, on the other hand, live by the principle that they should not partake in evil or in wrong things. They believe the law should prohibit wrong and should punish those who do wrong. Furthermore, as I quoted earlier, the mission statement of Jesus Christ's church demands that Christians teach and go into all the world, taking with them both a message and a behavior.

Now the obvious: What happens when both the Christian's message and his or her behavior conflicts with what becomes the law of the land? This is becoming a big problem.

But, before we go any further, what is the "law"? What does that word mean? I always like to use Webster's dictionary as a reference. Webster devotes a fourth of a page of the dictionary to the definition of law. Read carefully a couple of key phrases:

> Law is a binding custom or practice of a community. It is a rule of conduct or action prescribed and formally recognized as binding or enforced by a controlling authority.

So it's a binding entity on all those who live under it, enforced by a controlling authority. I always enjoy reading the alternate word definition, the one that may not be used much anymore, but still is in some dictionaries. "Law" once had this definition:

> The revelation of the will of God as set forth in the Old Testament.

That speaks for itself, but it's probably not the majority view for some of these people we're talking about who decide these cases.

Also key in this discussion are other definitions like "sovereignty" and "law-giver." Does it make a difference how the laws are created, handed down, and voted on by a legislature? Are they created by a bureaucrat, by fiat, or are they rewritten by judges? We must take all these into consideration.

Consider what the dictionary says about the word "lawbreaker." What's a "law-breaker"? "Lawbreaker" is defined by Webster as "one who violates the law." So the question of what is the law is pretty important. Is it *the Law* or the law? It reads the same.

Recently there has been a lot of discussion in public education about "shifting paradigms." There are also some major changes and shifts in the law and what the concept of law is. As it relates to human affairs, the law is capable of doing certain things. Remember our definition? It says that the law is what the community prescribes. There are rules to be followed and you can be punished for breaking them.

The Four "P's"

Traditionally, law does four things in America. I call it the four P's. First of all, the law can **prefer**. It can prefer certain behaviors and activities. This is done by creating certain rewards and incentives. The simple example of a preference of a law is in the tax code. If you do something the lawmakers in Congress want to encourage, like go out and buy a house and get a mortgage, then you get a reward. You get to write off the interest payment. That's a preferred behavior in our society. Traditionally, there were some other behaviors that were preferred behaviors in our society, such as marriage between a man and a woman.

Secondly, the law can simply **protect** something. When you protect something under the law, that means that you don't create any special advantage. You don't give people a special tax break (as you did in the tax code for the house). But you punish people for interfering with it. A simple example are land-use laws. If you wish to stop somebody from interfering with the use of your property, the law will give you a way to do it. It may not prefer your use, but it will protect it. And it allows you to protect what's yours.

Third, the law can **permit**, or allow, certain behaviors and activities. This is when we let things happen, but they're not necessarily approved of. That's the status of the case I addressed earlier regarding Florida and sex between children. If a 17-year-11-month-old boy wants to do something with a 13-year-old girl, the law will permit it. It doesn't prefer it, but it won't punish it anymore.

Fourth, when the law doesn't prefer, protect, or permit something, it can **punish**. Basically, we all know when the law moves in to punish things. It means that they are illegal. It is outlaw behavior. An example of that, the most obvious example, is criminal law: murder. Normally, if you kill somebody without a legal excuse, you face severe consequences.

Now remember, when we talk about the law, we're talking about the four P's — what's preferred, what's protected, what's permitted, and what's punished. Christians, and those who believe in an unchanging God and an unchanging law from God, believe that those things don't change, even over time. Christians simply believe that God's law prefers certain behaviors every day and always will. They believe that God's law prohibits and punishes certain behaviors and always will. I know we have those in every age who want to rewrite the text, but to the average person, the unchangeable remains unchanged. So what God said a long time ago, longer ago than 1892, might be the same in 1992 and in 2092 and in 1492.

Now how does all that compare to man's law? When we talk about the incredible battle for religious freedom in America, we're not just talking about something for Christians, we're talking about people of all faiths, all religions. Let's look at the differences, the unique differences that apply to those who follow an unchangeable God with an unchangeable law.

When things change from being protected to being punished and vice versa, what happens to those people who will not change and will not change their behavior? That brings us to the cases and what we're now going to look at more closely.

It's not uncommon historically for man's law to conflict with God's law. We all remember the story of Daniel and the den of lions. Daniel had determined that he would pray as always, regardless of what the decree by Darius said. Examples like this are numerous in the Bible. But there are some real differences in our present-age legal system.

America is, as you know, a unique nation. And among nations, it once had a legal heritage that lined up with a world view that would be consistent with the faith of most Christians today. And it was a world view that was unchanging. That world view said, "We'll write a Constitution that will have two things to say about religion. First of all, it will say that government can never establish a state church." And that's all that that clause meant. "We'll never collect taxes and set up a state church like the one in England." And the other thing the Constitution said was, "We'll allow free exercise of religion." That's pretty simple English. Free exercise of religion shall not be abridged by the government. And with the world view of those who drafted that document, they didn't see that there was going to be any particularly big problem down the road. If you read the history of what they did for the next 30 years, as they worked in state legislatures, went to their home states and began to write and enforce the laws, and served as judges, it gives us a very clear picture that their world view was consistent with the unchanging world view that we've talked about.

But as we enter this present age, the world view is constantly on the move and is shifting from the favored to the disfavored, from the protected to the punished. Consider these verses in Isaiah 5:20-24:

> Woe to those who call evil good, and good evil;
> Who substitute darkness for light and light for darkness;
> Who substitute bitter for sweet, and sweet for bitter! . . .
> Who justify the wicked for a bribe,
> And take away the rights of the ones who are in the right!
> Therefore, as a tongue of fire consumes stubble,
> And dry grass collapses into the flame,
> So their root will become like rot
> And their blossom blow away as dust;
> **For they have rejected the law of the Lord of hosts,**
> **And despised the word of the Holy One of Israel.**
> (Emphasis added)

Ask yourself, as we review these cases, how these verses apply and what will happen if we don't engage in this battle.

I'll give you one example as I get into this issue and apply the rule. The case is called *Lilly v. City of Minneapolis*. The city of Minneapolis some months ago decided it would re-define marriage. It adopted a city ordinance to allow people who had any kind of a relationship that lasted six months or longer to come in and create the legal equivalent of a marriage. In addition to that, they said that they would subsidize it with taxpayer money because "if you work for the city, we're going to pay all your benefits, your insurance, and so forth, just like you were a traditional married couple." This was potentially very explosive because they were saying that they would subsidize people's sexual appetites with tax dollars.

Some of the people in Minneapolis who had the world view that the rules don't change, protested. But their protest fell on deaf ears. So they decided to bring the issue to light in a court of law. They enlisted the help of a volunteer attorney who was interested in religious freedom issues. They also contacted the group that I'm with, the Alliance Defense Fund, which funded the case. They sued the city of Minneapolis and guess what happened? The homosexuals and other groups that wanted to change the law brought in all their experts and attorneys for a full-blown hearing. But we found a judge who would listen to the rule of law. And, by the grace of God, the judge went through the law, went through the historical tradition, and determined, "Marriage is between one man and one woman." She wrote this, believe it or not, in 1994, in a legal opinion. So she wrote 28 pages, striking the city's ordinance down. It's illegal to re-define marriage and to make the taxpayers pay for that re-definition.

That case was followed by another in Georgia, where they tried the same thing in Atlanta. Portions of the Minnesota ruling that applied were used and they struck down the Atlanta ordinance in the same areas.

The homosexual movement is just one of many legal issues Christians face today. It is, as you know, a very well-organized, well-funded movement. On their legal agenda, they want to change what was prohibited (homosexuality) and punish that which is preferred and protected (heterosexuality). In most areas of the country, people who engage in homosexuality are in what we might call the "in-between stage." Their behavior is allowed or permitted. It's not protected, it's not preferred, but it's allowed.

Accompanying their attempts to change, they also want city, county, state, and federal government to pass "anti-discrimination" laws to allow them to be deemed a "protected class." Such a classification would make those who would do anything contrary to their agenda criminals. They could then call for punishment for those who would oppose the homosexual movement.

For example, what if a person who was a practicing homosexual wanted to work in the Christian school, pastor a church, or to lead a Boy Scout group? What if a Christian didn't want to rent an apartment to a practicing homosexual? Or, what if a young man in a college dorm didn't want to live with two homosexual roommates? All of these people would be lawbreakers and criminals, because by law, they are defined as lawbreakers. What was once punished for 200-plus years of American legal history has now moved to the "permitted" phase and would then move to a "protected" phase.

The homosexuals have had some setbacks in the courts. They've been in several major fights recently and they've lost almost every case, overwhelmingly. As usual, you never hear about their losses. You only hear about those that advance their agenda, when the so-called "progressive agenda" moves forward. The clash with the religious groups is supposed to be a tidal wave you can't stop. But you're not hearing all the news.

Forced association is a big issue. I discussed earlier the immigrant lady who's got a room to rent. She lives on Social Security and wants to improve her income and advertises the room for rent. A couple answers the ad and decides to accept her offer. She questions, "Where are the wedding rings?" They answer, "We don't have wedding rings. We don't believe in them." The little lady then offers a compromise, "Well, could you bring me the paper that says you're married?" They respond, "We'll bring you the paper." Instead, they go to City Hall and file a complaint. The next thing she knows, the little old lady is being hauled into court. She is deemed an outlaw because she has engaged in a violation known as "marital status discrimination." Did you know it is against the law, in many states, to discriminate on the basis of "marital status"?

Many Christians were probably supportive of those laws when they were passed because they were originally written to protect single mothers who wanted to find decent places to live. Whether the government should be in that business or not is another debate. But many people supported those laws, having no idea where the train would go once it got out of the station.

But, because these laws were passed, this woman is an outlaw because she refused to let people engage in what she believes to be a sin of fornication on her private property. The story continues. She gets into more trouble because even though the couple has already found another place to live and she's not going to offer the place for rent anymore, the officials want her to sign a statement declaring that she won't refuse to rent to non-married couples again. Naturally, her views are the same and she declines.

The Alliance Defense Fund funded legal counsel for her. We found a volunteer lawyer to defend her. The same kind of case is going on in Alaska. Christian landlords have won cases in both California and Massachusetts recently. In Massachusetts, of all places, the Supreme Court ruled 7-0 in favor of the Christian landlords who said "We're just not going to allow this sin on our property." So if you do stand and have the resources you can win many of these cases.

You may have read about the Boston parade case with the veterans. It was funded by the Alliance Defense Fund. That case was covered in the media, although they totally missed the main point of the case. The reporters consistently referred to the case as a homosexual agenda case. Technically it was. But that wasn't the big issue. The big issue was "forced association," "forced expression," and all of these other items on this bigger agenda.

The case was about a group of veterans in Boston that organized a St. Patrick's Day Evacuation Day parade each year. Evacuation Day is the day that George Washington's troops drove the British from Boston. The veterans marched every year on Evacuation Day and the parade featured all kinds of pro-family groups, carrying banners that said things like, "Jesus Christ: the Way, the Truth, and the Life." To counter this, a homosexual group was formed specifically to harass them. The gay/lesbian/bisexual whatever-they-are of Boston came in and said, "We want to march in your parade." The veterans said, "No. You're not going to march in our parade. We've worked very hard. We raise $35,000 every year by the sweat of our brow, going door-to-door, selling programs, raising nickels, dimes, and quarters to put on this parade for family values and patriotism. We're not going to let you in our parade."

The homosexual groups weren't satisfied. They said "We're going to march in your parade and we're going to put our signs up." They went to court. The government backed the homosexuals. It said this was illegal discrimination. All the lower courts agreed. Every single court. Even the Massachusetts Supreme Court said this was illegal. They ruled that the veterans had to let the homosexuals into their parade, pay all the costs, and let them show their signs.

All this infuriated a 65-year-old lawyer in Boston by the name of Chester Darling. He believes that it's just wrong. And he takes this case on pro bono, which means for no fees. He cashes in his IRAs and his own future to finance this litigation. He came to the Alliance Defense Fund and we were able to get funding to him when he needed it.

We also helped to train him. We sent him to Washington before he went to court to meet with and get advice from some of the best lawyers in the country. With the law and history solidly on his side, he won the case 9-0. The Supreme Court of the United States ruled that the government cannot force association and expression on other people in their private affairs. That's a big principle, and a great victory for Christian rights.

That precedent also was applied to the National Day of Prayer. An atheist group wanted to come in to the city park where the National Day of Prayer people were standing on their podium and use their platform. This ruling on the right of who we choose to associate with has sent a thunderclap across the country for righteousness and stopping part of the homosexual agenda.

On the University of Virginia campus in Charlottesville there is a beautiful statue of Thomas Jefferson, who was a secularist. He had a different view of Christ than most Christians today, and nobody on earth knows his eternal fate. But Jefferson understood the critical importance of religious freedom in this country. From a secular viewpoint, he probably understood more about the importance of religious freedom than most Christians in America today. He realized that without this basic freedom there was no way that this country could continue as the founders had devised it to be. He founded the University of Virginia and understood that the university had to have a sacred place for religion.

Jefferson said that the Bible is a good book and that every student should study it. He also felt that it should be part of the mandatory curriculum in the state university. That shocks people when you tell them that because they like to talk about Jefferson's comments on the "separation of church and state." At the school Jefferson founded, 118 groups applied to get student activity funds — private money, not tax dollars. Those groups included the gay and lesbian group, the animal rights group, the environmental group, the Muslim group, and the Ghandi peace group. Some Christian students there got together and decided to publish a little newspaper. They felt that a 119th view would be good for people. So they put out some issues of this little paper. In it, they talked about how racism was wrong. They talked about overeating. In one of my favorite attacks on the paper, somebody said, "Those guys apply Christianity to everything in life." Those kids really had guts.

Then they went to the university and asked to be treated like the other groups. They requested to have some of the student funds to use for their newspaper. The university said "No. That's religion and you can't have any money." The Christians argued that they were no different than the other groups that were receiving money. The university's representative contended that these other groups, Muslims, homosexuals, etc., are different because they are part of America's culture and that Christianity is not. We included that statement in the brief to the United States Supreme Court and let the nine justices of the Supreme Court read the opinion of the University of Virginia. Five of those nine judges were not amused, and in a 5-4 decision in June 1995 struck it down, saying that the university had engaged in illegal discrimination, that it was unconstitutional. This ruling is going to have an unbelievable impact in the future.

Equal Access

The Bible says "Go ye therefore." How do you "go ye therefore" if you can't go? A friend of mine lived in the Soviet Union for a while under Communist rule. He lived in the embassy building and was told when he went there that it was okay to believe anything you wanted, it was okay to have any religion. But when you left that embassy compound, you kept your mouth shut. You didn't give anything to anybody, you didn't show anything to anybody, and you didn't talk about anything to anybody. There are many people in America who would like to see religion treated like that. They would allow Christians to believe anything we wanted in our own minds, or inside the walls of our own church so long as the walls are in a place so we won't bother anyone else. But they would not allow crosses and manger scenes outside of the walls because it's irritating, and they destroy the environment! Believe it or not, that's one of the arguments they're now using on churches. They're calling them "environmental polluters." There is a case on the East Coast where they're telling a church group up there that all their traffic brings noise pollution, air pollution, and (my favorite) the smell of cooking from the kitchen is disturbing. Incredible.

A couple of years ago in the Lamb's Chapel case involving one of James Dobson's films, the Supreme Court ruled that you must treat Christians just like the rest of the world. If you open your school, your forum, or your public building and rent it, you've got to let Christians have the same access and privileges.

Unfortunately, there are a lot of people who just haven't

gotten the message or they are very deliberately discriminating. One of the things that happens in these cases, before these suits are filed, is that a lengthy five-page letter is sent to these school districts explaining the law, that they're violating the Constitution and pointing out that the Supreme Court of the United States has ruled on this point already. You'd be amazed how many school districts still say they refuse to allow Christians in the school.

Pastor Don Kimbrough went to a senior center in Albuquerque, New Mexico, and said, "You let all these other groups come in here — Eastern meditation, Oriental, and so forth. We'd like to come in and show the film *Jesus* and give a Bible to all the seniors. We will not take an offering. In fact, we will refuse to accept a love gift from anybody because we want no misunderstandings. We're just here to give the gift of Christ." The senior center refused. So on and on and on these suits go. Literally across the country, there are scores of these battles involving the very ability to spread the gospel itself.

There is a college in the Northwest that told the Christian students they have to take down the posters that advertise their faith from their private dorm room walls. Their contention is that it's offensive for people because students are compelled to live in the dormitory. Even though these are private apartments the students pay rent for, they feel that there is a danger of making someone feel uncomfortable if they should walk in a room and see one of these posters. This is hard to believe, but true.

The Battle for the Family

What is the definition for "family" today? We have a case where we are funding a defense where a mother is suing the father for custody of the children. The mother alleges that the fact that the father allowed a child to be baptized as a Christian shows that the parent is unfit and engaged in child abuse. There is another one about a father who decided to become a woman, and is now fighting over custody of the children. He's admittedly homosexual and is HIV positive — active AIDS. He wants custody of the boys to bring them into a household with

two other men who also have AIDS. These cases are unbelievable.

These cases are going on all over America today but,
praise the Lord, there is something that's being done. In 1994,
Bill Bright, James Dobson, Chuck Colson, James Kennedy,
and several others joined together to form what is now the
Alliance Defense Fund. It acts as a servant to all of the existing
legal groups, to the volunteer attorneys across the country.

We have three missions: First of all, to develop *strategic
plans* in each of the areas that are critical in the fight for
religious freedom. We are developing a plan and road map to
know how to get from where we are to where we want to go.
Not just to win a case here and a case there, but a strategy to take
these to the next level and the next level and the next level, until
Christians have the rights and access they are entitled to under
the laws of the land.

Second, we bring together volunteer attorneys. We've
got a lot of men and women out here who would love to give
their time, but they don't have a clue how to do it. We're
training those people, giving them the resources they need,
like Chester Darling, who argued the Boston case and won at
the Supreme Court. He attributes his win to our help in training
and preparation.

Thirdly, we provide *funding* to make sure these cases
have the resources they need. Most of the cases Christians lost
through the years were for one of two reasons. We either never
showed up for the battle at all by letting some government
official or somebody else defend our positions, or, if we did
show up, we showed up without enough horsepower. We
showed up with inadequate counsel, with inadequate resources.

God has given us a great asset in a free nation. A nation
that allows us to determine our own laws. As stewards of this
asset, how long should we permit ungodly actions to continue
to be imposed on us? How long before we take a stand for those
who cannot take a stand for themselves? I ask you to consider
becoming involved in the legal battle for religious freedom. So
much is at stake and we need all the help we can get. And most

of all, remember the source of all our strength. We ask you to undergird all of our work with what really counts — with prayer and with thanksgiving for the victories when they come.

For more information call or write:

Alliance Defense Fund
7819 East Greenway Road, Suite 8
Scottsdale, AZ 85260
(602) 953-1200

6

The World Financial Picture: Facts Every Christian Should Know

Tom Cloud

Most Christians need a better understanding of the basics regarding world financial interaction. You can't understand where we're going unless you understand where we've been. Once you understand these foundational truths, you can begin to manage your investments by looking at the way things actually are, not the way you wish they were.

To be a profitable investor, you've got to look at trends according to an economic indicator analysis, not from the standpoint of what you're reading in the newspaper or what your stockbroker is telling you. It's imperative that you analyze indicators because all investments are eventually driven by them. You've got to manage your money as if you have just moved to Japan, you didn't know anybody there, you didn't know how the psychology ran, you didn't know what was good or bad, and you didn't know what people thought about different investments. The only way to assess investments would be to look at the issues strictly from economic indicator analyses to determine where different investments had been and the likely direction to move in the future.

Timing Is Everything

People are always curious to know what I think has been the best investment of all time. My answer is simple, "everything." Since 1974 when I started my business, until today, every conceivable item or stock you could invest in has gone up and down. Therefore, there is never a "bad" investment; only bad times to get in or out. There are also no "good" investments. Simply a good time to get in or out.

During the great oil embargo, oil went from $3 a barrel to $40 a barrel. And we've seen gold go from $32 an ounce to $850 an ounce, then back to $328 an ounce. How about the stock market? It hit 1,000 in 1968 and it didn't hit 1,000 again until 1982, when it quadrupled. The bond market lost over 80 percent in the 1970s, then made a three and a half times progression in the 1980s. Any of these investments could have been good or bad, depending on your timing.

A major difference between many other people and myself is that we track buy-and-sell signals. People shouldn't be told to buy into something when they have no idea when to get out. For instance, I recommended staying out of gold from 1980 to 1987. I didn't see one buying signal during those seven years that suggested I move into gold. But from 1987 to 1993, we recommended going in, and out, twice. And we've been recommending buying gold again since March 1993.

I want to back up and bring you forward to where we are today. Some of what I'll explain will seem elementary to some of you, yet for others it will be the first time you've really heard an explanation of how economics and cycles work together.

What Drives the Economy?

In the United States there is a $5.5 trillion dollar economy — the largest economy in the world by over two times. Four sectors drive the economy: the consumer, the corporation, our government, and foreign sectors. Today, the United States is the only country in the world where two-thirds of the gross domestic product (GDP) is driven by consumer *spending!* If we don't spend a lot of money, our economy doesn't grow. Of course, we achieved this by spending borrowed money. And we are borrowed to the max and lead the world in total debt.

Many national stock brokerage firms are recommending investing in stocks because baby boomers are now saving money. Yet others are saying that it's a great time to invest in stocks because baby boomers are now in the position to buy big items and they are spending money. We can't have both. Compare Japan, an economy that's 48 percent driven by the consumer, with our country, which is 66 percent driven by the consumer. Can the United States continue to borrow at that pace? Of course not.

In addition to the consumer's influential 66 percent, the corporate sector has remained steady at about 17 percent throughout the past five years, and it's unlikely to change much in what it will spend into the GDP. The government sector's share has come up from about 11 percent to 14 percent, leaving the foreign sectors with a balance in the range of 10 to 17 percent over the past five years. By far, the most important gross domestic product influence is you, the consumer, driving the economy of the future, or for as long as it can continue to live beyond our means on borrowed money.

Even if the flat tax rate is somehow passed, it will be wonderful for our children and grandchildren, but not for you and me in the next five years. We're going to have to tighten our belts so that future generations won't completely collapse from our stupidity. Properly tightened, it could be very deflationary. For instance, if a flat tax rate and balanced budget amendment were passed prohibiting the government from spending more than it is taking in, you better understand how to invest in a deflationary cycle. We must also realize that this type of belt-tightening cannot be without pain. We will have severe pains in economic markets and investment markets if this scenario ever actually is implemented. In the long run it will be good, but in the short run unemployment will go up and salaries will flatten out. A lot of bad will go along with it on the short term. All of that is very bad for equity markets.

We should also be very concerned about the influence of Japanese investors. Japan is a country with 12 percent of the landmass of the United States. Yet back in 1980 they owned about 34 percent of our securities here. And their real estate was valued at more than the United States' only five short years ago. What happened was that Japan began a recession in the early 1990s and came close to a full depression. Real estate prices fell 50 percent. We are standing at a crossroad at which the fragile Japanese economy could literally collapse. I can assure you that it would have great repercussions on you and me in America. The Japanese would be forced to sell their U.S. Treasury bonds and Treasury bills which, by and large, are financing the debt of the United States of America.

The United States has doubled the size of the Treasury in the last few years. The Treasury is the only department in the United States that runs 24 hours a day, 365 days a year. It never stops printing money. It prints money to replace old bills and also for the additional increase to the money supply. If Japan's economy were to fail, and the Treasury had to create an extra 17 to 30 percent overnight, it just couldn't be done. So keep an eye out for what's going on in Japan because it does have a lot to do with what goes on in the United States. If Japan's situation doesn't get better, it could cause a very bumpy road for all Americans.

The United States Debt

In 1980 we elected Ronald Reagan, primarily on the promise that he could get the tax rates down and balance the budget. Jimmy Carter had exploded the U.S. debt. Reagan did get the tax rates down, but unfortunately, he never balanced the budget. We went from $2.6 trillion in total debt in 1980, to $8.49 trillion in 1988 when Reagan left office. Under Bill Clinton, it's continued the same upward climb, despite what he says. The total debt includes the federal debt, plus the corporate, consumer, municipality, and real estate debt.

In the same time period, interest rates fell from 21.75 percent to 10 percent. Financing and refinancing was the rage. Interest rates were falling, bonds were going up, and it was a great time to borrow. But we were running up debt for the future that had to be paid back. Unfortunately, it is now near the time when that debt will come due.

Until the 1980s, the 30-year bond was the bellwether bond, an index by which to gage interest rates. But the "live-for-today" attitude has driven the maturities on Treasury bonds and Treasury notes shorter and shorter. We now see 6-month, 12-month, 18-month, and 3-year securities in place of the 30-year bond. Today, the 30-year bond only trades twice a year. There's no demand for it. Who wants to put their money out there for 30 years with the kind of economic scenario that we have in this country and the world today? No one.

The Rule of 72

One of the first things you learn in any financial course is the "rule of 72." You can take any rate of return and divide it into 72 to determine how long it takes the investment to double in value. For example, if you were receiving a rate of interest of 6 percent a year on an investment, you would divide 6 into 72 and get 12. Therefore it takes 12 years to double the investment at 6 percent per year (disregarding taxes). If you have $1,000, it increases to $2,000 in 12 years. But, if you're receiving 12 percent interest, it increases to $2,000 in only six years.

Your bank understands this principle very well. If you borrow money from the bank, roll it over, and don't pay the interest; the principal and interest keep compounding. That's what has happened to this country: the debt has climbed from $8.49 trillion in 1988 to $17.1 trillion in 1995. We have doubled the debt in seven years. Divide the increase into 72 and we're compounding our debt at over 10 percent! We're experiencing double-digit growth of our debt in this country! Yet we're told by our Congress that they are busy cutting government. In the past 95 years, we haven't had one year during which the federal budget (the business of running the country) was less than it was the year before. But they're telling us that we're supposed to stand up and applaud because they cut the growth from 9.2 percent to 7.7 percent.

But don't forget that 7.7 percent compounds very quickly. We currently have $17 trillion of debt out there in a $5.5 trillion economy. At some point that debt has to be dealt with or our whole economy will fail. And we have less and less options as time goes on. Depending on what you're holding in your portfolio when the curtain closes, you win or lose. It's that simple. You may currently be in a $200,000 home. But if major employers begin to lay off people in your area, your home quickly drops in value to $180,000. If a few more executives get laid off, it drops to $160,000. Where did that $40,000 equity in your home go? Did anybody really lose it? Now if they had cashed in and sold their $200,000 house, they would have had their money. But now they're getting $160,000, so $40,000 has disappeared. It's happened before, all across the country, especially in California. Bottom line: the debt has to be dealt with, probably in the next recession. Prepare for a major devaluation of the dollar.

The Trade Deficit

The USA's trade deficit is caused because we are importing more than we're exporting with our world trading partners — currently more than $160 billion a year, an all-time high. The trade deficit has continued to average over $12 billion a month and has been as high as $16 billion a month. This means an annual trade deficit of around $160 billion per year. If we continue to send $160 billion per year out of this country, to countries like Japan, Taiwan, Korea, China, Singapore, etc., they will eventually come back and buy up our securities and real estate.

In the future, during the first wave of the fall of the dollar, I would recommend that you put your money market in the yen. We saw the yen fall from a high of 297 yen to the dollar to 82. It's been engineered higher but the dollar will resume its downward spiral sometime in the future. If we keep sending our dollars out at 160 billion a year, we're filling the world full of dollars. We're giving a glut of dollars around the world because we're buying more goods than we're selling. We can't continue on like this or America will not be owned by Americans anymore. There are many, many cities in the United States where the Japanese own more of the downtown areas than the Americans, and all that's happened in the last 10 years.

The Budget

We hear a lot of talk about the budget. As I said earlier, that's the cost of running this country. The budget year covers the period from October 1 through September 30 each year. Our government is very pleased if the budget deficit for a year is only $160 billion. Each year, to get the deficit "down" to the "low" target number, they conveniently borrow from our pension plans, our Social Security plans, and our government military retirement. By calling it loans they don't count it in the federal budget deficit. The real deficit *each* of the last few years, counting all the "loans": between $325 and $350 billion dollars! This is easily found in the government's own published documents. Therefore, if they are not willing to admit to the true deficit each year, do you really think they can balance the budget in seven years? Hardly.

The Gramm/Rudman/Hollings Act was a balanced budget amendment. Our senators said they would go to prison if they didn't balance the budget by 1990. There's not a single one of them in prison to my knowledge. Our representatives simply said, "We cancel the law. We're going to vote it out. We haven't even come close to balancing the budget." That could very easily happen again if we move into a recession or depression in the next few years and the Republicans lose control of the Congress and Senate. Nobody is happy in a recession, much less a depression, and it would be easy for the Democrats to sweep back into control. Of course, the first thing they would do is cancel the balanced budget amendment. (If it ever is passed!)

Future Scenarios

Let's consider some possible economic scenarios we may face in the future. Unfortunately, some of these possibilities we don't know much about because we haven't seen them very many times in history. But let's talk about the one we've seen the most; inflationary contraction/ recession.

Inflationary Contraction/ Recession

When prices go up and the economy goes down, it's termed an "inflationary contraction" or "inflationary recession." The adjective is inflation; the noun is contraction or recession or depression. All recessions in this country since 1934 have been an "inflationary contraction/recession" resulting in the gross national product reflecting a negative growth rate. Prices go up even though the economy is sinking. Many people believe we're headed for inflationary growth. Whether it's 1 percent or 10 percent inflation, at least the economy has some growth in it — rising prices and a growing economy.

Stagflation

"Stagflation" is a term that was coined in the early 1980s, when we had inflation, but the economy wasn't growing much — it was growing at rates between .5 percent and 1.5 percent. Experience has shown us what to expect if that scenario develops.

Deflationary Growth

But what we have never experienced is "deflationary growth," where prices go down and the economy still grows. However, we have had a "deflationary contraction." I believe there's a good chance we may be on the horizon of seeing the second one in the history of our country.

The Most Likely Scenario

What is the most likely scenario that this country is facing? I believe that we are on the verge of a *deflationary* contraction. Of course, I hope and pray it's not as bad as the 1928-1934 period. We're in an economy today in which debt is not a factor, because it's repudiated or forfeited (because the people don't pay it). But this debt must be dealt with before this country can grow again. It must somehow evaporate and go away. It's going to be a difficult time for many people because jobs are going to be lost and investment portfolios will go down. (Some of them more than others, depending on what they're invested in.) But we must burst this huge debt bubble so that the economy can grow again. The only way that I see this can happen is for us to go through a deflationary contraction, in which prices are actually contracting and the economy is going down the drain.

Depression

What is a depression? The textbook definition says that it's more than six quarters of economic contraction. So a depression is no more than a bad recession if you look at it from a financial world standpoint. And I believe that we are headed toward an economic contraction. Hopefully it won't last for over six quarters. Consider it a necessary recession/depression because we want the future generations of this country to have life as good or better than our generation. They certainly can't inherit $17 to $20 trillion dollars of our debt and improve. Think ahead seven years from now, when the budget is supposed to be balanced. We could have $35 trillion in debt if it compounds the same rate as it has for the past seven years. We understand rationally that we can't have $35 trillion in debt. It's impossible. Yet it is possible. Don't rule it out! Your investment plan should include a "what if" scenario.

What To Watch & What To Do?
Inverted Yield Curves

Inverted yield curves are a topic not seen in the economic world for 20 years, until 1994. In an Inverted Yield Curve, you have yields that are higher on short-term securities than they are on long-term securities. Investors can receive a return of 7 percent short-term when the 30-year long-term bond is only 6.8 percent. Inverted yield curves are historically very deflationary because they're an indicator that interest rates in the future are going to go down. Investors prefer to take the higher rate now, while the economy is still growing at a moderate pace.

The inverted yield curve problem is not going away. The longer it hangs around, the more likely we will move toward a deflationary contraction of the money supply.

How about 1995? An incredible year. We saw the lowest rate growth in M-1, M-2, and M-3 money supply indicators.

Every gauge the government uses to measure growth of our economy had been growing at unbelievably low rates — 1.5 percent on an annual basis. Companies were announcing future price increases. This low growth rate in the money supply is very contracted and is a deflationary signal.

Understanding Inflation

The definition of inflation is "the creation of money." It's "more-currency-by-decree." When enough money gets in circulation it causes prices to go up because we have more paper money chasing the same amounts of goods or services. We gauge inflation in this country by consumer prices, which are really a by-product of inflation, the creation of money.

Velocity of Money

Another thing to consider is the velocity of money as it moves through the banking system. The 1980 Monetary Control Act, Jimmy Carter's biggest blunder, gave the Federal Reserve the right to drop the reserve requirement from 15 percent to 6 percent and to zero in case of emergency. Why would our government pass that law if they weren't planning on using it sometime in the future? Prior to 1980, if a bank wanted to loan you a dollar, then it would be required to take 15 cents and deposit it with the Federal Reserve. Therefore every dollar on deposit could be loaned out six times (15 cents divided into a dollar). So banks are in the business of creating money, just like the government creates money on the printing presses.

In 1979 this country was in a recession. President Carter decided that the government couldn't create money fast enough and it was hurting his re-election chances in 1980. He felt his only hope was to end the recession, so he railroads through congress new rules for the FDIC. The result was that a bank only had to have 6 cents on deposit for every dollar on loan, meaning every dollar could be loaned out 16 times (6 cents divided into a dollar). This drove us to 19 percent inflation by the last quarter of 1980.

Today, banks have tightened up and have contracted in

number through interstate banking. In June of 1995 the money supply velocity slowed to its lowest level since 1981-82. So the money is not spending through the system as fast as it was in the past. This slower movement of money through the banking system is another deflationary signal.

Derivatives

Derivatives, which is speculation on the interest rate of government-issued instruments to go up or down, first came into the news when Orange County, California, defaulted on its debt due to losing large sums of money on leveraged derivatives. Because of the competition between mutual funds and money market funds, these fund managers have decided to take a little higher risk to increase their portfolio return percentage. In just a few years, losses from derivatives escalated from $15 billion to $30 billion and then to $45 billion.

I believe interest rates will soon go down a little bit. We're not going to hear much in the news about derivatives. But let me tell you right now that I will guarantee you the minute interest rates turn back up, derivatives will be back on the front of our newspapers. I think that the long-term interest rates may come down, but we may have an inflationary interlude beforehand.

Interest Rates

Alan Greenspan has been given the right to drop interest rates any time he feels it's necessary. The mentality was, "The ball's in your court, Alan. When you feel the economy is getting too slow and needs to be brought forward a little bit, you can drop interest rates." This way the White House will have a scapegoat when something goes wrong. So when interest rates spike back up, watch for the derivative problem to be back in the news.

We also have to hope that the Japanese stock market recovers, because the potential loss in the real estate mortgage in Japan could easily affect the American economy.

Inflation

The January 1994 issue of the *Economist* concluded that

"inflation is zero; inflation is dead." Is it dead? This depends on what you mean by inflation. For example, the government's figures are wrong when they list, in the Consumer Price Index, a hand-held calculator for $32. They don't cost $32. That's what they cost in 1968. Now you can buy them for $2.99. Something is wrong. We all know that inflation is not 2 percent, as the government reports. And it's not 10 percent or 12 percent, as some people have claimed. The real inflation rate is somewhere *around 2 percent below the prime rate,* where it has always been historically. So inflation is running between 4 percent and 7 percent, not 2 percent, even though that's what they want us to believe.

The Federal Reserve

Andrew Johnson "smelled a rat" in the 1860s and asked, "Why should the American public pay interest to a private company?" So basically, he booted out the world bank from controlling American banking. It stayed out for some 60 years before it came back in the form of the Federal Reserve. Most Americans don't realize that the Federal Reserve is not a government agency. It's privately owned by a few influential families. The Federal Reserve authorizes the U.S. government to print money and we pay this private company interest on the money we just printed!! Their billions get bigger as our middle class gets smaller. And it's going to keep going in that direction until we elect someone who will abolish the Federal Reserve.

Interest Rates and Business Cycles

There are many investors who speculate on whether or not interest rates will go up or down. There is an argument in the economic world as to whether interest rates have been in a cyclical decline for ten years — from 1982 until 1992. Most people understand interest rate cycles. A typical cycle begins with low interest rates at the local bank, say around 7 percent. Then it eventually moves to 8 percent, then 9 or higher. Then the competition to find funds to borrow heats up between the government, the corporation, and the consumer. The economy begins to grow too fast and the interest rates get higher.

Eventually, too many people can't make a profit, so they quit borrowing investment money. That causes the economy to go into recession, the interest rate comes back down, and we start over again. These are normal business cycles that have gone on for 200 years.

With this in mind, it's interesting to analyze the period from 1982-1992. There we had interest rates going down continually, which indicates a cyclical decline. There was one small rise in the fall of '87, when interest rates went up 1.5 percent. Many economists believe that this could be a cyclical interruption of a cyclical decline. If this is the case, it is rare because there have been only four in world history. If you go back in history and study the South Sea bubble, the railroad mania in 1812, the Civil War in the 1860s, the Great Depression in the 1930s, you find that not one had a cyclical decline where interest rates went down continuously for over 10 years.

There are more and more people in the financial arena who are pointing out the uniqueness of this period with more than 11 years of declining interest rates. If they are correct, and I believe they are, then this is a very deflationary signal.

Investment Tips for Deflation

I've been in this financial planning/consulting business for over 20 years, starting my practice in 1974. I did full-service financial planning for six years, but then changed because I saw a need and a niche that nobody was filling. We use sophisticated trend analysis to determine when to buy and sell gold, historical documents, and diamonds. We meet with investors, one on one, and design a portfolio strategy. We give them advice on when to buy *and* sell, and update the portfolio quarterly. By the grace of God, we have been very fortunate in our recommendations.

Our advice only helps people with 10-20 percent of their portfolios. We've become a specialist in a tight investment group. There are other financial planners that can consult for the big picture. So some of these things I'm going to cover — stocks, bonds, real estate, oil, and gas — you'll need to deal with your own broker/consultant/expert. I'm only sharing trend analysis and where I think they're pointing.

I have a responsibility, biblically mandated, to multiply my assets. Consider Ecclesiastes 11:2, a very simple piece of wisdom. Solomon exhorts you to divide your wealth into seven or eight different areas, because no one knows what may befall the land. Today we call that asset allocation, or, spreading your risk among several different areas of investment. That is as wise today as it was in the time in which Solomon lived.

I also like what James 1:5-6 says: "But if any of you lacks wisdom, let him ask of God, who gives to all liberally and without reproach, and it will be given to him. But let him ask in faith, with no doubting, for he who doubts is like a wave of sea driven and tossed by the wind." There are many out there today who have been in that position. The three billionaires that I work with are no different than those of us out there who are making $1,000, $5,000, or $10,000 investment decisions, because it's God's money and he has given us responsibility for it.

I apply the same biblical principals and understanding when dealing with my clients.

If you have any doubts about an investment, simply wait and pray for wisdom. Each financial decision is one you have to live with and for which you are accountable. It's amazing to me that people actually make major buying decisions using advice from telemarketing firms. I once consulted with a doctor who had purchased $245,000 of gemstones through a telemarketing firm in Toronto, Canada. They kept telling him the stones were worth $350,000. It took us 18 months to get him $16,000 for them. The most he could get anywhere else was $12,000. It was junk and he lost a bundle. But I was able to work with him and I watched him grow as a person and in the Spirit. He's now funding ministry work in South America. It's hard for me to believe anyone would make that type of investment, especially over the phone, but it happens every day. So remember James 1:5-6. If you have any doubt about an investment of any kind, wait and pray. If you are feeling pressure to purchase something, don't.

Stocks

I've been very bullish on stocks in general for the last few years. I personally have invested heavily in stocks. I've recommended that clients invest in stocks. I've had as much as 40 percent of my portfolio in stocks. But, I think the stock market may be topping, and I look for negative returns in the foreseeable future. It is easy to determine that the market is overvalued. You need to be very careful and know very well every stock you own.

Bonds

If there is a deep recession, a deflationary contraction, bonds are going to be a good place to have part of your portfolio. But you must be careful on the grades of those bonds you purchase. Best bet: buy general obligation bonds with the highest interest rate you can find.

Junk Bonds

Up until now they have had some big returns. But as the economy slows, they could cost you dearly. If you own any, it's time to sell. They are coming to an end, no more double-digit returns. We're going more to our preservation point. I see no need to liquidate bonds. I see no need to be in a hurry — as you see interest rates going up, you may want to liquidate some of your position in bonds.

Real Estate

I have grave concerns for real estate. Somebody asked me recently if I had any real estate holdings. My answer: "Very little." I've sold my vacation condo on the beach, my office building, and my farm. I'm down to zero in real estate except for a home that I own, thank the Lord, free and clear. That's the lowest percentage of real estate in my investment portfolio that I've had in my entire investment career.

Now is all real estate bad? No. Rental properties can be good during recession. Rental properties were one of the best investments during the Great Depression. Behind gold, it was the best investment. People were losing their homes and they had to live somewhere as an intermediary before they could buy another home. So rental properties in good locations are good investments.

Also, well-located strip shopping centers will be good investments because no matter how bad the economy gets, you're still going to have to buy groceries, hardware, etc. You may stop spending entertainment dollars, but you'll always have to purchase the basics.

Most resort property could be in trouble. With no interest rate deductions and the peak of stocks and bonds, there's not going to be as much money around to buy those properties. And I do expect a moderate recession and corresponding drop in the resort property values.

Gold

Gold has good possibilities. There are problems in South Africa as 30,000 miners could go on strike. The largest country in the world for gold supply, South Africa, is now having double-digit inflation. The living standards are deteriorating as President Mandela is publicly pushing for capitalism while privately bringing Communism in the back door.

Concerning the second-largest gold producer in the world, in 1994 the United States went into a decline in supply for the first time in 15 years. So the supply and demand factor has shifted dramatically in favor of higher prices. This warrants a careful analysis of the world's oldest currency.

If you invest in gold, there are several options that are beneficial to different investment portfolios. Unfortunately, definitions within the gold industry itself may widely differ. What I call semi-numismatic, somebody else may call a rare coin. Yet, these distinctions are very important. Unfortunately, there are no standard legal definitions to guide new investors. So you have to know the terminology, and *characteristics*, of what you're investing in.

First and foremost you must determine why you're buying gold in the first place. For instance, are you buying gold coins for domestic barter, or are you buying gold to trade in Europe in case of a depression here in the United States? Do you want coins that have an acceptance worldwide or do

you want popular American coins which are more suscep-
tible to the American economy and drop faster in times of
recession?

I've recently attended world gold conferences in Hong
Kong and Zurich. It's amazing to hear people like Sir Harry
Schultz, the highest paid financial consultant in the world, who
has been out of gold for 13 years, talking about gold going to
$1,000 in the not too distant future. Or Peter Lynch, the great
money manager of the highly respected Magellan fund, predict
$1,000 per gold ounce by the year 2000. And how about John
Pugsley, who did not invest in gold for seven or eight years,
investing heavily and becoming very bullish on gold. And then
Bob Prector and Elliott Wave expect gold to reach $450 - $480.
These are major statements from major investors

The most basic approach to gold is that it will always be
there when you need it. That's something you can't say about
dollars. But it's imperative to know exactly what you're
buying and have a clear purpose: barter, world hedge, confi-
dentiality, profit?

Silver

Silver figures are a somewhat misrepresented — it's not
as rare as some people are claiming. Silver is not in a bull
market right now. In fact it could go down. It may climb to
$6.75–$7.00 but not $10. The problem is, there is an ample
supply and the only thing that would make it go higher is
inflation. No inflation exists in a contracting economy. Also,
it only trades in six world markets, whereas gold trades in all
27 financial markets in the world.

Gemstones

This is one of two areas of investments that we've seen
the biggest profits in recent years. Not many people have
tracked gemstones because they're not regulated and you can't
look up the price everyday in the *Wall Street Journal*. We
recently entered into a deal with Banco de Brazil, the seventh-
largest bank in the world and larger than any bank in the United
States. Several Brazilian mines have lost the inventories that

were collateral for loans to banks. We have the contract to bring those stones to the United States and sell at below wholesale prices.

These stones include green tourmaline, topaz, golden beryl, aquamarine and kunzite, all available for one-seventh of retail or less. And all very rare. For instance, there are only seven acres of topaz mines in the history of the world and they are being quickly depleted. You can buy them for $80 per carat and appraise anywhere between $500 and $700 per carat by the top gemological labs in this country. I don't recommend that anyone invest more than 2 or 3 percent into this area, but it's something that I think can make significant profits for the mid-to-long-term.

Rare Documents

This interesting area is the most exciting market that we've been involved in. To date, we've never had an investor lose a penny. That's an unbelievable statement, considering the millions of dollars that we've handled in investments. This is not autographs from Mickey Mantle or Willie Mays. These are extremely rare and unique documents like the original lease to Mount Vernon that has George and Martha Washington's signatures. Only three of Martha Washington's signatures are known to exist, and one client owns all three of them. This original document has increased in value over six figures.

We also handled a document called "General Order Number Nine," 1 of the 11 copies citing Gen. Robert E. Lee's surrender to Ulysses S. Grant at the Appomattox Courthouse on April 15, 1865. Of the 11 documents in existence, six are in museums, and five are in private hands, and four of those are owned by my clients. The highest amount anyone has paid for one is $92,000, yet all have had offers for more than $140,000.

Occasionally, we run into what those in the autograph world call a "virgin find." Something on par with the Declaration of Independence is found in the back of a $15 frame and it goes to auction at Christy's and sells for $3.6 million. That happened in 1993.

Last Thoughts on any Investment

Regardless of the investor, attention to spiritual matters should always be the first priority. The Bible says in Mark 8:36, "For what does it profit a man to gain the whole world, and forfeit his soul?" Never lose sight of what really matters, the *real* long-term investment — Jesus Christ.

For more information on Tom Cloud call or write:

Tom Cloud
Cloud & Associates, Inc.
8735 Dunwoody Place, Suite 0
Atlanta, GA 30350
1-800-247-2812
email (cloudtgl@pop.atl.mindspring.com)

7

Public Education: Don't Be Deceived!

Anita Hoge

America is asleep and the enemy is truly within — within our schools and within our communities. The "Steeling the Mind" video entitled "The Truth about Outcome-Based Education" was the first to expose the vast deception going on in public education and gave credibility to our movement. I want to continue in that vein, to be a messenger, someone shining light into the darkness — the darkness of deception. My hope is to gently pierce your heart to awaken the sleeping angels so that we may weep for our children and be prepared to fight for them.

Let us begin with a clear picture of the deception. This new reform speaks often of something called a paradigm shift. Now this is not a new continent, nor is it a geological fault in California; this is a theoretical concept that we need to understand. A paradigm shift is a re-definition, a re-engineering. It is about starting over again. It's starting with a clean sheet of paper, rejecting all the conventional wisdom and received assumptions of the past. It is a new reality, a new world view.

Let me give you a couple of examples to drive the point home. When I say the word, "Special Education," traditionally, what are you thinking of? You think about the little child in the wheelchair, about children who have disabilities, physical disabilities. That is the traditional paradigm. In the new paradigm, who is a Special Ed child? In the new paradigm, it's any child who is at risk, any child who does not meet an outcome-based education goal, outcome, or graduation requirement.

Let me give you another one: "Character Education." We all want our children to have good character, but in the traditional sense, what are we talking about? We talk about Character Ed, teaching true honesty, teaching morals — there is a right and wrong and there is a standard. In the new paradigm, character education is, "I'm okay, you're okay." It is diversity — something called "universal values."

So as parents, we have to ask the question: Do we want character education that teaches moral absolutes, or do we want character education that teaches situation ethics and universal values? There is a difference and the difference is in the definition. The difference is what techniques will be used on our children and what the outcomes will be.

The goal of the education elite is to break down any barriers that interfere with their goal to create a New World Order, to create good global citizens of tomorrow — the future workers of this New World Order that we're talking about. And when they talk about resistors to this movement, who are they talking about? It is most of you who are reading this and it is me. Why? Because we're still in the traditional paradigm. We're still teaching our children biblical principles of right and wrong. So who do you think the education elite are going to go after? It's the people with the strongest belief system. It is us. It is the Christian community.

As we move forward, what I would like to do is give you a little bit of background about myself — where I began and why I believe this whole entire paradigm shift is a deception. They are lying to us and I am a testimony, a witness. I am the parent who experienced this whole traumatic four-year federal investigation in the state of Pennsylvania where I filed against the state. And when I found out what was going on, first I cried.

Then I prayed. It should have been the other way around, but nothing is as close to you as your children, so the impact was tremendous. They can take away your money, they can take away your house. But when we talk about your children, what I have to say will really hit home.

My son, an eighth grader, came home from school one day and said, "Mom, I've just taken the weirdest test in the world."

I said, "Gee, what type of questions were on the test?"

He said, "Well, all the eighth-graders were taken down to the assembly and there was a sample question. 'If you saw an old lady standing on the side of the street, what would you do: A) Push her in the street; B) Throw rocks at her.' "

I wasn't overly concerned, but I thought, *Gee. I'll go down and look at the test and see what I can find out.* I thought I was really involved in my child's education at that time. I was in the PTA, I was writing a grant for the Artists in Education program in my district, and I was working very closely with the superintendent, Elizabeth. So I called her, and said, "I'd like to see this test my son just took, the Pennsylvania EQA (Educational Quality Assessment)." She said no one was allowed to see it, but that "We're having a PTA meeting. You can come; I'm going to be talking about it."

So I went to that meeting and basically she said, "You know, the kids are not scoring very well in comprehension, but they're doing so well in higher order thinking skills."

So I put up my hand, dumb mom: "Well, doesn't comprehension mean that what they are reading they understand, and higher order thinking is beyond comprehension, meaning just their opinion, so they're guessing? So you're saying that they're not understanding what they read, but they can guess really well?"

And she slammed her book down on the table and she said, "You and I are not going to get along anymore."

I said, "Well, okay. I want to see that test."

And she says, "You're going to have to go to the state."

That was where my story begins. I started writing letters,

started calling my senator and my state representative, demanding to see that test. It took six months before I really got any kind of response. I got a lot of letters back saying that I couldn't see the test. This concerned me so I started expanding my list of what I wanted to see. I wanted to see the test, I wanted to see how it was scored, I wanted to see the resources for improvement — what they were doing with the information.

Then one day, probably because I called these people every other day, a legislative aide sent me these resources for improvement for every quality goal of education. Understand that the quality goals of education in Pennsylvania were things like citizenship, self esteem, getting along with others, creative activities, flexibility. There's nothing wrong with those, is there? And then come the resources for improvement, one for each goal. And when I opened it up, there were all these little computer codes.

So guess who found out how to use the computer? I went to the depository library at the University of Pittsburgh and found out there was another network out there that I could get into. I tapped into the United States Department of Education computer banks and the Pennsylvania Department of Education. Everything that I talk about is information from actual documents from either the Pennsylvania Department of Education or the United States Department of Education. Now I was prepared.

So when I called the state, I called the testing director and I said, "Mr. Coldiron, do you realize that you are about to give a test that is in violation of federal law?"

And he tried to walk around the definition. "Oh, well, this is a cognitive test. We're not testing attitudes." I had the paper in front of me. He said, "You know, Mrs. Hoge, you are going to be sued for libel if you continue to tell people that you found federal funds involved with this test."

Now most normal parents, when they say they're going to be sued, gasp. Right? But when you have the document in front of you that says yes, indeed, they are testing attitudes, yes, indeed, they are lying and lying big-time, then you have a little bit more strength to stand on because that knowledge becomes your armor.

And I said, "Mr. Coldiron, you are going to be sued for libel personally if you continue to violate federal law." And I hung up on him. At that time I filed my federal complaint. Again, it took four years to resolve it in which the Feds did agree this was a psychological test that measured the attitudes and values of the children. It consisted of 375 questions on attitudes, values, opinions, and beliefs of children, 30 questions on math, 30 questions on reading analogies.

Now there are two very important things that I found out about the law that protects us and basically about what the government was doing with our children in public schools. First of all, I found out that, yes, the federal government was using our children for psychological research. The other thing I found out was that they were collecting a great deal of personal and sensitive information. They were forming psychological profiles of not only the children but what the parents were teaching their children. So it was a psychological profile on the family. Do they know who the resistors to non-traditional values are in this country? Yes, they do.

The first thing I realized is that the law protects only the invasion of privacy. When they give this test, they test attitudes. What that does is violate your privacy because they're asking for a lot of personal and sensitive information.

But there's a second point to consider, because the government was scoring this test to what they called a minimum positive attitude — they were scoring this test to the liberal educators view of political correctness! So, it was an invasion of privacy. But when government decides to score the attitudes and values of our children, that's an invasion of our freedom, no matter who you are. The United States government cannot score the opinions and values of our children.

Let me tell you about one of the test questions. There is a club called the Midnight Artists. They go out late at night and paint funny sayings on buildings. You are asked to join the club. The question is whether or not you would join, even after your best friend asks you to. The state-desired response was yes. You got one point for yes, you got 0 for no. So if a child said no, he would not go out and vandalize, that was a behavioral weakness according to a sub-scale that said that they would honor self-made commitments to individuals of the group.

Now in the evaluation that I pulled off of the computer, it said, "citizenship." And that is what the parents were told. Citizenship is having quality values and attitudes associated with responsible citizenship, and all the parents in Pennsylvania are in agreement with that. Remember, parents, think in the traditional paradigm. But in the evaluation, it said that they were measuring the psychological notion of threshold by reward and punishment. That was the B.F. Skinner model saying, "Would you comply if we did this? Would you comply with your best friend?" So it was a stimulus response, it's just the rat in the maze type of thing. If a child does something, give him a reward at the end.

I read that and I thought, *I'm in the Twilight Zone.* I told my husband to read it. "It says they're testing the psychological notion of threshold." They're lying to you and they've lied to us all. What were they measuring when they measured self-esteem? Was the student an individual or did he go along with the group? What were they measuring when they measured flexibility? At what point the child would change without protest. Reward and punishment. So what do they have? What they have is a psychological profile of what your child might do in the future. Predicting behavior, that's what it's all about: performance, behavior, actions. What will your child do in the future under certain circumstances?

So now they have a psychological profile of a family, of your beliefs, of what you taught your child, what you believe in. Remember, cognitive is not two plus two equals four only. Cognitive is, "I believe Aunt Mary makes the best apple pie in the world." Or "I believe in God." Cognitive is what you taught your child to be true. It is truth. The whole idea of re-mediation is to take the belief system of the child and create a conflict to change the child to the desired response. Remember that the test was just a temperature-taking device to see where the children were in their attitudes and values. The next step would be the re-mediation.

So when I found out that this was going on, I then filed my federal complaint. They resolved it by saying that yes, it was a psychological test. They had to issue a policy to all 501 school districts saying that they would never issue this test again. But what did they do to get around the law? They changed the name of the test. Because by law, my child had to take the Pennsylvania EQA. So now they changed it to the Pennsylvania Assessment System. But we refused to give up.

Remember, at this time, the whole idea was to change curriculum, to bring in controversial programs. They designed drug and alcohol abuse programs, like 'Here's looking at you 2000.'" But how do they validate a self-esteem program? They validated it in Pennsylvania under the Pennsylvania EQA. And where did they validate the character education program — from the Thomas Jefferson Research Institute? They validated it in Pennsylvania under the Pennsylvania EQA. After I got lists and lists and lists where all of these different states were validating all of this curriculum under the Pennsylvania EQA, I began to realize that Pennsylvania was very important to the nation. We were a national pilot in the testing for the National Assessment of Educational Progress, which is the national test to test the attitudes and values of all United States children. Results would validate specific teacher methodology and specific curriculums to be sure that the children were going to change.

So what happened? They brought in this controversial piece of curriculum. A teacher looks at it and says, "This is a bunch of junk. I'm not going to teach this." Or maybe there was a child, very strong in his attitudes and beliefs, who just wasn't going to change. There was no way to force change. There were teachers and children falling through the cracks.

So what came on the scene five years ago? Outcome-Based Education. The new education reform. Remember the slogans: All children can succeed. Success breeds success. Schools control the conditions for success. It's all simply untrue. We need to use common sense when we read their marketing slogans. Because none of it really makes sense.

There's one important thing I want you to understand about Outcome-Based Education, actually, *the* most important thing. Because then you won't fall for all the tactics that are coming onto the horizon.

Outcome-Based Education was a major shift in power. Who created the educational standards under traditional education? It was Mrs. Smith. Remember Mrs. Smith in the fifth grade? She gave those spelling tests every Monday morning, so you had to study all weekend. She said, "If you're going to make an A, you're going to have to get all these words right." It was the teacher who created the standard. I have great respect for teachers. I think they were doing their jobs. But what happened? The state took away their academic freedom to teach in Outcome-Based Education. Why? Who controls the standard now? The power shifted from the teacher, the local school board and our local schools — those who traditionally determined graduation requirements — and it moved to the state. So now the state is saying, "Johnny, you have to meet this outcome or you're not going to graduate." That's the most important thing to understand. What we have completely lost is local control. Under Outcome-Based Education, we allow the state to control the standards.

Many of you have heard about compromises and you think maybe that will improve the situation. Now William Simon and Bill Spady are saying "Academic Outcomes — don't you want academic outcomes?" And a lot of Christians have said, "Okay; well, I can go with that." Why shouldn't we do that? Because if they have the power to change outcomes from values to academics, then they have the power to change the outcomes from academics to values. They shouldn't have that power at all. Don't allow them to have the power. Your power is in your locally elected school board. That is who should create the standards with your teachers and your principals. It's local control. It's not the state. Don't give up your representative power that was given to you by the Constitution. Your elected representatives should be creating the standard. So when you sit down in these groups and they say "academic outcomes," emphatically say no!

In Outcome-Based Education, in which the Goals 2000 legislation created criteria for your states and your local districts to get the money for implementation, all of those criteria are performance-based with what is called Total Quality Management Alignment. You are required to have an assessment that measures it and you have to teach it and you have to have a system of accountability. Basically, this is what Goals 2000 is saying, so each state is back there creating standards and performance-based or outcome-based education. So, let's look at really what happened.

Under traditional education, what you had was the Carnegie Unit. What's the Carnegie Unit? It means you take so many hours of math, so many hours of science, so many hours of English, so many hours of history, and you had to pass so many classes in order to graduate. That was the standard. So time was fixed. You had to go to school 180 days. And ability levels were flexible, right? Because you had different IQs, you had a whole lot of different types of people, so time was fixed and ability levels varied.

What happens in OBE? They've taken tradition and they've turned it on its head. They said, "We don't like that traditional education anymore." The education system that was the foundation of this century's world accomplishments like men on the moon, computers, etc., is summarily being dismissed. In its place they have a better idea. They now want *abilities* to be fixed instead of time. And time will be flexible. "We don't care how long it takes you to meet these outcomes as long as you all meet these outcomes." Time is fixed. Everyone needs the same standard, so time is your new variable. Don't let all the jargon fool you. This is pure socialism! This is socialized education, where everyone has to meet the same standard.

Let me give you an example. We'll play OBE basketball. Maybe some of you have heard of it. It's kind of fun. I'm going to take a whole group of people over to a basketball court and on this date I'm creating the standard. None of you can leave this court until you all do a slam dunk. Nobody can leave. Two days later, what's wrong here? Everybody has to meet the same standards or we don't go home. So what happens to the 6'7" who goes over and just plops the ball right in — what are we going to do with him? Well he has to go and help that lady over there because she can't jump at all. And we've all got to help each other because we want to go home for dinner. In order for everyone to meet the standard, what do I have to do? Lower the hoop. I've got to lower the standard. This is what we're talking about when we say all must meet the same outcome.

Key Questions to Ask about Outcome-Based Education

First of all, Outcome-Based Education is major double-speak. What they are saying is that you have to have specific outcomes in order to graduate. Now a lot of the states say they're moving toward academic outcomes. But you realize they're still saying things like "You have to have cooperation with others, you have to relate meaning to art. You can't have prejudice and you have to be flexible." So you still have all of these hard-to-define, subjective outcomes.

I have created five questions that will help you win any debate involving a vague outcome that is being set down as a standard. The first question: How do you measure that? If you have a goal like interpersonal skills, if you have a goal like relating meaning to art, if you have a goal like honesty or integrity, how do you measure honesty? Number two: How do you score it? So when you're in a school board meeting and they're saying, "Well, you just want your evaluation on this sort of thing," you'll say, "Well, gee — how are you going to score it? Right here in our strategic plan it says we have to measure these outcomes, right? So if we have to measure them, how is it measured? How much is too much and how much is not enough in order to graduate?" We're talking about honesty, not an easy thing to measure. Would they be willing to use the biblical measurement? Number three: Who decided the standards? Was it our local community or was it the state? Number four: How will my child be re-mediated? What are you going to do with my child if he has one set of moral absolutes and you think he should change, or use situation ethics? And the fifth and most important question: What if a parent disagrees with the state? Who has the ultimate authority over the child — the parent or the state? If these are state-controlled outcomes, can a parent opt out of a graduation requirement? Can your local district opt out?

These are the questions to ask, and I can guarantee you they're not going to answer any of these questions. When you get to number five, start again with number one, with another outcome. But do not allow them to move forward on any of these outcomes until you have that criteria.

The second major problem with OBE: This whole system contradicts traditional American education. Why? Traditional American education was built on content standards. It was built on curriculum. This new transformational Outcome-Based Education is based on global citizens. The Department of Labor, through a commission called the Secretary's Commission on Achieving Necessary Skills, created standards for the human capital of the future. They refer to your children as human capital and you, the parents, as the suppliers. Human capital. Your child is a statistic. And when they do an assessment, I challenge any of you to go to the dictionary and look up the word assessment. Assessment is the value, like property, of your usefulness to society. These new assessments will determine your child's usefulness to the New World Order, and that's what we're talking about.

Mark Tucker is with the new standards project and he is also with the National Center for Education in the Economy. They changed the name of the national center, as it used to be the Carnegie Forum on Education and the Economy. He is working on the new standards project, which is the new assessment. Why do we need a new assessment? Because they're not measuring content anymore, they're measuring attitudes. So we need new tests in order to measure the attitudes. His quote is "We must break the traditional education system root and branch and to do that *we must change the culture of society, the attitudes and values of our communities.*" And that's what they intend to do.

The third problem is that OBE trivializes knowledge. Knowledge has made this country the greatest country in the world to live in. Why? Because we've had the intellectual freedom. What gave us that freedom? Our Constitution, our right of concept of belief. It was the First Amendment. That is what has made this country great. But they have said, "We don't want this any more. What we want is process, not content." So imagine. Your children are going to be put through processes. They're going to be recycled until they meet the new objectives.

The fourth problem: OBE really conflicts with the competitive nature of American capitalism. I have debated William Spady of the High Success Network a few times, and I have all his training tapes. This is what he says.

> I do not like competition. I do not like grades. I do not like ability levels. I do not like class rank. I do not want to differentiate between one child who is smart and one child who is not.

He doesn't want competition, so in order to do away with it, what has to be done? Most of you are familiar with the bell curve. A bell curve means that if I gave a test on OBE to a large group of people who are reading this, some would score 90 percent, most would score in the middle — 60-70 percent — some would score below 60 and some would fail miserably. This is a bell curve and its called natural phenomena of random distribution. It's natural that some people are very bright, well read, conditioned to really keep up with everything. Most are in the middle and some could not care less or do not have the IQ to keep up. What William Spady says is, "I want a straight line. I don't want competition."

What do we have to do to children in order to eliminate competition? Think about it. Previously, children were rewarded for getting A's on their tests. Rewarded for doing the best they could. We tried to motivate kids. We wanted to encourage them to do their very best, to do something with their lives. But William Spady, the nation's number one influence on public education today, is saying we've got to change that concept because it's the group that matters, not the individual or his or her beliefs. Not you, Johnny, as an individual. Not you, Susie, as an individual. But the group. Because everyone's plotted on the same line. So now we're going to change the award system to rewards. So what are they doing to accomplish this? Cooperative education, group goals, group grades. We want Johnny, who could make A's, to be motivated and think about Susie who only has a C. She didn't study because she went to the party the night before and we should feel sorry for her because she just can't keep up. What happens to the child who is in the 99th percentile when his grade is averaged with two C's? The group might get a B-minus or a C-plus, and he gets a B-minus when he has gotten a 99th percentile on the test. And what happens to the child who failed miserably and then got a C on his report card?

This is what's happening today, all over America. It takes unnatural situations to create that kind of change in the system. In the past, you may not have understood that when you send your kids to public school, and even many private schools, you are sending them to war without even realizing it. Your children are challenged daily. And these teachers have the most influential hours of the day with children.

Now understand, there are extremely good teachers out there. Not all states are in the same position as others and not all school districts are the same even in the same county. But eventually, who holds the standard? The state. So eventually teachers will be monitored to be sure that the children are meeting the outcomes. Basically what we're talking about is pure socialist surveillance systems that monitor everyone in the system.

Another misconception: All children can meet high standards. That contradicts biological science. It's just not true. If you have a child with an IQ of 80 and a child with an IQ of 160, there's no comparison. Can they make the same standard? It's just not true.

Another thing that's very interesting about the outcome-based system is that we are moving to an individualized education plan for every child. Why? Because every child must meet the state's objective. Originally, individual education plans came from special ed. The whole idea was a plan for each child to help them meet their potential. It sounds good. We want each child to meet his or her potential and the teacher's going to push them on and that's the way it should be.

But not in Outcome-Based Education. In Outcome-Based Education, you have an individual education plan to meet the state's objective. It has nothing to do with potential, it has nothing to do with IQ. It has nothing to do with anything except what the state controls. This is a very important piece and I'll discuss it more later.

The next misconception is about local control. Because who controls the standard? The state. The other new piece that's coming into play is called the new diploma. The new diploma is called the Certificate of Initial Mastery and is controlled by the Department of Labor. The Department of Labor has set criteria for what your child will be, in a specific job criteria for the future. So this Certificate of Initial Mastery is the new diploma. In order for your child to graduate, they will have to meet all the subjective outcomes which are integrity, honesty, responsibility, self-esteem — all of which are part of the Certificate of Initial Mastery. Of course, all of the definitions are just the opposite of Christian definitions. It's all part of the national agenda, the national coding for the computer retrieval system. In all of the 32 states that I've been in, the outcomes are almost word-for-word the same as Pennsylvania. This Certificate of Initial Mastery will determine if the child graduates, go on to college, and get a job. This will be total control over their lives. Big brother is closing in rapidly.

Now the eighth major problem is that these standards are indeed based on vague and subjective outcomes, which will require behavior modification or social engineering in order to change the child. What we are talking about is mental health. These children will have to have the political correctness of the appropriate mental health outcomes in order to graduate. Remember the slogan: "You cannot change a country until they're psychologically ready for that change." You can't just control the certificate and say "We're going to control which job you have" without conditioning the minds to say that it's okay, because Americans would never sit down for that. It's going to require social engineering.

Now I want to give you a quote from Benjamin Bloom because I think it's very appropriate at this point. He wrote all the taxonomies, the original legislation that got the federal government involved in education, like the original Title 1. Bloom's quote is, *"Good teaching is challenging the child's fixed belief."* That statement should scare you to death! He's the father of mastery learning. He's the father of OBE. So the key, especially for Christian parents, is knowing that your children will be challenged daily by a non-Christian environment. Are you willing to send the children God has entrusted to you into that kind of situation on a daily basis?

The ninth problem — schools will no longer be the neighborhood schools. They will become the cradle-to-grave concept with on-site, school-based clinics. Goals 2000 mandates on-site health services. I know you've all heard this slogan, and I hate it. It just makes my skin crawl. *"It takes a village to raise a child."* You know what my response to that is? Not unless you live in a commune. My neighbor isn't going to discipline my child, I am. The grocery store down the street isn't going to tell me what's best for my child. It is God, through my husband and me, who will determine what is best for our child! This new community intends for the school to become the hub for technology, health care, education, job training, and the elderly.

The tenth problem concerns the issue of privacy. You

know what they've been saying. There are no such things as data banks. They're not monitoring individuals.

I have ten of the federal handbooks outlining how they monitor every move that people make. The teacher, the individual child, the entire family, the medical records, the performance. Is this a conspiracy? Absolutely not. This is a plan that has been in effect for a long time. I have the documents to prove this is a plan to monitor the American citizen's every move. This isn't just to scare you — this is to tell you. Privacy will be a major issue.

I was asked by the National Center of Education Statistics to testify at the Department of the Interior. One of the people there said we need to have an opposing view on privacy on the Internet. So when I was asked, they thought I was going to be the parent who was going to testify on all of the pornography on the Internet. I went in and testified on Outcome-Based Education and Medicaid, and it totally blew them away. I spoke one hour and 15 minutes. When I was done, one of the people from NASA came up and said that the problem is not the hacker out there who is illegally getting into data, it is the government-authorized use of data that we have to be concerned about. And I said, "Yes. Thank you!" They understood.

My comments were challenged as "opinion" by Barbara Clements who is head of Speedy Ex Press, in charge of the electronic portfolios for our students. I responded by saying, "Folks, guess what? If this was about reading and math, I wouldn't be here today. I challenge any person in this room to go to their education reform regulations and I can guarantee you that everything that I'm telling you is going to be in the regulations. Because if your state wants federal money from Goals 2000, your state must pursue Outcome-Based Education. They must pursue the teaching of ideology. They must pursue the new assessments. They must pursue the technology to monitor individual children in the system. It isn't an option."

What's in store for us in the future? Consider this quote: "Universal coverage will be achieved under Medicaid by January 1, 2000." This is from the White House Health Care

Interdepartmental Working Group, Hillary Clinton, Medicaid. Medicaid will be the national health care initiative that is being forced through the schoolhouse door. How is this going to happen? The national health care reform effort has tried to redefine the shape and financing of health care. A diverse array of health care providers recognized students and their families as a vulnerable new market and are positioning themselves as school-based, on-site, health care providers.

How are they doing this? Different steps have been taken. Pennsylvania and Georgia are pilots. Orange County in California, with their Medical, is a pilot. There are different states which are requesting waivers from Donna Shalala and Health and Human Services in order to implement this agenda.

Hillary Clinton proposed this as option number three, if her national health care did not pass, which it didn't. Medicaid is going to be the national health care industry, believe it or not.

This is how it's going to work. Schools have been targeted first for partial hospitalization, licensed to become Medicaid providers, and they will bill for medical and mental health services. The first step was to push for the schools to be able to provide Medicaid services. Originally it was for those "other" children, not your children. Those children over there who need health services. So the schools began to apply for partial hospitalizations. Special education, particularly IEPs, have been expanded to include OBE at-risk objectives. Any child who does not meet an OBE objective will be eligible for Medicaid funding and labeled with mental health wraparound services. So when we talk about not meeting these vague and subjective outcomes, we're talking about mental health. And who's going to pay for it, who's going to fund OBE? Medicaid.

What's the downfall of this? Your child will have DSM codes on his or her permanent records. What's a DSM code? It's the Diagnostic and Statistical Manual for Mental Health Disorders. Children will be coded if they didn't cooperate, or if they didn't meet this or that political correctness, or they didn't get their certificate of initial mastery. If you taught your children to adhere to Christian values, they will be politically incorrect and have permanent black marks on their records. DSM code — oppositional deficit disorder, 313.81. Do you know what it says? If this child argues, disobeys, and doesn't go along with what he is being told, he has an oppositional deficit disorder. That's every child in the whole world, especially if they're 4, or 3, or particularly if they're 16.

So what's going to happen to these kids with DSM codes? There is a space on the driver's license application that says that if this child has a mental disorder, they will fail the physical. So as we move to HMOs, and your doctor doesn't really know your child and they pull up the child's electronic portfolio and it comes up that they have a certain DSM code, your child will not drive. If you have a certain DSM code you can't get into the military. What does that mean? A politically correct Army. In other words, the United States will no longer have the best fighting force in the world. We can't even imagine the impact of DSM codes on our children's records.

Tracking? Well, what about the teachers? I've recently written an article entitled, "Teacher, Teacher, I Declare, They Know the Size of Your Underwear." Why did I write it? Because they monitor the teachers just as closely as the children. It's not all in place yet, but think about the ramifications. You have the cross-referencing capability of computers, and you have on one side all the children, all their attitudes, all their values, all their background, everything on the child and their testing results. Then on the other side you have everything on the teacher, children that they're teaching, everything on the curriculum. You simply cross-reference.

We're going to call up Mrs. Smith. It shows that all of her children failed the state assessment. This computer system can trouble shoot instantly who is not in compliance. So Mrs. Smith has to be re-mediated. If she refuses, she's out. A new teacher who goes along with the state will take her place. What about Johnny in the classroom? It's easy to re-mediate Johnny. He'll get an IEP. He'll have a "support team" that will come in and test him for problems. It's a fishing expedition. These teams go into the cafeterias and watch the children eating breakfast and they watch the children out on the playground. There was one actual case in which a child pushed another child down in front of the slide. That child was targeted for mental health rehabilitation because he had criminal tendencies. So we have to ask, what is normal behavior? What are we talking about with Outcome-Based Education? It's performance, it's behavior, it's discipline. Watch for the clues within the curriculum: anger management, conflict resolution, stress management, self-esteem, coping, decision-making.

How much influence will Medicaid have in all of this? Poverty guidelines have been dropped in Pennsylvania. If Medicaid is no longer a program for the poor, then it becomes the national health care program for everyone. All they have to do is expand the definitions of who is at-risk, who is eligible, and begin to target children. Once these children are targeted, they're going to call in the parents and implement case management under Medicaid.

Now you have a case manager who comes into your home. If you, as a parent, say "I don't like what you're teaching my child," then you have to go to Parents as Teachers training because you're an uncooperative parent. If you disagree, then you're an abusive parent. And if you become an abusive parent, social services will come in and take away your child. This is what the future holds. It is parents versus health care, which is really mental health. Understand what direction we're going and get down on your knees.

Let's hear the good news. First of all, we have all this information in Pennsylvania. We are the first to explode a whole entire state. We started with 30 people. Now there is an army. When we began, we were dedicated. No matter what differences we may have had, we pulled together 30 people who were dedicated to fight the system, fight the state control, and keep our freedom.

We went to our legislature. On Valentine's Day 1995, our legislature passed a resolution to investigate the Department of Education in the Medicaid connections. We've been having public hearings for the last six months. I testified just recently for four hours on the Medicaid system, the fraud, the fraud of teachers acting as psychologists in the classroom, and the idea of identifying normal children in fishing expeditions. So we're exposing the whole system.

We have good news in Pennsylvania because we are exposing everything we can, but we couldn't have done it without the knowledge. The knowledge is your armor. This knowledge will help you, it will give you strength, and your faith will help you to stand and be committed.

There was a man who called me from British Columbia. He said, "You know, the eyes of the world are on the United States and the parents in Pennsylvania. They are depending on the parents in America. The eyes of the world are upon you." And I have to ask you, ten years from now, what do you want people to say? "Oh, those are parents who didn't care. They let the children go to the state." Or are they going to say, "Those are the parents who fought and won because they care about their children. They care about America. They want to always be able to teach their children Christian principles without fear of reprisal"

The Lord our God does not give His people a vision without the ability to work it out. Nor does He give them a job without the strength to see it through. The Lord is with us, truly. We must be committed to save our children. My job as messenger is to tell you what I know. My responsibility is to give you that knowledge. Now that responsibility rests on the shoulders of everyone who reads this. We must be committed. We must become very close to our children. Our children are at war. The enemy is within and some of us didn't even know it. Let us be watchful shepherds, caring for the flock, protecting our children. Let us preach all of God's plan to the powerful and to the humble, to the rich and to the poor, the men of every rank, the men of every age, as far as God gives us strength for now, tomorrow, and forever.

Above all, we must pray diligently for our children's protection, as well as spiritual discernment for parents. May God bless your efforts.

8

America's Mass Media Deception

Dale A. Berryhill

Is there media bias in America?

You probably remember Shannon Faulkner, the young lady who was accepted to the Citadel Military Academy because she deleted her gender from her transcript. When Citadel officials found out she was female, they withdrew her admission. The national media leapt to her defense, the ACLU defended her free of charge in court, and a federal judge ordered the Citadel to admit her immediately.

You've probably never heard of Raymond Tittman, a young man who moved with his family to America from Tanzania, in Africa, while he was in college. When Tittman applied to go to law school at Georgetown University, he naturally listed himself on his application as African-American. But when he got to Georgetown, the officials were shocked to learn that Tittman is white, so they expelled him from law school. They not only expelled him, they sought sanctions with the national accreditation board to keep Tittman out of every law school in America. It took a lawsuit to force Georgetown to back down and re-admit Tittman.

Raymond Tittman's case exactly parallels that of Shannon

Faulkner, and it happened the same school year that Shannon Faulkner was applying to the Citadel. Yet everyone has heard of Shannon Faulkner and virtually no one has heard of Raymond Tittman. Why? Because Shannon Faulkner's case makes feminism look good, while Raymond Tittman's case makes affirmative action look bad. So the national media simply blacked out Tittman's story.

Is there media bias in America?

Rush Limbaugh has two of the best-selling books in American history, yet virtually no major newspaper reviewed his books. The *New York Times* did not review his first book even though it was number one on the *New York Times* best-seller list for months. A *New York Times* spokesperson said, "Well, it's just not the kind of book we usually review."

Is there media bias in America?

The late Ron Brown, Bill Clinton's secretary of commerce before his death in a tragic plane crash, had been accused of ethical and legal violations, including alleged payoffs. The national press hardly touched the story. They were too busy covering the fact that Newt Gingrich had signed a book deal. The Democrats said Gingrich's book deal was a violation of ethics, and the media repeated the charge, even though politicians on both sides of the aisle regularly receive advances on book deals. Vice President Al Gore had received a lucrative advance for his recent book *Earth in the Balance*. We did a computer search of news stories, and guess what we found? Newt Gingrich's book deal, in which no law was violated, in 6 months generated four times the stories that Ron Brown's scandals had generated in 18 months. Four times the stories in one-third the time, even though Ron Brown was accused of breaking the law while Newt Gingrich had broken no law.

Yes, there is media bias in America.

Now, it's one thing for the media to be slightly biased one way or the other. In fact, the media will probably always lean a little bit to the left, just because of the nature of the business. But what we are seeing today is media complicity with government officials to hide facts.

When I was growing up in the late sixties and seventies, in the days of the Watergate scandal, the national media told me that it had a duty to go out and discover the truth, to uncover scandal. And I believed them. I agreed that the media should be a watchdog of the government.

Is the media a watchdog of the government today?

Former Secret Service agent Gary Aldrich's recent book, *Unlimited Access*, gives the inside story of the goings-on in the Clinton White House. George Stephanopoulos, a senior staff member of the Clinton administration, actually called around to the television talk shows and asked them not to interview Aldrich. Did the media howl at such a blatant attempt at government censorship? No, shows such as "Larry King Live" and NBC's "Dateline" canceled interviews already scheduled with Aldrich. That's not acting as a watchdog; that's acting as a lap dog.

The same thing happened when David Brock wrote a book exposing Anita Hill. And there was a similar example back in the 1992 campaign, when Floyd Brown, the man who had produced the Willie Horton commercials in 1988, produced some new commercials against Clinton focusing on Gennifer Flowers. Ron Brown, at that time head of the Democratic National Committee, sent letters, of which we have copies, to every cable operator in the country saying, "Please do not run these ads. They are in bad taste. We do not need a divisive campaign in this country." And Brown was successful in his effort. The cable operators didn't run the commercial. Now imagine if a Republican had sent a letter asking any portion of the media to censor something. What do you think the reaction would be?

Much of this is simply politics, and it's obvious that the bias is against one particular party. Now, I should make it clear that, as a Christian, I don't believe the Republican party is going to save America. No political candidate is going to save America. Don't forget that the disciples thought that Jesus Christ was going to overturn the Roman domination of their country and that He was going to usher in an earthly kingdom. Christians today should not fall into the same trap. The Republican party today represents many of my values, and it may represent many of your values. But don't look for Bob Dole, George Bush, Ronald Reagan, or anyone else, to usher in a Christian nation. Only God will usher in a Christian nation. And He will do it not through the voting booth, but through the heart.

Why, then, am I talking to you about media bias? Because our society has turned away from God, and the media has been the greatest instrument of those who wish to discard biblical values. The Bible tells us that truth will set you free, and the corollary to that is that lies will imprison you. Well, our national media has been spreading lies for 30 years, and our country is now imprisoned by crime, welfare dependency, drugs, unwanted pregnancies, sexually transmitted diseases, and the negative effects of broken homes. As Christians, we have an obligation to refute the lies of the media, and to show the truth behind the moral teachings of the Bible.

Playing the Game

In 1980 a couple of young guys created a Monopoly-like board game called "Public Assistance: Why Work For A Living?" The game mercilessly lampooned the welfare establishment and government liberalism. Players in the game are either Able-Bodied Welfare Recipients or Working Persons. There are two tracks going around the board, the Able-Bodied Welfare Recipient's Promenade and the Working Person's Rut. Both players receive a check each time they circle the board, but the Working Person must pay taxes out of his. Whenever the Welfare Recipient receives a card labeled Out-of-Wedlock Child, every player in the Working Person's Rut must give him $50. The Able-Bodied Welfare Recipient then receives a higher amount every time he circles the board.

The two inventors later added a second game called "Capital Punishment," in which Liberals come out of the Ivory Tower to spring Prisoners off the Path of Justice and back onto the Street until one of the players has lost all of his Innocent Victims to crime.

If you've never heard of these games, it's because of an orchestrated, government-funded campaign to ban them from the marketplace. This campaign was spear-headed by the American Public Welfare Association, the professional organization of welfare bureaucrats. Members of the APWA, using their official government authority, intimidated retailers and called on other liberal groups to denounce the games and threaten boycotts. For example, Virgil Conrad, the South Carolina welfare commissioner, told the APWA, "We have contacted the chief investigator for the South Carolina Consumer Affairs Commission, and he advises us that legally, the game cannot be stopped from being sold. However, he promises that he will encourage retailers not to include the game in their inventory." This government official is going to use your tax dollars to go around asking retailers not to carry a certain game. Even the New York City welfare commissioner felt compelled to send an official letter to the presidents of the 13 national chain stores headquartered in the state of New York in which he said, "Your cooperation in keeping this game off the shelves of your stores would be a genuine public service." That's your tax dollars at work.

Did the media report this campaign of government censorship? On the contrary, the national media cooperated with it. The head of welfare, Patricia Roberts Harris, gave a speech to the National Association of Broadcasters in which she spoke out against the game and specifically asked the media not to give it any publicity. Where was the outcry from the media over a government official telling them how to shape the news? There was none and, in fact, the media did exactly what they were asked to do. Again, they acted as lap dogs, not watchdogs.

A liberal bias is one thing, but examples like this show that we are talking about a real danger to freedom. Board games and people getting into law school are one thing, but what else have they kept from us? I think it's interesting that the press is the only for-profit industry granted freedoms in our Bill of Rights. Most reasonable, mature people would say that with those freedoms come responsibilities. We grant the media freedom because it will help the country. But when they advocate their responsibility to report the truth, they end up hurting the country.

Where Does Media Bias Come From?

If you don't believe me when I tell you that the media is biased, perhaps you'll believe the journalists themselves.

Bernard Goldberg of CBS News recently wrote an article for the *Wall Street Journal* in which he admitted that the media is biased. "No, we don't sit around in dark corners and plan strategies on how we're going to slant the news," said Goldberg. "We don't have to. It just comes naturally to most reporters."

Sidney Stark of the liberal *Boston Globe* said on March 16, 1992, at the beginning of the presidential race between Clinton and Bush, "Many reporters may truly believe a Clinton victory is essential for the good of the country. Still, the question is whether the coverage, as a whole, has become so one-sided that the mainstream press is not giving the public the whole truth. That clearly has happened."

By August 23, 1992, Mickey Kaus of the very liberal *New Republic* magazine had to agree. "The media are already incredibly pro-Clinton," he wrote. "I get embarrassed watching the news these days. Every story is twisted against Bush."

According to a recent survey, 43 percent of the voting public voted for Bill Clinton in 1992, but 89 percent of the journalists covering Bill Clinton in Washington, DC, admit that they voted for him.

Of the writers and editors of *Time*, *Newsweek*, the three networks, and PBS, 75 percent identify themselves as being liberals, 97 percent say they are pro-choice, 80 percent believe homosexuality is normal, and 51 percent see nothing wrong with adultery. Do you think this group is going to accurately portray Christians and their values in America? Not a chance.

Should homosexuality be discouraged by our society? Fifty-three percent of the general public says "Yes," but only 4 percent of the media agrees. What about the media executives? Not a single media executive believes that homosexuality should be discouraged by society. Perhaps that explains why the media is always promoting homosexuality.

And here's the most telling statistic. When directly asked, "As a journalist, is it okay to try to shape public opinion to fit your views?" 66 percent of journalists said, "Yes." These people actually believe it is their responsibility to bias the news.

Does Media Bias Have an Effect?

Are they succeeding in their efforts? Well, as an example, 68 percent of Americans don't believe the rich pay their share of taxes. But, what's the truth? *USA Today* (April 15, 1996) looked at IRS figures for 1992 and found that:

- The top 1 percent of income-earners paid 27 percent of all income taxes paid.
- The top 5 percent paid 44 percent of all taxes paid.
- The top 10 percent paid 58 percent of all taxes paid.
- The bottom 50 percent of income-earners paid only 5.1 percent of all taxes paid.

Those are the facts, yet 68 percent of Americans believe just the opposite. Why? Because the media constantly and consciously repeats the lie that the rich do not pay their fair share of taxes.

The media also constantly and consciously repeats the lie that Ronald Reagan's policies ushered in a "decade of greed"; that the rich got richer and the poor got poorer. But, according to official figures of the United State Census Bureau, the real income of every income group rose by double digits between 1980 and 1990. Furthermore, IRS figures show that the relative tax burden of the rich went up during the so-called "decade of greed." The top 5 percent of income earners, who paid 44 percent of all taxes in 1992, paid only 37 percent in 1980. The 58 percent of all taxes paid by the top 10 percent of income-earners in 1992 was up from 50 percent in 1980. And the bottom 50 percent of income-earners saw their burden drop from 7 percent of all taxes paid in 1980 to 5.1 percent in 1992.

Following the Clarence Thomas hearings, the majority of

Americans believed that Anita Hill had lied about her allegations of sexual harassment from Thomas. Two years later, only 27 percent thought she had lied. What had changed in those two years, other than the media's constant repetition that she had been unfairly treated? Yes, the media does have the power to shape public opinion.

Political Deception

How did Bill Clinton win in 1992? What was his number one issue? He focused on the economy. And what happened to economic reporting during that period? It increased fourfold from the same time a year before, even though the recession had been worse in 1991. Isn't it odd that the content of the news reports just happened to correspond with the message of the Democratic presidential campaign?

Bill Clinton first started attacking George Bush in the first quarter of 1992, claiming the economy was in terrible shape. Yet, during that first quarter, the economy grew by 4.7 percent. In 1996, under Bill Clinton, first-quarter growth was only 2.8 percent. When Bush had a 4.7 percent growth, Bill Clinton called it "the longest recession since the Great Depression." When Clinton was running for re-election, and he had only 2.8 percent growth, did he call it an even worse recession? No! A White House economic advisor called it "plain and simple good news for the American economy and more evidence that the present economic strategy is paying off." Sounds to me like his strategy of not requiring drug testing of his economic advisers is paying off.

Has the bias continued into the 1996 presidential campaign? On the "Today" show, on February 20, 1996, Jane Pauley, talking to Bryant Gumble, said, "Didn't you say 'Senator Nole' earlier in the program?"

Bryant Gumble laughingly replied, "Yes I did, yes I did, yes I did. And I also said, 'Mr. Puke-anan.' " Does that suggest that Mr. Gumble is an objective journalist?

So Much for Conventional Wisdom

During the 1996 Republican National Convention in San

Diego, you heard over and over that the convention was "scripted" and it was just a big put-on for TV. Of course, that's better than what the media said about the Republican Convention in Houston, Texas, in 1992. There they were saying it was full of hate, divisive, and intolerant. Supposedly, President Bush let all the wrong people speak and, as a result, he lost the election. They have repeated that line so many times that they even believe it themselves. R.W. Apple of the *New York Times*, a veteran reporter for what is supposedly one of the best papers in America, had this to say in August 1996 in reference to the 1992 Republican National Convention: "Houston, after all, was followed by the defeat of George Bush, who entered his hometown convention a favorite for re-election, yet lost." This is what the media has been telling us since the convention occurred in 1992. What's the truth about the Houston Convention? Here are four different polls:

CBS Poll — Voter Support

	Before Convention	After Convention
Bush	35%	46%
Clinton	58%	48%

LA Times Poll — Voter Support

	Before Convention	After Convention
Bush	32%	41%
Clinton	52%	49%

Harris Poll-Voter Support

	Before Convention	After Convention
Bush	33%	45%
Clinton	63%	50%

ABC Poll — Voter Support

	Before Convention	After Convention
Bush	29%	42%
Clinton	58%	27%

Did the Houston Convention cause George Bush to lose? No, he lost partially because of the way the national media mis-characterized that convention, something they are doing to this very day.

As you'll recall, they also mis-characterized Bill Clinton's election, calling it a "LANDSLIDE!" Here's your landslide:

	Electoral Votes	States Won	Percent Popular Vote
Bush — 1988	426	40	54%
Clinton — 1992	370	32	43%

USA Today pointed out that in 1988, not one of the top 50 newspapers in America referred to George Bush's election as a "landslide."

This bias continued into the 1996 campaign. The national media told us that the Republican "Contract with America" was a failure. There was a big story in *Newsweek* the month of the 1996 national conventions saying that Newt Gingrich's Republican revolution had failed. What's the truth? Eighty-one bills and resolutions were introduced concerning Contract with America elected promises. Every one of them were voted on by the house, 57 percent have been enacted into law, and 27 percent were vetoed by the president. Had President Clinton not vetoed these bills, 84 percent of the Contract with America would be law. That doesn't sound like a failure, that sounds like the most massive change in government in decades!

Much of this material comes from my book, *The Media Hates Conservatives*, which was researched in the offices of Accuracy in Media in Washington, DC. I wrote this book so that people will have the facts to counter the lies being spread around by the mainstream media. We need to tell our friends, relatives, and co-workers the facts so they won't be fooled again. Only the truth will set us free.

Accuracy in Media videotapes every prime time news-cast every day. Let me share with you the transcripts of a few of these news stories from the 1992 presidential campaign, so you can decide for yourself whether there is media bias in

America. First, here's the complete transcript of a story by Dan Rather of CBS News that aired the night the Republican Convention opened in 1992. You would think that the lead story that night would be about the convention. But notice how CBS News cleverly ties the convention in with bad economic news:

> Dan Rather: "From the Astrodome in Houston and the Republican National Convention, Dan Rather reporting. Good Evening. A tremor shook the dome here today. It was in the form of facts, new figures about business, jobs, and the American economy. Money correspondent Ray Brady has the story."
>
> Ray Brady: "The one week he didn't need it, President Bush was hit today by more downbeat economic figures. An unexpected drop in the number of new homes being built. Housing starts fell 2.8 percent in July, the second month in a row they've been down, leaving builders gloomy."
>
> Builder: "Since April it's been tailing off and July was pretty slow, and August so far has not picked up yet."
>
> Brady: "It's been housing that's led the U.S. out of every recession since World War II. This time, though, Americans aren't buying, even though mortgage rates are at their lowest level in nearly 20 years."
>
> Economist: "Low interest rates is not the only game in town. We need more than that."
>
> Brady: "Builder Bill Gilligan says buyers are simply afraid to make a long-term mortgage commitment."
>
> Gilligan: "The overriding factor is job security. There aren't many industries in which there is a real stable environment that the buyers can feel comfortable that they're going to have a job next year or several years down the road."
>
> Brady: "Just today a jolt from the job front

from Wang Laboratories: The one-time giant manufacturer of word processors filed for bankruptcy. The toll among workers? About 5,000 jobs lost. Economists say continuing corporate layoffs and today's housing figures are both signs time may be running out for President Bush, that it would now take a near miracle to turn the economy around by election day. Ray Brady, CBS News, New York."

That story ran more than two minutes, an awfully long time for any news story. You'll notice in this story one of the media's favorite tricks — if it helps liberalism, talk to individuals. Find horror stories that people can be quoted as saying, "I'm being hurt by this." But if it's something that helps conservatism, just quote the statistics and move on. Have you ever heard the media interviewing someone saying, "I am a male and I was harassed by homosexuals?" Have you ever heard any story about homosexual harassment? You hear it all the time about heterosexual harassment. What about, "I suffered from an abortion," "I had a friend who died while getting an abortion," or "I am suffering psychological stress because of the abortion I had"? We never see stories like that. They only give statistics on abortion, then they move on.

Now, we just looked at a two-minute-long story on the fact that housing starts were down by 2.8 percent. But the very next night, there was good news about the economy. But instead of being the lead story, this was buried two-thirds of the way through the newscast, and look how much time Dan Rather gives it:

Dan Rather: "Some good news about the economy made it into the Astrodome today after the tremor of yesterday about housing construction being down. The government reported today that the U.S. trade deficit fell last month as exports, it is said, hit a record high. More U.S. exports could mean more jobs for Americans."

That took about 20 seconds. Worse, let's look at a story

with even better news, which took place on October 30, 1992, just four days before the election. Again, this story was buried in the newscast:

> Dan Rather: "The Commerce Department says sales of new homes fell one percent in September, the first outright drop in five months. For the first nine months of the year, sales are more than 20 percent above the same period of last year."

When housing starts are down 2.8 percent, it warrants two full minutes at the top of the newscast, but when new home sales are up 20 percent, it rates 14 seconds later in the broadcast, and even then it is prefaced by the 1 percent drop for that particular month.

Need further proof that there is media bias in America? The next transcript has to do with Floyd Brown, who produced the infamous Willie Horton ad in 1988, and who came back in 1992 planning to run commercials against Clinton. Look closely at how this story was put together. Notice also that you hear from several Democrats but you don't hear one word from a Republican. You'll even hear guilt by association, in which someone involved with the commercial used to work for someone who used to work for the Bush campaign:

> Dan Rather: "Get ready for more negative advertising in the presidential campaign. The whole campaign may be about to get a lot dirtier. The man behind the ad that helped destroy Michael Dukakis in 1988 said today he's preparing a new assault on Bill Clinton. Bill Plant is at the White House:"
>
> Plant: "If you liked the 1988 presidential campaign, you're going to love 1992."
>
> Voice from 1988 ad: "Dukakis not only opposes the death penalty; he allowed first degree murderers to have weekend passes from prison. One was Willie Horton."
>
> Plant: "Floyd Brown is back. Brown heads the conservative political action committee which paid

for the Willie Horton ad. And just like four years ago, he can't wait to help George Bush, especially if his opponent is Bill Clinton."

Brown: "Every time I pick up the morning newspaper, I feel like a kid in the candy store. The fact is that he is just very vulnerable."

Plant: "Brown says he will raise $10 million to make what he calls comparative ads for the '92 campaign. He says there is no connection with the Bush campaign. The White House was alarmed enough to send assistant press secretary Judy Smith door-to-door in the press room today to disallow Brown's committee and demand that he stop soliciting funds. They may be a little sensitive at the White House because of what happened in 1988. One man who worked on the Horton ad was working at the same time for the official Bush campaign. The producer of the Horton spot had previously worked for Bush media advisor, Roger Ailes. This time around, Democrats don't buy the idea that there is no connection."

Woman speaking: "I would bet there's not a viewer tonight who believes that this isn't connected to George Bush and his effort to win re-election."

Plant: "Bill Clinton wasn't buying it either:"

Clinton: "George Bush said on David Frost that he would do anything it took to win. I'm getting sick and tired of people who are too weak-kneed to take him on."

Plant: In case there's any doubt about what kind of campaign lies ahead, a senior official said today that the president will make family values a key campaign issue, but that he won't be doing any ads attacking Clinton's character. "No," said the official, "the president will let others do that." Bill Plant, CBS News, the White House."

What we had in that transcript was the Democratic candidate and one of his campaign officials explicitly accusing the president of the United States of lying. Instead of investigating to find out if there was a connection to the Bush campaign, the media simply let unsubstantiated allegations of specific legal wrongdoing be aimed at the president of the United States without calling them into question.

Next, let's look at a story regarding Bill Clinton's draft-dodging, which aired the the day the draft-dodging allegations broke. The letter that Bill Clinton had written to his ROTC lieutenant 20 years before had been given to the media, but not by anyone connected with the Bush campaign. Notice that the story from start to finish is not about the allegations, but about who gave the letter to the media. Notice also that this story is told from start to finish from Bill Clinton's standpoint. Bill Clinton accuses the Republicans of a smear campaign, and not a single Republican is quoted to balance things out:

> Dan Rather: "In the presidential campaign, Democrat Bill Clinton says Bush-Quayle reelection forces are using a smear campaign to constantly raise questions about his past, and as Richard Threlkeld reports tonight, Clinton had to deal with those questions again today, just six days before the New Hampshire primary:"
>
> Threlkeld: "At a hastily called news conference, Clinton accused the Republicans of trying to wreck his presidential campaign by leaking the contents of a letter he wrote as a young man about his draft status during the Vietnam war."
>
> Clinton: "We may never know the motives of the people who leaked this letter. But I think it's a fair guess to presume that they did not wish my campaign well, and that they were willing to violate the law to derail it."
>
> Threlkeld: "For a week now, Clinton's been on the stump here in New Hampshire, charging that Republicans are behind allegations that he'd had an

extramarital affair, and that he tried to avoid being drafted for Vietnam."

Clinton: "We know their game plan. They've run it against me for years in Arkansas. We've seen it in America before. Define and destroy before people really get to know the candidate."

Threlkeld: "Clinton produced as evidence a letter he said was leaked to another broadcast network, and Clinton said his aides were told by the network that it was their impression the letter came from someone at the Pentagon. It was written in 1969 to the head of the University ROTC unit Clinton had then agreed to join, but never did. He received a draft deferment as a result, but later changed his mind and declared himself eligible, although he was never called up. After first accepting the deferment, he writes, his 'anguish and loss of self-regard and self-confidence really set in.' "

Clinton: "Like so many people in my generation, I felt a profound ambivalence. I loved my country but I hated the war."

Threlkeld: " 'But,' Clinton writes, 'I decided to accept the draft in spite of my beliefs for one reason: To maintain my political viability within the system.' If recent polls are to be believed, Clinton support here has been hemorrhaging because of what he insists are Republican dirty tricks played on him because Republicans fear he is the most electable Democrat."

Clinton: "It represents a pattern of behavior by people desperate to stay in power and willing to impugn the motives, the patriotism, and the lives of anyone who stands in their way."

Reporter: "Both the White House and the Bush campaign deny any involvement in releasing the letter. Clinton, meantime, says he will publish it in tomorrow's newspaper so that in next Tuesday's primary, New Hampshire voters can judge for themselves. Richard Threlkeld, CBS News, Manchester."

Bill Clinton produced as evidence against Republicans a letter that he had written. How can a letter he wrote be evidence of anything other than his desire to dodge the draft? And Clinton says that he will publish the letter the next day? It was already in the hands of the media, and they were going to publish it the next day. This story represents a truly ingenious manipulation of the truth that could hardly be accidental.

Please notice, I am not commenting here on Bill Clinton and George Bush and who should have won. I'm only commenting on what the media did with the information it had. And what it did in that case was absolutely shameful.

So was what the media did to Dan Quayle. The next story has to do with Dan Quayle's comments about Murphy Brown. Notice that Dan Rather introduces the Dan Quayle/Murphy Brown story by saying that President Bush has flip-flopped and is now trying to "distance" himself from Quayle. Notice that in the story there is not the slightest evidence to support this idea.

Rather: "Good evening, Dan Rather reporting. The Bush-Quayle re-election campaign appeared to be in disarray today over the fray created by Vice President Quayle's carefully orchestrated attack on the Murphy Brown TV show. The vice president insisted again today that the fictional character of Murphy Brown's fictional, single motherhood, promoted bad values. He originally said it in the context of what has happened in Los Angeles. President Bush first seemed to agree, then he suddenly disagreed, and then began distancing himself. Bill Legatuda has more about President Bush, Dan Quayle, Murphy Brown, and campaign '92:'

Murphy Brown: "I'm not going to be like other mothers."

Legatuda: "Who would have thought one of

TV's favorite comedy stars would give birth to the day's hottest political debate."

Quayle: "Hollywood doesn't get it."

Legatuda: "Campaigning in California, Quayle charged that because Murphy Brown is an unwed mother, she is undermining traditional American values."

Quayle: "A character who supposedly epitomizes today's intelligent, highly paid professional woman mocking the importance of fathers by bearing a child alone. . . ."

Legatuda: "That stirred up a storm. Today, the vice president spoke to kids at an inner city school in Los Angeles, and wouldn't back down."

Quayle: "I don't believe that we should glorify illegitimacy. There are too many children born out of wedlock."

Legatuda: "The creator of "Murphy Brown" fired back, saying if Quayle believes women can't adequately raise children without fathers, 'He'd better make sure abortion remains safe and legal.' Pro-choice advocates seized the moment."

Woman: "Murphy Brown went on to choose pregnancy over abortion. Now, Vice President Quayle criticizes her for having that child."

Legatuda: "At the White House today, the president seemed to squirm a bit as he tried to balance his anti-abortion stand against a growing tide of sympathy for women left alone with the kids, though he would not directly comment on the popular television show."

Bush: "One of the things that concerns me deeply is the fact that there are an awful lot of broken families."

Legatuda: "But his critics were asking, 'What has the administration done to help?' "

Woman: "If they really were sincere about

families and family values, then the infrastructure would be in place to support families."

Legatuda: "But for all the criticism, the Bush-Quayle administration is striking a chord with the constituency it needs the most, the conservative middle class, which has been defecting lately."

Woman: "God wanted us to be together as man and wife so we could raise children."

Man: "I think family values is clearly being moved out as a new Republican campaign thing."

Woman: "I feel that the vice president should stay in South Central for one night just to see how it is."

Legatuda: "And that was how many of the kids who are fans of Murphy Brown and children of single mothers themselves reacted.

Woman: "My mother raised me fine, as good as any married couple could."

Legatuda: "The administration may have better luck generating a new dialogue on family values than changing America's TV habits. This week, 38 million viewers watched as Murphy Brown became the country's most famous unwed mother."

The White House did not try to distance itself from Quayle. In fact, Bush's comment was that he was also concerned about all the single mothers. That is exactly what Dan Quayle had said in his speech. Quayle's speech was 45 paragraphs of concern for single mothers in the inner city, saying that we have failed them. He had one sentence about Murphy Brown, and that's all the media focused on.

But here's the kicker to this story: Quayle gave his speech on May 20, 1992. Ten days earlier, the liberal *Washington Post* ran an article by a liberal writer named Barbara Defoe Whitehead entitled, "What is Murphy Brown Saying?" The article directly attacked the television show for "glamorizing single motherhood." Does that phrase sound familiar? Dan Quayle's staff used Whitehead's article as one of many sources for writing his speech, and they lifted that one phrase, the very phrase the media attacked him for. The obvious question is, why didn't Barbara Defoe Whitehead get some of the same ridicule that Dan Quayle received, and, why did the *Washington Post* join in attacking Quayle when they had said the exact same thing ten days before? The only possible answer is that the issue was being used as a political weapon in an election year to discredit one particular party. That is not the proper role of the media.

And in the ultimate act of hypocrisy, the slogan of the 1996 Democratic National Convention was "Families First." Oddly, the media had no problem with this.

Finally, let's look at Connie Chung's infamous interview with Newt Gingrich's mother:

> Connie Chung: "Mrs. Gingrich, what has Newt told you about President Clinton?"
>
> Mrs. Gingrich: "Nothing. And I can't tell you what he said about Hillary."
>
> Connie Chung (whispering): "Whisper it just between you and me."
>
> Mrs. Gingrich (whispering back): "She's a bitch. Really, that's the only thing he ever said about her. I think they had some meeting and she takes over. But when Newt is there, she can't."

The kicker to this story is that the interview was taped early in December 1993, but was not aired until January 1994, on the day that Newt Gingrich was sworn in as house speaker. Again, this wasn't news, it was a conscious effort to discredit a specific party.

Connie Chung's only defense for her actions was to say that Mrs. Gingrich "should have known" that Chung didn't mean what she said. In other words, because Chung is a journalist, Ms. Gingrich should have known she was lying. Great defense, Connie.

It's Not Just Politics

The bias in the media goes far beyond politics. It goes to

anyone who opposed the progressive vision, the liberal world view. It especially targets Christians. We've heard a lot recently about the burning of black churches. According to the Department of Alcohol, Tobacco, and Firearms, the total number of churches burned from January '95 to July '96 was 98. Forty-six were white, 52 were black. Yet the media never talks about the white churches that are burned, and they report the story only as one of racism. The real story is that there is a rash of church burnings. Not black church burnings, just church burnings! It's not racial prejudice; it's anti-Christian bigotry.

That's hardly the only example. Beginning in 1989, pro-life demonstrators in Los Angeles began complaining about the unnecessary brutality being used against them by the police. They specifically complained about Police Chief Daryl Gates. For three years, the liberal media that claims to be so much against police brutality was totally silent — until Rodney King got beat up by those same police. Are liberals really against police brutality, or does it just depend on who's in the choke hold?

Johnny Hart, the cartoonist who writes the "B.C." comic strip, is a devout Christian. Sometimes he works Christian themes into the strip. In the strip scheduled to run on Palm Sunday of 1996, the character named Wiley writes a poem called "The Suffering Prince." "Picture yourself tied to a tree, condemned of the sins of eternity," goes the poem. "Then picture a spear parting the air, seeking your heart to injure despair." The poem ends with the words, "For he is not lost, it is you who are found." The *Los Angeles Times* would not run the cartoon. "B.C." didn't appear in the *LA Times* that day. They just censored it.

Two weeks before, the *LA Times* had run an editorial cartoon picturing Bob Dole being crucified, with his crown of thorns reading, "Christian Coalition." It seems that if it's anti-Christian, the *LA Times* will run it, but if it's pro-Christian, they won't.

The Real Problem and the Real Answer

The real conspiracy here is not by men; it's from the

forces of darkness. As Christians, we know the problem is actually from Satan. The Bible tells us that Satan is the father of lies, and that there is no truth in him. The liberal media has to lie, because the values it believes in are ungodly. That's why our job is to spread the truth to the best of our ability, both truth in the divinity of Jesus Christ, and truth in the reality of God's moral plan.

Paul encourages Christians not to be dismayed or upset with what people do, "For our struggle is not against flesh and blood, but against the rulers, against the powers, against the world forces of this darkness, against the spiritual [forces] of wickedness in the heavenly [places]" (Eph. 6:12).

The people who run the media today could disappear tomorrow and they could be replaced by more of the same, because their numbers are legion. Satan tries to convince people that right is wrong and that wrong is right, and he is using the American media to do so. It doesn't matter who controls the companies. What matters is that we can trust only one thing — the Word of God. And we should be suspicious of everything else.

There is some good news. Not only the Good News that Jesus Christ will triumph in the end, but also the good news that the American people are getting wiser. In 1985, 30 percent of Americans believed the media was doing a good job. In 1993, after the 1992 campaign and the examples of blatant bias that we just examined, only 17 percent of Americans believed they could trust the media. That means that, for the first time in history, journalists are rated lower in the American mind than Congress. That's at least a step in the right direction.

9

How to Explain Jesus to Your Non-Christian Friends

John Ankerberg

Dealing With Atheists

I've had the privilege of speaking on over 75 university campuses to very non-Christian crowds. One of the first things that people say is "I don't need to listen to your stuff about religion because I'm an atheist." You may have had a friend say to you, "Hey, I don't care about Jesus. I'm an atheist."

What do you say to that person? What's your answer? Here's my advice to you. First, pray for wisdom. Then focus on simply getting them to be open to listening to your evidence. I usually say something like, "If you're an atheist, prove it to me."

Then the guy says, "Well, let's see. What information would I need to prove to you that there is no God?" You know what you would need? You would need to have all knowledge. You would have had to search every corner of the universe to make sure that God was not there. And you know right now that we're very limited. You don't even know what the person behind you is thinking, or what he's talking about. And if we don't know what's going on behind us, how could we know about what's going on in London, Hong Kong, or Chicago? We don't have that information. We're not there. We're limited in time and space to right here.

And what if God's not bound to this planet — what if He's out in space somewhere? Our space scientists tell us that even traveling 22,000 miles per second, you can't get out of our galaxy in a lifetime. Assume your starting point was around the sun. You were born, then you got into a spaceship that was going 22,000 miles per second. By the time you were 75 years of age, you wouldn't even be outside of our galaxy. And then scientists say that out there beyond our galaxy there are billions and billions of other galaxies in this thing we call the universe. If we don't know what's going on in this room and if we don't know if God's in Hong Kong, and if we don't know if God's hiding behind some planet in our own galaxy, how in the world could anyone say that God might not be out there in the universe?

You cannot say as a fact that there is no God — and most of the intellectuals will never say that. It's your village atheists that say that. Your village atheists do not know enough to realize that they cannot say, "There is no God." But I would advise you to say to your friend, "Look, would you admit that you don't have all knowledge, that there's the possibility that God's out there?" He'd have to admit to that if he's honest.

Dealing with Agnostics

Another person comes along with the argument that he is an agnostic. An agnostic is a fellow who is brilliant in the area of not knowing anything. Thomas Huxley coined the term and it basically means that you simply don't know if God exists. There are two kinds of agnostics that I've met every place that I have traveled. First of all, there is the ordinary agnostic. The ordinary agnostic is the fellow that says, "Listen, John. I don't know if there is a God. But I'll tell you what. If you've got some evidence, I'm open. I'm willing to listen." I love that kind of a person. If you're an agnostic and you're open to listening to the evidence, you can learn a great deal.

But then there's the second kind of agnostic who is what I call the ornery agnostic. The ornery agnostic is the fellow who says, "I don't know if there is a God or not, but I know that you don't know."

Of course, my next question is, "How do you know that I don't know?"

And he says, "I just know." Whatever you show them, they disregard it or try to make it fit into their world view. They're not going to look at the evidence. Their minds are closed.

Hopefully, if you're an agnostic, you're not an ornery agnostic, you're an ordinary agnostic who is open to any evidence.

What Is Christianity?

So what is the evidence? What is our case? What are we presenting? What is Christianity? Well, let's start off with a quick definition. Christianity is not a system of ethics, although it encompasses that. It is not a philosophy and a world view, although it certainly encompasses that. Christianity is totally based on a person, a real person who lived in history. He did certain things, He said certain things. And if He didn't do those things, if He didn't say those things, then Christianity is a fake. The one person that Christianity is based on is Jesus Christ, a real, historical person. Furthermore, it's not only based on Jesus Christ, it's based on a "personal relationship" with Him.

When you say that Christianity is based on an actual person in history who lived and breathed, this gets us out of this fairy tale realm and into the world of factual data. For example, we have evidence about Jesus Christ that is similar to evidence about other people. Let me ask you a question. Do you believe that Abraham Lincoln was the president of the United States at one time? Did you meet Lincoln personally? Most of us would say we have not met Lincoln personally, but we agree that he was the president of the United States. How do you know that he was the president of the United States if you've never met him personally? You know it because you were taught in school by your teacher who said there was somebody who saw what Lincoln did, and there were people who wrote down some of his speeches, etc. Both pro and con came down to us as historical records telling us that Abraham Lincoln was the president of the United States. He was shot in Ford's Theater, he didn't slip on a banana peel in Peoria and die. We know these things from historical information.

Going on back, you find other people such as Shakespeare, Charlemagne, and Julius Caesar. At the time of Julius Caesar, somebody else who actually lived in real history was Jesus Christ. If you go to the *Encyclopedia Britannica*, you will find 20,000 words listed under the person of Jesus Christ—without a hint that He didn't exist. Why? Was it because those guys at the University of Chicago are such warm-hearted Christians? Did they just want to load up the encyclopedia on Jesus Christ? Did they simply want to give Him more space than anybody else in the encyclopedia of world history? Of course not. Anybody who has ever written a history of the first 100 years A.D., whether they be a Buddhist, Muslim, Hindu, atheist, agnostic, or believer, has put Jesus Christ in there. Why? Because He was a real, historical person. How do we know that? We have eyewitnesses and historical reports about Jesus and His life on earth.

What Schools Teach Our Children

Many parents tell me that they raised their daughters and sons in Christian homes, took them to church every Sunday from a small child through grade school and all through high school. But then they sent them away to college where they lost their faith to some ungodly professor.

It's easy to understand why they lost them. Let me read to you a quote that is the standard fare at 99.9 percent of the universities of this country. This is the standard line that is given to your sons and daughters when the professor talks about Jesus Christ as a historical figure. This is an actual quote from a professor, Dr. Avrum Stroll, at the University of British Columbia. "Jesus probably did exist. But so many legends have grown up about him that it's impossible for scholars to find out anything about the real man. The Gospels of St. Matthew, St. Mark, St. Luke, and St. John were written long after Jesus was crucified. They provide no reliable historical information about him. It is almost impossible to derive historical facts from the legends and descriptions of miracles performed by Jesus." That is what your son and your daughter will hear at 99.9 percent of the universities in this country. This type of information is often reprinted by such magazines as *U.S. News & World Report* with titles like "Who Was Jesus?" When you read the article, the answer is always that they don't know who He was. Why is it that they don't know?

Let me play the role of a secular professor and try to trip you up on your beliefs. You're the Christian telling me about Jesus. I ask you about the age-old scenario about the party game where you whisper something into a person's ear — a sentence, a paragraph, or even a word. And it goes from one person to another, until we come to the last person and say, "Tell us what that sentence was." What has happened to the sentence? It becomes completely distorted; it's not even close to the original statement.

What Information Can You Trust?

If I'm am a secularist coming to you as a Christian wanting an answer, here's my dilemma: Jesus lived and taught a long way from here, across the ocean, in Israel. There's no problem with the fact that Jesus really did live. But what He said and did was seen and heard only by people who were standing around Him. They passed it on from that point orally — word of mouth — down through the years. My contention is that we have no way of finding out if it matches what actually happened. Therefore, we are left with only the faith of the church. Faith which people sincerely believe, but have no way of verifying. The people who finally wrote about Jesus were removed from Him by the time it was written down. Just like at the party, we have no way of finding out whether it really happened.

It's important to have a good response for this professor because that's what all the professors are saying to your kids when you send them to school.

If in fact that's how we got the Gospel accounts, then we are in deep trouble as Christians. I would agree with the professors. But, what if the truth was different? If I went to you as a professor and I whispered one sentence into your ear, and then said, "Professor, would you stand up and repeat what I said please," do you think we'd have a shot at getting it right? Yes, those people have it absolutely, word-for-word, in paragraph form, just the way it was given to them. The question is, did this historical information come down from people who were right on the scene, who were eyewitnesses, or, like some of the others have said, came down hundreds of years after the time of Jesus as legend and myth?

When I use the Bible with a secular crowd I say it is a book. I'm not going to argue it is inspired and inerrant, delivered to us from God. I believe that it is, but that's not the point here. All I want to find out is whether we have accurate information in this book about Jesus. There are a lot of writers who write who don't claim inerrancy; they don't claim inspiration from God, and yet we believe what they say. We bring people into courts of law all the time. We ask "Did you see the guy pick up the gun and shoot the person?" If the guy says "Yes," and he's a credible witness, the testimony will be used. So we want only want to find out whether we have accurate information.

Aristotle said every time you open up a historical document, you must give the benefit of the doubt to the person who wrote it. Therefore, giving the benefit of the doubt intellectually to the writer, our first question is "What do they claim?" Did they claim to be 200 years after the fact? Or did they claim to be eyewitnesses who saw it and stood up and repeated what they saw?

In Luke 1:1 we read:

> Many have undertaken to draw up an account (NIV).

Many critics today say it was oral and that it was only

delivered word-of-mouth and wasn't written down until 200 years later. Luke disagrees. He says "many" had undertaken to draw up an account. What's drawing up an account? It's an historical narrative, it's a written account. An account of what? "Of the things that have been fulfilled among us" — namely, Jesus' life.

In other words, Luke was saying in the beginning of his book that when he came along, there were other people who were eyewitnesses, other people who had personally seen Jesus. Even before he got a chance to write, others had written accounts of what had transpired when they had been with Jesus. "Many," he says. I don't know how many "many" is, but it's more than one.

"Many have undertaken to draw up an account of the things that have been fulfilled among us, just as they were handed down to us by those who from the first were eyewitnesses."

So he is explaining that the people who wrote these accounts were just like the eyewitnesses who have given us other accounts. They were right there, in person, on the scene.

Luke goes on to say in verse 3, "Therefore, since I myself have carefully investigated everything...." In the King James Version it's translated, "has a perfect understanding." "Perfect understanding" means carefully investigating everything. That's exactly what you do when you do research. You get all the information available, look closely at the details, sift through the evidence, then you write your conclusion. Luke says that they claim to be eyewitnesses. They claimed, and they put it into writing, that Jesus did certain things. He's saying that he didn't just accept what they said but "carefully investigated everything from the beginning."

How did he investigate? The Bible says, in several places, that he was the traveling companion of the apostle Paul, and he also had access to the other apostles. It's very probable that he had access to several different written documents about Jesus' life. He could question Peter, John, and others about what they were saying. In other words, Luke is saying, "I checked it out,

I have carefully investigated everything from the beginning."
It's interesting that he used the word, "beginning." The Gospel
of Luke is the only one that mentions Jesus' birth. That's where
the Christmas story is recorded. When he said that he checked
it out from the beginning, he wasn't kidding.

Luke 1:3, continues, "It seemed good, also, to me, to write
an orderly account for you, most excellent Theophilus [prob-
ably a governor], so that you may know the certainty of the
things that you have been taught." That's why Luke says he
wrote his Gospel. Why? He wanted him to be certain of the
facts. He's saying, "I had eyewitness testimony, I was basing
it on that, but I just didn't accept it, I checked it out carefully.
I investigated all of it before I wrote it down for you."

You may have seen the movie, *The Last Temptation of
Christ*. It upset many Christians at the time because of the
biblical inaccuracies that it contained. I tried to have the
director, Martin Scorsese, on my television program with
some Christian conservatives like Cal Thomas, but unfortunately it fell apart at the last moment. But we were able to fly
out to Hollywood and actually see the film. We also obtained
a copy of the movie so we could write a book and quote
accurately. Martin Scorsese was taking the information from
Nikos Kazantzakis' book, *The Last Temptation of Christ*. They
were simply taking an extremely liberal and distorted view of
Jesus and distributing it in story form.

In one scene, sitting around a fire, Peter says to John,
"Hey, John. We've got to talk to the people tomorrow. We need
a good miracle from Jesus. What could we have Him do?"

John says, "Well, let's see. I know — people are hungry;
why don't we have him feed 5,000 people?" What they were
implying was that Jesus didn't really do those hundreds of
miracles; it was cooked up around the campfire by His disciples.

Apparently Nikos Kazantzakis, Martin Scorsese, nor any
of the people at Universal ever read 2 Peter 1:16 to understand
what Peter himself said about those miracles:

"We did not follow cleverly invented stories when we

told you about the power and coming of our Lord Jesus Christ, but we were eyewitnesses of His majesty."

Luke was saying, "We based what we wrote on eyewitness reports. These are not cleverly invented stories; we didn't think this up over a campfire. We were there, in person!"

Look at what John says in 1 John 1. He was obviously awed by what he saw. Five times in these verses John says "We have seen" something. Three times he says "We have heard" something. Six times he says, "That which we have heard and seen we proclaim or testify to you." He also says, "That which was from the beginning, which we have heard [talking about the apostles and other eyewitnesses], which we have seen with our eyes, which we have looked at [that word 'looked at' means 'carefully scrutinize,' to really examine carefully] and our hands have touched. . . ." Why did he say they had to touch Him? I believe it was because God knew that at some point in the future, there would be a cult called Gnosticism that would contend that Jesus was a ghost. John says, "We touched Jesus," hence, He's not a ghost.

First John 1 continues:

This we proclaim concerning the word of life. The life appeared. We have seen it and testified to it and we proclaim to you the eternal life, which was with the Father, and has appeared to us. We proclaim to you what we have seen and heard so you also may have fellowship with us. And our fellowship is with the Father and with the Son, Jesus Christ. He commanded us to preach to the people and to testify that He is the one whom God appointed as judge of the living and the dead. And this is the message we have heard from him and we declare to you.

Do you get the idea that John saw something, heard something, and that's what he's telling the people about? Of course! It's as if he's saying, "We were there at the party, we saw Jesus do these things, and we wrote it down." It was not recorded 100 years later, it was an eyewitness account. In Acts 1:1 it says:

> In my former book, Theophilus, [referring to Luke] I wrote about all that Jesus began to do and to teach until the day He was taken up to heaven after giving instructions through the Holy Spirit to the apostles He had chosen.

And it was Jesus who chose His own Apostles. Then, after suffering, He showed himself to these men and gave many convincing proofs that He was alive. He appeared to them over a period of 40 days, and spoke about the kingdom of God. There are 10 appearances of the resurrected Christ after He was crucified. Why did He continue to appear all these times? John says it lasted for 40 days. Jesus kept showing up and showing himself to these people. Why? To make absolutely certain that they didn't miss the point! He was alive again. If you went to a funeral and watched them close the casket and bury the body, but the body showed up at your home later, very much alive, you wouldn't know what to think. But if he continued to show up and talk and eat for 40 days with you and your friends, you would be convinced that He was alive. Jesus proved He was alive over and over again to these guys.

According to Acts 1:1-3, Jesus chose these men. Look at what He commissioned them to do.

> But you will receive power when the Holy Spirit comes on you and you will be witnesses in Jerusalem, all of Judea, Samaria, to the ends of the earth.

Did they receive power through the Holy Spirit? Turn to Acts 2:22. Peter is preaching:

> Men of Israel, listen to this. Jesus of Nazareth was a man accredited by God to you by miracles, wonders and signs which God did among you through Him as you yourselves know.

Don't miss the point that when Peter preached, he was preaching to other eyewitnesses. As F.F. Bruce at Manchester University said about the New Testament gospels, one of the reasons that we know that they hold true information is that you can't pad the case or lie when you're preaching to an audience of people who were at the same scene that you're describing. Bruce points out that not all those people were friendly. They had killed the very person they were talking about. They were hostile witnesses. If you said one word wrong, your life could be in jeopardy.

Turn to Acts 2:32. Peter is preaching again and says:

God has raised this Jesus to life. We are all witnesses of the fact.

They didn't say that they heard about it 10, 15, or 100 years later. No. The fact is, they were present at the scene. They saw what Jesus did. They were witnesses.

Acts 3:14 says:

You disown the holy and righteous one and ask that a murderer be released to you. You killed the author of life, but God raised him from the dead. We are witnesses of this.

Turn to Acts 4:19. Peter and John replied:

Judge for yourselves whether it is right in God's sight to obey you rather than God, for we cannot help speaking about what we have seen and heard.

That's a typical remark by John. They were saying, "What we're talking about is what we saw. What we heard." They were witnesses.

Acts 4:33 says:

With great power the Apostles continued to testify to the resurrection of the Lord Jesus and much grace was upon them.

Turn to Acts 10:38. Peter is preaching how God anointed Jesus of Nazareth with the Holy Spirit and power, how He went around doing good and healing all who were under the power of the devil, because God was with Peter. Then he says:

> We are witnesses of everything He did in the country of the Jews and in Jerusalem. They killed him [Jesus] by hanging him on a tree, but God raised him from the dead on the third day and caused him to be seen. He was not seen by all the people, but by witnesses whom God had chosen.

Remember, Luke said in Acts 1 that Jesus chose him "by us who ate and drank with him after He rose from the dead." He's simply saying, "We are witnesses of everything he did."

In Galatians 1:20, the apostle Paul, who was inspired to write a lot of the New Testament, says:

> I assure you before God that what I am writing you is no lie.

Now when you hear this, you wonder if any of those liberal professors ever read the New Testament. Apparently not.

When Was the New Testament Written?

Our next question is, when were these accounts written? Liberal scholars say they were written 200 years after Jesus died. Let's look at a couple of quotes.

William F. Albright at Johns Hopkins University, who died just a few years ago, was the foremost biblical archaeologist in the world. Anyone who majors in archaeology in college, especially if you study biblical writings such as the Dead Sea scrolls, will have to deal with Albright. Before he died, he said that every one of the books that we have in our New Testament — from Matthew to Revelation — was written by a baptized Jew between the time of A.D. 40 to 80, most likely between A.D. 45-75.

John A.T. Robinson, a bishop and one of the greatest critics of the New Testament in England, was challenged by his scholarly friends to re-examine the facts to determine when the New Testament documents were written. Before he died, he came out with a book called *Redating the New Testament* which stated that every book of the New Testament was written before A.D. 69, and the Gospel of Mark probably went to A.D. 40.[1] When did Jesus die? A.D. 33. If you want to see the documentation for that, look at *The Chronological Aspects for the Life of Christ.* It's a book that takes archaeology and the New Testament and links them together in terms of dates.[2] The first biblical record, "The Book of James," according to the critics, came out in A.D. 40. This date is by people who didn't even believe the Bible is accurate. That means that seven years after the death of Jesus, the New Testament documents were beginning to be circulated around Jerusalem, and you don't come up with a myth or legend in seven years.

Let me give you an illustration. Where were you, what were you feeling, and what were you thinking when you heard these words: "The president of the United States has been shot." Most of us remember where we were and what we were doing. How long ago did the Kennedy shooting happen? Thirty or so years ago. If you were born after 1963, you have no memories of the shooting. But what if somebody said, "Now here's how Kennedy died. He was driving down the street in his limousine, and there was an Indian standing on the sidewalk. He had a bow and arrow, he took the bow, shot the arrow, and got Kennedy right in the head."

You'd say, "No, because we've all watched the replay of the shooting on TV and there were no Indians involved. We know he didn't die by an arrow in the head." Why? You were an eyewitness via television or maybe you were actually on the streets in Dallas.

My point is this: You can remember what happened. And if somebody came out with a phony report of how Kennedy died, he would be quickly corrected. You were an eyewitness. These books of the New Testament came out only seven years from the time Jesus had died. Kennedy was shot over 30 years ago and you could remember that clearly. You had no problem.

Do you think it would be possible for those people, in that day, to say to those Apostles who were standing up in Jerusalem and saying "He's alive, we saw him," if it were not true? Of course not. They were the ones who killed Jesus.

Let's look at a biblical example in Mark 2. This is a story that many of us learned in Sunday school class — the story of the paralytic who was let down through the roof. Let me show you something you may never have seen. Mark's account of this event explains that the room was extremely crowded, and the scribes, the Pharisees who were the leaders of the Jews, are also seated there. These poor guys who had carried the paralytic to the meeting got there and couldn't get in. Why? Because the whole town was there, including many important Jewish leaders. So what did they do? One guy said, "Hey, let's go up on the roof. We can make a hole and let him down." So they lower the guy down through the roof and land him next to Jesus.

Did you realize this guy had never walked? They obviously wanted Jesus to heal him. What did Jesus say to the guy? He said, "My son, your sins are forgiven." They were expecting Jesus to tell him to "rise and walk" instead of forgiving his sins. In Matthew 9, when you look carefully at the original Greek, it translates, in effect, that this guy didn't want to go to the meeting, that they forcefully picked this guy up and threw him on the mat. And now he was being lowered down through a hole in the roof in front of all these people and Jesus said, "My son, your sins are forgiven" and immediately the place went into a frenzy.

What caused the uproar? You've got to know a little bit about Jewish background. Josephus, in his history of the Jews, tells us there was a man by the name of Theudas who wanted to impress the people that he was God's Messiah. And if you were to be God's Messiah, you had to do a miracle. So he decided to try to part the Jordan River. That was a big mistake. Everybody looked, but nothing happened. Josephus says a crowd stood at the river for about four hours in the hot sun while this guy was yelling for the Jordan River to part. When nothing happened, they concluded that it was blasphemy and they stoned him to death, which is the biblical commandment for dealing with false prophets. You didn't go around saying "I'm the Messiah" or "I'm the son of God." You didn't say any of that kind of stuff because they'd kill you if you couldn't back up your claims.

Jesus said in front of the scribes, the leaders of the Jews, "My son, your sins are forgiven." These scribes were thinking, *We're going to have to stone this guy.* Jesus knew that they were thinking, *There's only One that can forgive sins. That's God alone.* The Pharisees and the scribes weren't always wrong, and they were right about this. There is only One who can forgive sins. They knew Isaiah recorded in the Old Testament that God said, "I am the only Saviour, I am the only God, I am the only One who forgives anybody's sins" (Isa. 43:10-13).

As things were getting tense in that room, it's interesting to notice what Jesus did. He asked them a simple question. He said, "Which is easier for me to say to the paralytic: 'Your sins are forgiven,' or 'Take up your bed and walk'?"

What was Jesus doing? Why did He ask them that question? What would be the easiest thing for Jesus to do in that situation; "Take up your bed and walk" or "Your sins are forgiven"?

Let's put it this way. They were saying, "Who do you think you are? God?" And basically, Jesus, by saying, "Your sins are forgiven," was claiming to be God. But in order to make a claim, you'd better back it up with a miracle. Now let's say that Jesus was a fake and a phony. The scribes were saying, "Jesus, you're not God." So Jesus was saying to them, "But in order that you may know that the Son of Man has authority on earth to forgive sins, that which you cannot see, let me do something for you that you can see." He said to the man, "I say unto you, take up your bed and walk," and the man stood up and he walked, and he walked out of there. Jesus was saying, "When you see me heal his inability to walk, you'll know I also can forgive sins."

How Do You Introduce Your
Friends to Jesus Christ?

We have said that Christianity is based in history on a real person who actually lived. If you look in the *Encyclopedia Britannica*, you can find 20,000 words listed about Jesus and they never hint that He didn't exist. Why? Because anybody who does a history of the first 100 years has to include Jesus Christ because people gave us historical information about Him. As we have already established, there were at least eight eyewitnesses, or people who claimed that they had contact with the eyewitnesses, who wrote the books of the New Testament: Matthew, Mark, Luke, John, Paul, James, Peter, and Jude.

But then we came to what the universities are teaching today: "Jesus probably did some things, but by the time it was written down 200 years or so later, it couldn't have been historically accurate." That's what we're dealing with in our universities today. But Paul says, "I assure you before God I am not writing to you a lie."

But what else can we find to back up the claim that we have accurate information about Jesus? First of all, do we have accurate information about Jesus? If we can conclude that we do, then we want to see in those documents what Jesus claimed about himself. Did He ever say that He was God? Again, I am not taking the Bible as a book that dropped out of heaven, inspired and inerrant. I believe that it is without error, but I'm not using that assumption here. If you're a non-Christian, I'm simply asking whether I can look at these books and trust that these authors give me accurate information. A guy who creates road maps doesn't claim to be inspired by God, but we assume he gives us information that's accurate. So all I want to find out is whether we have evidence that shows these books are accurate in what they depict about Jesus. Next, we'll find out what they said about Jesus and what Jesus said about himself, and then we'll draw some conclusions.

Dating Proofs

Consider this argument in dating the books of the New

Testament. Let's say I want to start with the Book of Acts and date it as to when it was written. Then I want to work back to the Gospels and date them also. I think you'll find this interesting. Here are four reasons why the Book of Acts must have been written at least no later than A.D. 62.

Reason Number One

The fall of Jerusalem is not mentioned in the Book of Acts. Most of us know that Christianity began in, and then spread out from, Jerusalem. It's the primary city where the Apostles were based, and the Book of Acts records the first happenings of the church in Jerusalem and how it grew. Now history tells us that Jerusalem was destroyed in A.D. 70 by Roman soldiers. The emperor Nero first dispatched a man named Vespasian to this area. Then Nero committed suicide in A.D. 68. Therefore, Vespasian became the emperor, and subsequently gave his son Titus the responsibility of conquering Jerusalem.

In A.D. 70, Titus took four legions of Roman soldiers and laid siege to Jerusalem. He conquered the city, then burned it, and finally slaughtered its inhabitants. The whole world heard about this. And if the Book of Acts talks a lot about what happened in Jerusalem, why didn't Luke put the destruction of Jerusalem in there? Because it hadn't happened yet! Therefore the historical account of the fall of Jerusalem proves that the Gospels were written before A.D. 70. Otherwise, the fall of Jerusalem would have been recorded in them.

Reason Number Two

The historical account of Nero's horrible persecution of Christians is not mentioned in the Book of Acts. There were two Christian persecutions that Nero was responsible for — one was in A.D. 64 and the other one in A.D. 68. There are some words in the Book of Acts concerning some of the local persecutions, but nothing about the emperor's edict across the whole Roman Empire that Christians should be hunted down and killed. None of that is mentioned in the Book of Acts. Why? Because the Book of Acts was written before that. So, logically we've dated Acts before 64 A.D.

Reason Number Three

The third reason is that the apostle Paul was still living when the Book of Acts came to an end. He was one of the central characters in the Book of Acts. It's almost his biography. You can't spend that much time on one person's actions, talking about what he did, what he taught, what he said, and so on, and not deal with his death! Most people think that Paul died in the first Neronian persecution of A.D. 64. Because Luke does not record Paul's death (Paul is still living in the Book of Luke — he's confined to jail at that time), then this proves Acts had to be written before A.D. 64.

Reason Number Four

We know that Peter died in approximately A.D. 65 and James is said to have died in A.D. 62. But they're still alive at the conclusion of Acts. Luke felt it important to record the fact that Stephen and James, the brother of John, died. So if Peter, Paul, and some of the others were much more important, Luke would have recorded the facts related to those deaths. The reason these facts weren't recorded was because Acts was written before A.D. 62.

That's four good reasons for the Book of Acts being written prior to A.D. 62. So we begin with that premise. Now what do we know about Acts? Acts is Book Two of Luke. We know that Luke first wrote the Gospel of Luke, then wrote Acts. He tells us this in Acts 1: "In my former book, Theophilus, I wrote about all that Jesus began to do and to teach." That's what the Gospel of Luke is about. But if it's the "former book," that means it came first. So now we have A.D. 62 as the date when Acts was written. If the Gospel of Luke was written before that, we must date it before A.D. 62. But how far back? Well, let's try dating it A.D. 58, just a few years before Acts was written. Most scholars accept that date as fact.

Most also believe Matthew was written before Luke. People like William F. Albright and Dr. Johnny T. Robinson conclude that Matthew was written between A.D. 50 and 55, before the Gospel of Luke. Also, almost all of the scholars would say that Mark had to have been written before Matthew because there are sections of Mark that show up word for word in both Matthew and in Luke. These scholars say that they obviously used some of the material from Mark, and therefore had to come even before Matthew. Well if Matthew's at 50 to 55, many conclude Mark was written around A.D. 45. Both William F. Albright and Johnny T. Robinson put Mark as being written as early as A.D. 40.

Now what's the significance of all this? Well, Harold Hoehner's book, *Chronological Aspects of the Life of Christ*, documents archaeologically how Jesus died at A.D. 33. Sometime around A.D. 40, Mark had been recorded. By A.D. 50, Matthew had been written; by A.D. 58, Luke; and then by A.D. 62, Acts had been recorded.[3] What does that tell us? It tells me we've got accurate information. Because, again, if these books had been out 7 years, 15 years, 20 years — actually 29 years for all of the gospels and the Book of Acts, if the details weren't true, people would have protested. Remember, you have been living now for over 30 years since the time of President Kennedy's death. You know how he died. All of the gospels, if you were living in Jesus' day, would have already been circulated while you were still there. And just like you can remember the events about Kennedy, the people both pro and con could remember seeing Jesus. He was a controversial figure. Therefore, when you look at the Gospels, the dates on which they were written prove that we have accurate information.

Peter's Proofs

In the Book of Acts, Peter was preaching to two kinds of people. Those who loved Him and those who hated Him. If Peter was preaching to those who loved Jesus, they would obviously have scrutinized what he said. Maybe they were at the very place when Jesus originally said it. Peter couldn't get away with claiming anything that wasn't true.

On the other hand, if you had people in the audience who were hostile to Jesus, they would want to prove what Peter was saying was wrong. The Apostles were preaching to this kind of crowd constantly. The Apostle's books (Matthew, Mark, Luke, etc.) came out when those people, both those who loved Jesus and those who were hostile to Him, were still living. They could remember being there and watching Jesus as He spoke. That's why F.F. Bruce said it just can't be legend, it can't be myth. They couldn't have lied because there were too many people who were eyewitnesses and could have corrected them if they were wrong. That tells me we have accurate information.

Archaeological Proofs

Now another area that convinces us that we have very accurate information is archaeology. Sir William Ramsey from the School of Tubingen in Germany, was one of the higher critics of the "Book of Luke." He didn't believe that these men were eyewitnesses to Jesus' life. But he was one of the world's greatest archaeologists so he went to the Holy Land to prove his thesis. In Israel, he unearthed many stones with inscriptions that came from Jesus' time period. Reading them, he realized that his assumptions were wrong and that Luke was right. Many other archaeologists have done the same — all with the same conclusion — the biblical accounts are accurate.

Frank Peretti has written several best-selling books over the last few years. If the Lord tarries and Frank writes for another 30 years, the words that he'll be using in his book will probably reflect our culture and be a little different than the ones we used a generation ago. For example, during the 1960s, the teenagers used the word "groovy." If we read a book today and the characters are using the word "groovy," we would date the phrase to come from the mid to late sixties.

Today, we also use "dated" words like "awesome." Do you think that 100 years from now, when the historians are writing about America, that they will call President Clinton, "Slick Willie"? This term will not make any sense to someone reading history 100 years from now. Just like we use these nicknames for presidents throughout history, the people of the first century also had nicknames for their kings and rulers. And only the people who lived in that slice of history knew about it.

When Ramsey took his famous trip into the Holy Land, he believed that Luke was probably just a mythical figure — someone who used the name of Luke but really didn't know the events because he wasn't an eyewitness on the scene. But, Ramsey found that Luke, in naming the emperors, the rulers, the cities, and geographical areas, knew all of the secret names that were written on the stones that were excavated from that period. Ramsey concluded that Luke couldn't have known those things unless he had actually been there and lived during that period of time. Ramsey changed his mind completely about Luke and determined that Luke was one of the greatest historians of that time.

Luke mentioned 32 different countries in the Gospel of Luke and in Acts, 54 different cities, 9 separate islands, and several rulers. When they checked him out archaeologically, Luke never made one mistake; he was accurate in every one of those areas. Now if he is accurate in everything that you can check, then in the areas that you cannot check, you've got to give him the benefit of the doubt because he has already established his credibility. He has proven to be an accurate, historical writer.

What you may not realize is that if you will not accept the documents that we have in the New Testament then you can't accept Aristotle, Plato, Thucidides, and Homer. You're going to have to throw out the classics. Here's why. You've got Aristotle writing around 400 B.C. and they didn't have printing presses back then. So they would write it on material that would decay and fall apart. In order to preserve this material, usually papyrus, they would have to recopy it. And then as that copy got a little bit soiled and also started to disintegrate, they would have to copy it again. Do you realize how much time transpired between the time that Aristotle wrote his manuscripts and the date of the manuscript we have today? Fourteen hundred years transpired. Aristotle wrote about 384 B.C. and the oldest copy that now exists in the museums is dated at A.D. 1100!

Even though we have that big gap from the time of Aristotle to the time that we have a copied manuscript, no one in the world doubts the authenticity of Aristotle. Yet we don't have an accurate copy of what he said. Not one classical scholar doubts the accuracy of what we have, even though there is a 1,400 year gap.

We have the same problem with Plato. He wrote about 427 to 347 B.C. The oldest manuscript that we have found is dated A.D. 900. That's a 1,200 year gap. Thucidides wrote during 496-406; the earliest copy that we have found is A.D. 1,000, a 1,400-year time span. Sophocles wrote about 496 to 406 B.C. The earliest copy we have is dated at A.D. 1000, a 1,400-year time span. Yet they all agree that we have an accurate account of what these authors originally wrote and said.

Unfortunately, these same scholars, when confronted with the New Testament, claim that there is no accurate information available. But the truth is, there is incredible evidence. For example, in Egypt they found five verses from the Gospel of John which are dated as being written at A.D. 117. It's called the John Ryland's Papyrus. Obviously, these are copies, but if John wrote and ended his book in A.D. 80, that means from the time that he wrote it to the date of the copy they found is only 37 years. Compare this to 1,400 years for Aristotle! The Ryland's Papyri are dated around A.D. 175-225; it contains most of the Gospel of Luke and most of the Gospel of John. These are only 110 years away from the Apostles. The Chester Beatty Papyri are dated at A.D. 250, three codices that contain most of the New Testament. This would put them at 180 years from the time of the Apostles.

Major manuscripts that have the whole Bible, the Codex Vaticanus dated to A.D. 325, and Codex Sinaiticus dated to A.D. 350, would be only 255 years away from the Apostles. So, if you will not accept the New Testament writers as giving accurate historical information, what are you going to do with Plato, Aristotle, Thucidides, and Sophocles? I don't know of any classical scholar who is willing to chuck the entire classics, yet they continue to disregard the Gospels as fiction!

Let me give you another illustration. How many copies do we have for the New Testament compared to Aristotle and Plato and so on? When you are piecing together information to determine original writings, the more manuscripts that you have, copies that have survived through the years, the more accurate it will be. You can compare all of the different manuscripts. We have 49 copies of Aristotle, 7 of Plato, 193 of Sophocles, and 8 of Thucidides. Of the poets Cantullus and Lucretius, only three and two known copies exists. There are 643 copies of Homer's *The Iliad* in existence.

So, how many manuscripts or copies of the New Testament exist? At the present count, there are 24,633 manuscript copies that have been found. Hardly inferior information. They've got two copies of Lucretius. We have over 24,000. Who needs the proof? That's why Dr. Bruce Metzger at Princeton, in his text of the New Testament, states: "The works of several ancient authors are preserved to us by the thinnest possible thread of transmission. In contrast with these figures, the textual critic of the New Testament is embarrassed by the wealth of his material."

William F. Albright said, "Only modern scholars who lack historical method and perspective can spin such a web of speculation as that with which critics have surrounded the gospel tradition." F.F. Bruce at Manchester stated: "There is no body of ancient literature in the world which enjoys such a wealth of good, textual attestation as the New Testament."

What we have recorded in the Gospel are accurate, historical pieces of information about Jesus, written by eyewitnesses who were present on the scene. You can't doubt the information without throwing out ancient history.

Jesus Was God

The facts speak for themselves — we have very accurate historical information regarding Jesus. But then you have those people who say, "Jesus never said He was God." Major national magazines repeat this phrase frequently. I hear it on campuses all the time. Many, many professors teach this to kids at school. How do you answer them?

Some people insist that you need to know Greek and Hebrew. But that's not true, you can find answers without being a Greek and Hebrew scholar.

Consider the words that Jesus used in describing himself and who He claimed to be. John 8:12: "I am the light of the world." John 11:25: "I am the resurrection and the life; he who believes in Me shall live even if he dies." Notice the emphasis that Jesus puts on the personal pronoun "Me." No world religious leader has ever pointed people to himself. Mohammed said "Go to Allah." Ghandi and others all pointed people to someplace else. Buddha never said, "Come to me." In John 14:6, Jesus said, "I am the way, the truth, and the life. No man cometh unto the father but by Me." In Matthew 11:28, Jesus said, "Come unto Me, all ye that labor and are heavy laden. I will give you rest. Take my yoke upon you and learn of Me." Jesus also said in John 6:35, "I am the bread of life. He that cometh to Me shall never hunger. He that believes on Me shall never thirst."

John 8:56 records a conversation that Jesus had with the religious leaders of that day. Jesus said:

> Your father Abraham rejoiced to see My day, and he saw [it}]and was glad. The Jews therefore said to Him, "You are not yet fifty years old, and have You seen Abraham?" Jesus said to them, "Truly, truly, I say to you, before Abraham was born, I am."

Jesus and Abraham were about 1,500 years apart. John 5:46 says, "For had ye believed Moses, ye would have believed Me; for he wrote of Me." John 5:39 says, "The Scriptures bore witness to Him."

John 14:9 records His most blatant comment regarding His being God, "He that has seen Me has seen the Father." That would be easy for an Orthodox Jew to understand. If you've seen Jesus, you've just seen God. In Mark 2, Jesus claimed He could forgive men's sins. In John 11, He claimed

He could give all men eternal life. Jesus said:

> I am the way, and the truth, and the life; no one comes to the Father, but through Me.

If you take all of these statements that Jesus made, it's clear he was claiming to be God. And if you accept that, then you need to take the next step — a personal relationship with Jesus Christ, God of the universe and all that's in it. Christianity is not based on a person, it's a relationship with that person. When you die on this earth, and you will eventually die, you can know that the destiny waiting for you is eternal life in heaven. That's real peace on earth. Knowing ahead of time that when you die, you win. You go to heaven for eternity. Jesus said in 1 John 5:13, "These things I have written to you who believe in the name of the Son of God, in order that you may know that you have eternal life."

If you believe that Jesus is who He said He is, that He came to earth to pay the price for your sin so you can go to heaven and avoid the blackness and horrible heat of hell, and you have never become a Christian, pray this prayer to the almighty God of heaven and earth:

> Lord, I am a sinner and do not deserve eternal life in heaven. But I accept your death on the cross as your payment for my sin. Thank you for taking my sin away and its penalty of death and hell. I give my life to you. Please come into my heart and make me a new person. Guide me to the right teachers so that I can know and love you better. Amen.

---

[1] John A.T. Robinson, *Redating the New Testament* (London, SCM, 1976).

[2] Harold Hoehner, *The Chronological Aspects for the Life of Christ* (Grand Rapids, MI: Academie Books, Zondervan, 1977).

[3] Hoehner, *The Chronological Aspects for the Life of Christ.*

10

Exposing the Federal Reserve

Chuck Missler

If the press and the media in our country were doing their jobs, exposés like this would not be necessary. But there is a great deal going on behind the scenes that we're not told about because the press refuses to publish the truth about what's going on in our country.

For years, many authors have published writings suggesting that there is a hidden government behind the scenes that actually runs America. Most of us, I think, have dismissed these so-called conspiracy theories as extremist and unrealistic. But I had the opportunity some time ago to have lunch with Otto Von Hopsburg, who is a member of the European Parliament, and whose father ruled Europe until the end of the Austrian/Hungarian empire. During that lunch, he made two remarks — one that did not surprise me too much and one that totally shocked me.

He said the ignorance in America is overwhelming, and I knew what he meant, because I've traveled for 30 years in my corporate career with offices in Europe. I was always startled at how much the average Europeans know about our local politics and how ignorant we are of even the issues in our own country, let alone of the global scene. That was something I had encountered myself, and I understood his remark.

But he also made a remark that the concentration of power in America was frightening, and I didn't know what he meant. I spent most of my 30 years as an executive and, I thought, as a reasonably well-informed American who has a deep, passionate love for this country. I value the free enterprise system and our free democracy, etc. I had no idea what he was getting at, so I started to do some homework. The results of my inquiries are disturbing. I want to share some of those with you.

The Bible says we should not be ignorant of Satan's devices, and that's my excuse to get into some things that I want to call to your attention. I challenge you to do your homework. I'm hoping you will find what I'm going to talk about covered in the press in the coming months. If not, this country is doomed.

Andrew Jackson

We first need to have a better understanding of the forces that will shape the events in the coming few years. Let's back up to Andrew Jackson. He was the first president from west of the Appalachians. He was unique in that he was elected by the voters without direct support of any political party. And he vetoed the renewal of the charter of the Bank of the United States on July 10, 1832. By 1835, President Andrew Jackson declared his disdain for the international bankers with the remark, "You are a den of vipers. I intend to route you out and by the eternal God, I will route you out. If the people only understood the rank injustice of our money and banking system, there would be a revolution before morning."

Following that speech, there was an unsuccessful assassination attempt on his life. But he mentioned to Martin Van Buren, his vice president, "The bank, Mr. Van Buren, is trying to kill me." Was this the beginning of a pattern in our country? Would this pattern of intrigue plague the White House itself over the coming decades?

Abraham Lincoln

Abraham Lincoln worked valiantly to prevent the attempts of the Rothschilds to involve themselves in financing the Civil War. Baron Nathan Rothschild said: *"Let me issue and control a nation's money, and I care not who writes the laws."*

It's interesting that as Lincoln was struggling with the financing of the Civil War, it was the czar of Russia who saved the situation. The Union needed assistance because the British and the French were among the driving forces behind the secession of the South and subsequently gave them financing. The Russians intervened by providing naval forces for the Union blockade of the South in European waters and by letting both countries — France and Britain — know that if they attempted to join the confederacy with military forces, they would have to go to war with Russia. That may be a more relevant footnote in history than most people realize.

The Rothschild interests succeeded, however, through their agent, Treasury Secretary Salmon P. Chase. Chase forced a bill, the National Banking Act, through Congress, creating a federally chartered central bank that had the power to issue U.S. banknotes. When this happened, Lincoln warned the American people as follows:

> The money power preys upon the nation in time of peace and conspires against it in times of adversity. It is more despotic than a monarchy, more insolent than autocracy, more selfish than bureaucracy. I see in the near future a crisis approaching that unnerves me and causes me to tremble for the safety of our country. Corporations have been enthroned, an era of corporation will follow, and the money power of the country will endeavor to prolong its reign by working upon the prejudices of the people until wealth is aggregated in the few hands and the republic is destroyed.

He continued to fight against the Central Bank and some now believe that it was his anticipated success and influence in the Congress to limit the life of the Bank of the United States to just the war years, that was the motivating factor behind his assassination. Modern researchers have uncovered evidence of a massive conspiracy that links Lincoln's secretary of war, Edwin Stanton, to John Wilkes Booth and his eight conspirators, with over 70 government officials and businessmen. Not only were they involved in the conspiracy; they have now been linked to the Bank of Rothschild in Europe. When Booth's diary was recovered by Stanton's troops, it was delivered to Stanton. When it was later produced during the investigation, 18 pages had been ripped out. These pages contained the conspirators names and were later found in the attic of one of Stanton's descendants.

From Booth's trunk, a coded message was found that linked him directly to Judith P. Benjamin, the Civil War campaign manager in the South for the House of Rothschild. When the war ended, the key to the code was found in Benjamin's possession. The assassin Booth was portrayed as a crazed, lone gunman. That's where the myth was born. With a few radical friends, he escaped by way of the only bridge in Washington not guarded by Stanton's troops. "Booth" was located hiding at a farm near Port Wild, Fort Royal, Virginia. Three days after escaping from Washington, he was shot by a soldier named Boston Corbett who fired without orders. Whether or not the man killed was Booth is still a matter of conjecture and substantial historical contention. It remains that whoever was killed had no chance to identify himself. Secretary of War Edwin Stanton made the final identification. Some now believe that a dupe was used and that the real John Wilkes Booth escaped with Stanton's assistance. It's interesting how this myth of the lone assassin goes through Lincoln and both the Kennedy assassinations. It's always a lone, crazed gunman.

Mary Todd Lincoln, upon hearing of her husband's death, began screaming, "Oh, that dreadful house!" Earlier historians felt that this spontaneous utterance referred to the White House. Some now believe that it may have been directed at Thomas W. House, a gun-runner/financier and agent of the

Rothschilds during the Civil War, who was linked to the anti-Lincoln, pro-banker interests.

William Garfield

Let's move on to President Garfield. Our 20th president previously was chairman of the House Committee on Appropriates and was an expert on fiscal matters. In fact, upon his election, he appointed an unpopular collector of customs in New York, whereupon two senators from New York resigned their seats. President Garfield openly declared that whoever controlled the supply of currency would control the business and activities of all the people. After only four months in office, President Garfield was shot in a railroad station on July 2, 1881.

Myth of the Federal Reserve

One of the myths that we all live with is this charade that we call the Federal Reserve. It is neither federal nor a reserve. It comes as a shock to many to discover that it is *not* an agency of the United States government. The name, Federal Reserve Bank, was designed to deceive and it still does. It is not federal because it is not owned by the government. It is privately owned. It has stockholders. It pays its own postage like any other corporation. Its employees are not in the civil service; its physical property is held in private deeds and is subject to taxation, which, of course, government property is not. It is an engine that has created private wealth that is unimaginable, even to the most financially sophisticated. It has enabled an imperial elite to manipulate our economy for its own agenda and has enlisted the government itself as its enforcer. It controls the times, it dictates business, and it affects our homes and practically everything in which you and I are interested.

Few Americans realize this whole betrayal was destined to defraud Americans of their wealth and opportunity, and that it would eventually lead to the subjugation of the great democratic experiment to a centralized world government. The concerns of the leadership of the Federal Reserve and its secretive international benefactors appear to go far beyond just currency and interest rates.

Jekyll Island

In November 1910, after having consulted with the Rothschild banks in England, France, and Germany, Senator Nelson Aldridge boarded a private train in Hoboken, New Jersey. His destination was Jekyll Island, Georgia, and a private hunting club owned by J.P. Morgan. Aboard the train were six other men: Benjamin Strong, president, Morgan's Bank & Trust Company; Charles Norton, president, Morgan's First National Bank of New York; Henry Davidson, senior partner, J.P. Morgan; Frank Vanderlip, president, Khun-Loeb National City Bank of New York; Abraham Piatt Andrew, an assistant secretary of the treasury; and noted financial advisor Paul Warburg.

The secret meeting was described by one of its architects, Frank Vanderlip, as follows:

> There was an occasion near the close of 1910 when I was as secretive, indeed as furtive, as any conspirator. I do not feel there is any exaggeration to speak of our secret expedition to Jekyll Island as the occasion of the actual conception of what eventually became the Federal Reserve system. We were told to leave our last names behind us. We were told further that we should avoid dining together on the night of our departure. We were instructed to come one at a time, where Senator Aldrich's private car would be in readiness attached to the rear end of the train for the south. Once aboard the private car, we began to observe the taboo that had been fixed on last names, a discovery we knew simply must not happen or else all our time and effort would be wasted.

The goal was to establish a private bank that would control the national currency. The challenge was to slip the scheme by the representatives of the American people. Earlier it had been called the Aldrich Bill and received effective opposition. The devious planners of the revised bill titled it the

"Federal Reserve Act" to mask its real nature. It would create a system controlled by private individuals who would control the nation's issue of money. Furthermore, the Federal Reserve Board, composed of 12 districts and one director, the Federal Reserve chairman, would control the nation's financial resources by controlling the money supply, available credit, and by mortgaging the government through borrowing.

This kind of conspiracy would be unnecessary today, but in those days, the average voter was sophisticated enough to understand the issues. Today, I doubt all that would be necessary.

The conspirators had a problem because President William Howard Taft had made it clear that he would veto such a bill if it was introduced. They had to make sure that he did not win re-election. At first, they supported former President Teddy Roosevelt in the Republican primaries, but he failed to get the nomination. Then the bankers supported the Democratic contender, Woodrow Wilson. In exchange for their support, Wilson promised to sign their bill into law, but the problem was the polls indicated that Wilson would only draw about 45 percent of the vote. The bankers needed someone to draw a sufficient number of Republican votes away from Taft without harming their Democratic candidate. So they arranged for Teddy Roosevelt to run against both of them by representing a newly invented third party called the Bull Moose Party. Does that sound familiar? Using Ross Perot to defeat George Bush and get Bill Clinton elected is an example. Back then it was 45% percent; Clinton won with 43 percent. Interesting tactic.

The plan worked. The Federal Reserve Act was held to vote on until December 23, when everybody went home on leave except those who had been bribed to remain or who were somehow beholden to the power elite. Only those senators and congressmen who had not gone home, owed favors, or were on the payroll of bankers were present to vote on the legislation. It's interesting that involved behind the scenes in the election of Woodrow Wilson and Franklin Roosevelt was Col. Edward

House, son of the Civil War Rothschild agent, Thomas W. House. Col. Edward House was a representative of the interests of the Rothschild Bank. Originally he was a member of the Institute of International Affairs formed in Paris at the Majestic Hotel in a secret meeting on May 30, 1919. It's American branch was formed on July 29, 1921, and is now known as the Council for Foreign Relations.

The Federal Reserve Act was simply a way to pacify the American voters. They had been crying out for banking reform and held scores of elections, alternating one set of politicians for another, only to find themselves with the same programs and getting deeper in debt. A prominent congressman, Charles A. Lindbergh, Sr., had complained that it was a common practice of congressmen to make the title of a piece of legislation sound like a promise or a right, but in the body or text to actually take away that which was promised in the title. Lindbergh also pointed out that the government officeholders understood that if they joined with the banking interests to exploit the American people, their re-election was more certain than if they served the people who elected them. By joining the exploiters, their campaign expenses were paid, the support of the political machines and the Capitol press was assured, and — if by chance they should lose — they were appointed to an office or position that was equal to or better.

The same phenomenon is visible today. It seems that the same cast of characters emerges in key positions whether the nation goes Democratic or Republican. Both sides appear to have sold out. For example, the North American Trade Agreement and the GATT Agreement were both called "agreements" to avoid requiring the two-thirds majority of the Senate that the Constitution requires. If you have Internet, you know the day after they're passed, they're listed among "Treaties." Why weren't they called "treaties" up front? Because they wouldn't have passed. They only passed with a bare majority in a special session of a lame duck Congress that had just been swept out of office.

Even Woodrow Wilson felt that he had made a terrible

mistake in signing the Federal Reserve Act. He later wrote:

> Some of the biggest men in the United States in the field of commerce and manufacture are afraid of something. They know that there is a power somewhere so organized, so subtle, so watchful, so interlocked, so complete, so pervasive, that they had better not speak above their breath when they speak in condemnation of it.

Where Does the Money Come From?

How does it work? The Federal Reserve is nothing more than a group of private banks which charge interest on money that never before existed. Let me give you an example of a slightly simplified, but very accurate summary of a fairly complex flowchart. The U.S. government prints $1 billion worth of interest-bearing U.S. government bonds, sells them to the Federal Reserve for the cost of printing figured at $23 per $1000. The Federal Reserve places the $1 billion in their checking account, then writes checks against it for a total of $1 billion dollars. Question: Where was the billion dollars before they touched the computer to make that entry? Answer: It didn't exist. We allow this private banking system to create money out of absolutely nothing, then loan it to our government and charge interest on it forever. The Federal Reserve collects interest on the U.S. government's own money.

A communiqué from the Rothschild Investment House in England to its associate in New York remarked, "The few who understand this system will either be so interested in its profits or dependent upon its favors that there will be no opposition from that class, while on the other hand, the great body of people mentally incapable of comprehending, will bear its burdens without complaint."

The privately owned Federal Reserve is now the nation's largest creditor. In fact, the interest payments received each year account for over half of what the American people pay in federal income tax. Over $1 billion a day for the interest on the debt. The principle shareholders of the Federal Reserve are the

Rothschild Bank of England, the Rothschild Bank of Berlin, the Warburg Banks of Hamburg and Amsterdam, the Lasard Brothers Banks of Paris, Israel Moses Seiff Banks of Italy; Chase Manhattan Bank of New York, Lehman Brothers of New York, Khun Loeb of New York, and Goldman Sachs of New York. This profitable charade has been going on for 81 years. The Monetary Control Act of 1980 expanded the power and reach of the Federal Reserve system by giving them control over all depository institutions, whether or not the banks are members of the so-called Federal Reserve system. This act, among other things, gave the Federal Reserve the power to use the debt of foreign nations as collateral for the printing of Federal Reserve notes. What that means is now they can saddle American taxpayers with the foreign debts. This unseen ruling class enjoys imperial wealth, they know what they want, and they know how to obtain it. They even manage one of the ultimate luxuries in life — privacy. The real power is to remain invisible.

Why isn't somebody screaming? Louis T. McFadden, chairman of the House Banking & Currency Committee, as early as December 15, 1931, said, "The Federal Reserve Board and its banks are the duly appointed agents of the foreign central banks of issue and they are more concerned with their foreign customers than they are with the people of the United States. The only thing that is American about the Federal Reserve Board and banks is the money they use."

On Friday, June 10, 1932, McFadden again pleaded his case. "Mr. Chairman, we have in this country one of the most corrupt institutions the world has ever known. I refer to the Federal Reserve Board and the Federal Reserve banks."

Some people think that the Federal Reserve Banks are United States government institutions. They are not government institutions. They are private credit monopolies which prey upon the people of the United States for the benefit of themselves and their foreign customers, foreign and domestic speculators, and swindlers, the rich and predatory money lenders. In that dark crew of financial pirates are those who would cut a man's throat to get a dollar out of his pocket; there are those who send money into the states to buy votes to control our legislation; and there are those who maintain an international propaganda for the purpose of deceiving us and wheedling us into granting new concessions which will permit them to cover up their past misdeeds and set again in motion the gigantic train of crime.

Thomas Jefferson pointed out, "I believe that banking institutions are more dangerous to our liberties than standing armies. Already they have raised up a money aristocracy that has set the government at defiance, that issuing power should be taken from the banks and restored to the government to whom it properly belongs."

JFK

President John F. Kennedy planned to exterminate the Federal Reserve System and to ultimately eliminate the national debt — just as Andrew Jackson and Abraham Lincoln had attempted earlier. In 1963, by presidential order of John F. Kennedy, Executive Order 11 and also 110, the United States Treasury began printing over $4 billion worth of United States notes to replace Federal Reserve notes. When a sufficient supply of these entered circulation, the Federal Reserve notes and the Federal Reserve system could be declared obsolete. This would end the control of the international bankers over the U.S. government and the American people. Some of these bills are still in circulation. Keep an eye out for them. They are in $1, $2, and $5 denominations. Look carefully at your dollar bills and watch for a red seal on the black and white side. It's a seal on the right side, and it's typically green on your normal Federal Reserve notes. But on a United States note, there is a red seal and if you'll look closely, it says "United States Note." Douglas Dillon's signature appears as Secretary of Treasury. The reverse side, the green side, is identical to your regular dollar bill. There were $4 billion of these in circulation. Watch for them. But it's interesting, a few months after putting this plan into effect, John F. Kennedy was professionally assassinated by four rifle teams (three direct teams and one diversionary team).

We now know the names of the members. What's amazing is not the professional assassination. Anybody with the money and the connections could pull that off. The real mystery is the cover-up. Few Americans realize, even to this day, that a coup d'état was engineered to save the Federal Reserve system for the power elite.

Trail of Blood

The astonishing thing, of course, is the resources that went into the cover-up of Kennedy's murder conspiracy, because it involved participation at the highest levels of our government. But the trail of blood continues. In the seventies and eighties, Congressman Larry P. McDonald spearheaded efforts to expose the hidden holdings and intentions of these international money interests. The Federal Reserve has *never* been audited and *everyone who has pursued to have it audited has been murdered.* Congressman Larry P. McDonald was killed on August 31, 1983. Sen. John Heinz and former Sen. John Tower had served powerful banking and finance committees and were outspoken critics of the Federal Reserve and the eastern Establishments. On April 4, 1991, Sen. John Heinz was killed in a plane crash near Philadelphia. On the next day, April 5, 1991, Sen. John Tower was killed in a plane crash. The coincidences seem to mount.

Regarding all of this, we find a virtual media blackout. What amazes me about many of these issues isn't just the conspirators; it's the fact that you cannot get the participation of the Establishment media to deal with any of these issues. And yet the publications are available to anyone who does a little bit of homework — all of this is old news. As I research all of this, Otto Von Hopsburg's remark still echoes in my ears: "The concentration of power in America is frightening."

Vince Foster

On July 20, 1993, White House Deputy Council Vincent W. Foster was murdered. The ensuing cover-up by the powers that be in Washington continue to be aided and abetted by the establishment press. But little by little, more and more bits of information continue to leak into the public community. We now understand that he was under investigation for espionage. Apparently, a lengthy investigation by more than a dozen sources with connections to the global intelligence community have confirmed a shocking story of money laundering and espionage connected with the highest levels of the White House. Foster's first indication of trouble was when he discovered that his coded bank account at Banca Della Suizzeria Italiana in Chiasso, Switzerland, had been surreptitiously emptied of $2.73 million that he had stashed away. And he was further shocked when he discovered that it had been transferred to the U.S. Treasury. The CIA had Foster under serious investigation but someone in the White House tipped him off. He then, according to credit card records, canceled two-day, round-trip TWA and Swiss Air tickets to Geneva he had purchased on his American Express Card through the White House travel office on the first of July. Less than three weeks later, his body was found with remarkably clumsy arrangements to suggest a suicide.

For months, a cadre of CIA computer hackers armed with a super-computer had been monitoring Foster's Swiss bank account. They had located it while monitoring money flows, secretly snooping through the electronic files of Israel's government. Foster was just one of scores of high-level U.S. political figures to have secret Swiss bank accounts looted of their illicit funds. Over the past two years, over $2 billion has been swept out of off-shore bank accounts belonging to people connected with the U.S. government, with hardly a peep from either the victims or the banks involved. This adds another dimension to the determined efforts to dismiss Foster's affair as a simple suicide.

Foster is also suspected of being an invaluable double agent with access to high-level political information, sensitive code encryption and transmission secrets. He also apparently was a behind-the-scenes manager of a key support company that's involved in one of the largest, most secretive spy efforts on record: the silent surveillance of banking transactions both here and abroad. If you have a Swiss bank account, you'll be very interested in the following. These bank snooping efforts began in earnest soon after Reagan became president in 1981. The initial aim was to track money behind the international terrorist groups. With traffic of over $1 trillion a day through New York, monitoring this kind of cash flow around the world is a gigantic undertaking. But using super-computers, advanced electronic eavesdropping techniques, reconnaissance satellites, and van-installed special equipment, this effort was started and became a joint effort of a number of intelligence agencies, not in the United States, but abroad. The network included wire tapping, special chips in certain hardware, and on it goes.

PROMIS

A software system called PROMIS was developed for the United States government. It's an acronym built from Prosecutors Management Information System. Originally it was designed to manage criminal information. But it was easily adaptable to track anything, including massive amounts of complex monetary transactions. This brings me to a company that you will be hearing about if you haven't already. It's a Washington company called INSLAW Inc. They originally developed the software and they sold management software to courts and related justice agencies, to the insurance industry, and several large law firms. Its principal asset was its highly sophisticated computer and software system called PROMIS. In 1982, INSLAW received a $10 million contract from the Department of Justice to install this in the office of 42 U.S. attorneys. Our U.S. government very quickly failed to pay on the contract and therefore deliberately drove INSLAW into bankruptcy and absconded with the software.

The bankruptcy judge, George Basin, acknowledged that the government stole the PROMIS software by trickery, fraud, and deceit. Basin lived to regret his ruling when his reappointment was denied and he was replaced by one of the Justice Department lawyers *who had argued the INSLAW case for the government!* Shortly thereafter, the decision was reversed on technical grounds. If it wasn't for the diligence of the owners of INSLAW in trying to pursue their just interests, we wouldn't have found out the rest of the story. The injustice to INSLAW was just the tip of the iceberg. After several congressional investigations concluded the wrongdoing by the Justice Department, Nicholas Bua was appointed to investigate the INSLAW scandal in June 1993. The Bua report was released ostensibly clearing the Justice Department officials from any wrongdoing, but now is increasingly regarded as a superficial whitewash.

At some point the PROMIS software was modified to include a *secret* "back door" which permitted surreptitious monitoring of the data bases using it. The software was eventually sold to intelligence agencies in the Middle East. PROMIS has also been sold to numerous major world banks for use in their wire transfer rooms to track the blizzard of numbers, authorization codes, and confirmations required for each wire transaction. Since it was the dominant tracking software available, and because the United States government leaned on banks abroad in order to enhance their surveillance efforts, PROMIS soon became the international standard.

The installation and software support of PROMIS involved a small firm called Systematics Inc. in Little Rock, Arkansas, funded and controlled by an Arkansas billionaire by the name of Jack Stephens. Vince Foster was one of Stephens' trusted deal-makers in the Rose Law Firm. Other Rose Law Firm partners included Hillary Clinton, Webster Hubbell, and William Kennedy, whose father was a Systematics director. In the late 1970s, Vince Foster apparently was one of the silent overseers of Systematics in the intelligence community. The largest intelligence agency goes by the initials NSA, which some people say stands for "No Such Agency." Other people say it stands for "Not Secret Anymore." It's more commonly known as the National Security Agency and is the largest of our seven intelligence agencies.

Billions of dollars move around in black accounts. That's not a racial term, that's a term used for the covert community for buying and selling arms, laundering drug money, and other clandestine activities. As an outsource/supplier of data processing, Systematics was used to help manage the covert money flow. At the end of every day, using the secret "back door" and disguised as routine bank-to-bank balancing transactions, snooping would be out of visibility of bank regulators and often the banks themselves.

Now Systematics' unique position may also explain why Jack Stephens tried to take over Washington-based Financial General Bankshares, or FGB, in 1978, on behalf of BCCI. But according to a lawsuit filed by the Securities Exchange Commission, Stephens had insisted upon having Systematics hired to take over all of FGB's data processing. Now we know why.

When Bill Clinton was elected president in 1992, he brought Foster, Hubbell, and Kennedy to the White House staff, and Systematics' foreign business flourished. It announced data processing deals with major banks in Moscow, Macau, Singapore, Malaysia, Pakistan, Trinidad, and other places. Even domestic giants like Citibank signed big data processing deals. The book *The Puzzle Palace* points out that it's inconceivable that any U.S. company could be involved in these transactions without deep participation by NSA and the other intelligence community involvement.

Since 1993 the Bua report has been under more and more scrutiny. On July 12, 1993, INSLAW submitted a 90-page rebuttal of the report to associate Attorney General Webb Hubbell, offering evidence that the Bua report was false. INSLAW didn't realize at the time that Hubbell and Foster are both linked through covert operations to two Arkansas companies, Park-o-meter and Systematics, and the ultimate frustration now, the INSLAW people have put the Bua report on Internet. You can read it yourself searching under the keyword "Bua."

Trail of Blood

Paul Wilcher, a Washington attorney investigating the INSLAW scandal, wrote Attorney General Janet Reno a 105-page letter describing the evidence he had concerning the

INSLAW scandals. The first page of the letter read, in part, "The lives of key participants and other witnesses and even myself are now in grave danger as the result of my passing this information on to you. If you let this information fall into the hands of the wrong persons, some or all of those who know the truth could well be silenced in the very near future." A few days later, eight days after the Bua draft, on July 20. 1993, Vince Foster was found murdered. Three days later, July 23, Paul Wilcher was found murdered in his apartment. A number of mysterious deaths, all with apparent links to INSLAW and Vince Foster have occurred. Most of them the day before key evidence was scheduled to be given.

Alfred Alverez and two friends opposing the software modifications were murdered in July 1981. Paul Morasca began to expose the CIA activities and was found murdered in January 1982. Larry Guerrin, a private investigator pursuing information concerning the INSLAW case, was found dead in Mason County, Washington, in February 1987. David Meyer, a San Francisco attorney seeking to expose links between the Justice Department, CIA, and Iran-Contra, was shot the day before a key court date, February 6, 1989. Dexter Jacobson, attorney, August 14, 1990, prior to his scheduled FBI meeting. Gary Ray Pinnell, attorney, February 11, 1981, just prior to an FBI meeting.

Alan D. Standorf, an electronic intelligence employee of the National Security Agency and a key source to Danny Cassalaro, was found dead in the back seat of his car at Washington National Airport, January 31, 1991. David Eisman, attorney, April 1991, shot to death 24 hours before scheduled meetings in which he was to receive key evidence of corruption by Justice Department officials. Alan May, found dead in his San Francisco home under suspicious circumstances, June 19, 1991. Tommy Burkett, after a meeting with Cassalaro, found shot in the bedroom of his parents' home in Virginia, 1991.

Danny Cassalaro, to whom a lot of trails lead regarding the investigation of the INSLAW situation and possible links to BCCI, CIA, and related matters, told his brother, "If there was an accident and they die, don't believe it."

On August 10, 1991, Cassalaro received sensitive documents in the parking lot of the Sheraton Hotel in Martinsburg, Virginia. He had confided to a number of confidants that he had finally broken the INSLAW case after a year-long, full-time investigation. The next day, Cassolara was found murdered in his hotel room, his briefcase and notes missing. I also understand that an NSA employee was also in the room and murdered, but his body was removed from the scene.

Ian Spiro was assisting in the collection of documents to be presented to the federal grand jury in connection with INSLAW. His wife, Gail Spiro, and their three children, shot in their home ranch of Santa Fe, California, were found on November 1, 1992. Three days later, the husband was found murdered in the front seat of his Ford Explorer in the remote desert. Jose Aguilar, a workman occasionally involved at their home, was also found shot November 14, 1992.

Vali Delahanty disappeared on August 18, 1992. On April 13, 1994, her skeletal remains are discovered in Lake Bay, Washington. Peter Sandvugen, a former CIA operative assisting in gathering evidence against the Justice Department, found dead December 2, 1992. The list goes on and on.

Sherman Scholnick, who is a plaintiff with a citizens' group in Chicago called the Citizens' Committee to Clean up the Courts, has filed a lawsuit against Bua. He maintains that 40 witnesses have been murdered by agents of the Department of Justice. Last fall, congressman Jack Brooks, D-Texas, and Charlie Rose, D-North Carolina, tried to enact a bill that would force an investigation of the Justice Department and the death of Danny Cassolaro and the INSLAW scandal. On September 27, 1994, Attorney General Janet Reno issued a report stating that there was no scandal, no need for independent counsel, or further investigation. On October 7, the resolution was defeated.

But the mysteries multiply.

If Foster knew that the United States was spying on foreign banks through the "back door" in PROMIS software, why would he let himself be caught red-handed? Maybe he felt that, as an insider, he had some protection, or he was a bag man for somebody he was confident would cover him. Sources in the CIA indicate that Foster is not the only one in the White House under suspicion for peddling state secrets.

According to two separate sources, the documents relating to Systematics were among those that were taken from Foster's office immediately after Foster's death. We understand that Webb Hubbell has delivered those documents to special prosecutor Kenneth Starr. Let's hope the truth will come out. I've been told that Kenneth Starr is a Christian. I encourage all of us to put him at the head of our prayer list. The pressure on him has to be gigantic.

On July 20, 1993, about 1 p.m., Vince Foster left his office at the White House and said that he would return later at 5:45 p.m. His body was found in Fort Marcy Park. Most of the experts indicate this evidence had been moved at least four times. The more one learns the details, the stranger it becomes. Why was there no blood on the ground and no bone fragments or brain tissue found nearby? Why were rug fibers all over his clothes? Why was there no dust on his shoes, despite the long dirt path to get to where he was? There are over 40 discrepancies in the FBI account that make a suicide verdict virtually facetious. A cover-up of immense proportions is again taking place. The Clinton administration simply says, "For reasons of national security. . . ."

The good news is that there are a few media sources picking this up, namely the *Pittsburgh Tribune*. I've found out that if you want to find out what's going on, read the foreign press, like the *London Telegraph* and others. Much of the above data is available in a magazine called *Media Bypass*, which broke these stories. The stories are starting to leak out both in private newsletter types of publications and on the Internet.

How to Find Truth

The real issue here, to me, is the issue of truth. We live in a country that we consider a free society and yet our media, our press, is participating in the cover-up. Jack Davidson, who publishes strategic investing, has highlighted this over the last couple of years. He was hit with a lawsuit that was finally thrown out of federal court recently. But he had to spend the last couple of years defending himself at an enormous cost. The lawsuit was obviously contrived because he was one of the ones ringing the bell about what's going on. There's a major journalistic war going on between the *London Telegraph* and the *Washington Post*, accusing the *Washington Post* of not just spiking the truth, but deliberately publishing information they knew was not true to help hide these stories.

Where is the press when you need it? The press' mandate before our society is to tell the voters the truth. And yet Don Hewitt, the executive director of CBS' "60 Minutes" can brag on camera that they successfully hid the truth from the U.S. public in order to get Clinton through the New Hampshire primary.

The "Clinton Chronicles" tape was hand-carried to every senator and congressman and had a lot to do with Robert Fiske being replaced with Kenneth Starr as a special prosecutor. But where's the media when you need them? And more to the point, what's going on? Is it true? Is Skulneck and other people's accusations true that the Department of Justice from the top down is corrupt? Is the corruption so widespread on both sides of the legislative aisle that there is little chance of it being exposed? There are many people, the most knowledge-able people I know in Washington, who believe it's so wide-spread and so deep that both sides have a strong interest to have this all covered up. Is the free society that you and I have enjoyed these many decades over? Is it just a charade, a facade? Whether you look at the banking situation or the apparent corruption in the judicial process, it is very frightening.

What do we do about this? Well, one of the things I strongly urge you to do is learn your Bible. Armor yourself with truth so you will recognize what is false. Secondly, start developing your sources of information. Anyone who stares at the tube at the 10 o'clock news with ABC, NBC, CBS, FOX, or CNN is going to get spoonfed the same kind of managed rhetoric that the powers want you to have. And yet if you look around the world anywhere else, you realize it's managed and deceitful, either by incompetence or by bias or by something much more sinister. In any case, develop your sources of information.

In this day and age, it's so important for Christians to have access to more than one source of information. The monopoly on the news in this country is still not 100 percent, thanks to talk radio, newsletters, short-wave radio, faxes, Internet, and the foreign press. Some of the foreign press includes the most reputable papers in the world for centuries. We used to have some like that in this country; in fact, about 25 years ago there were 2,200 independent newspapers in the United States. Today, 95 percent are owned by less than 50 families. The venerated *New York Times* and *Washington Post* used to be trusted pillars of truth. Not today.

Despite the misleading information being disseminated through the mainstream media on a daily basis, God is still in control. Nothing is happening, or ever happens, that He isn't allowing. It's a great time to be alive, to serve God, and be used in the lives of others for the cause of Christ. The Bible encourages us to search the Scriptures and to pray for wisdom. I hope you do. God Bless.

11

The Truth Behind Outcome-Based Education

The following is a panel discussion by the most educated individuals in America on the topic of OBE and how it ties into the nationally orchestrated attempt to move America into the New World Order through influence and control of our children. This information, circulated widely across America on audio and video tape, has been credited to being a "wake-up" call to a sleeping generation of parents. When it first debuted it stunned the live audience at the Steeling the Mind of America Conference and the circulated audio and video tapes have since been shaking up school boards across the nation.

The panel members who participated in this eye-opening informational discussion were **Berit Kjos**, from Palo Alto, California, author *of Your Child and the New Age*; **Gen Yvette Sutton**, lecturer and legal researcher from Philadelphia, Pennsylvania; **Dwight Williams** of Denver, Colorado, author *of A Layman's Guide to Outcome-Based Education*; **Charlotte Iserbyt** of Bangor, Maine, formerly of the United States Department of Education; **John Loeffler**, Coeur d'Alene, Idaho, host of "Steel on Steel," a nationally syndicated radio talk show.

Loeffler: Berit Kjos, what are the stated goals of American education?

Kjos: To prepare students for a global work force and for

citizenship in the 21st century — a world that would be very different from the one we live in today. The person who probably said it best was Shirley McCune, former executive director of the Mid-continent Regional Educational Laboratory. "What's happening in America today," said Shirley McCune, "is a total transformation of our society. We have moved into a new era. I'm not sure we have begun to comprehend the incredible amount of organizational restructuring and human resource development. What we have to do is build a future. The 'human resource' to be developed, according to the new national-international blueprint, is our children. The National Education Association (NEA) and its 240 international affiliates agree that the whole world has to change, and that's really what the new education is all about. They're using the American system, which is part of the international education system, to actually create that new world." She said this at the 1989 Governor's Conference on Education, where people like former Education Secretary Lamar Alexander, and governors Clinton and Riley worked together to draft the six main education goals that summarized President Bush's America 2000 (1991), Clinton's Goals 2000 (1994), and the international plan adopted at the 1990 United Nations World Conference on Education for All.

Loeffler: When they say restructuring, we're not just talking about academics — adding, reading, writing. We're talking about emotional, sociological, psychological, everything.

Kjos: Yes, globalist-oriented educators are talking about a new set of beliefs, values, attitudes, and behaviors. They believe that children must learn to see themselves not as individuals, but as part of a greater whole — interconnected both with the planet and with every other person around the world.

They want children to become global citizens, willing to conform, compromise, and sacrifice in order to save nature and prevent war and other conflicts. It's a utopian vision.

Sutton: And I think the important thing is that it won't

happen naturally. This is not inevitable or necessary. There is nothing wrong with the educational system that we used to use in the United States. The real reason behind restructuring of education is to create or achieve the New World Order.

Loeffler: Because otherwise, if they didn't change the way people think and their world views, they wouldn't tolerate some of the sociological changes that are afoot right now.

Loeffler: How long has this project been underway?

Iserbyt: It's been underway for a long time. Basically, it started in the early 1900s with the Carnegie Corporation changing the social studies. I have a very interesting book called *Recommendations and Conclusions* on the social studies that Carnegie funded with the American Historical Association. In that book, they come right out and mention New World Order and they mention the need to change from the free market system to collectivism. So you follow through with that book which basically changed our social studies. How many parents out there have wondered why we didn't focus on the American system of government — free market and individualism and all — and they never really understood that this has been in the works ever since the early 1900s.

Then you move on to when the United States went into the United Nations in 1945, and the creation of the United Nations Educational Scientific Cultural Organization (UNESCO). Then you jump a bit to where the United States Office of Education was funding a lot of very controversial programs, even prior to 1965. That was the key year, however, when the decision was made by the top internationalists — don't forget: the same thing was going on in other countries, not just in the United States — to focus on changing children's attitudes and values to prepare them for what Berit was just talking about. The way they did that was through massive amounts of money going into the schools under the title of equity, basically, and they sold it to the American people because we are concerned about minorities and the poor. And they poured billions in. With the billions, they had to set up an accountability system.

Loeffler: When you say "equity," what do you mean?

Iserbyt: Equity is to bring the schools to the point that the minorities would have the same opportunities that our children had in schools that were spending more on education or focusing more on academics. They said they were going to do this for the minorities. But in fact, they poured the money into experimental programs, all of which, with the exception of the open classroom which was also experimental, there were two divisions. The experimental programs dealt with the changing of attitudes, values, and beliefs, and the open classroom, and doing away with the focus on academics. It also dealt with the use of mastery learning, which is now called Outcome-Based Education, based on behavioral psychologist B.F. Skinner from Harvard, who said, "I could make a pigeon a high achiever by reinforcing it on a proper schedule." And parents have got to understand that *is* OBE. They use the minorities.

They spend millions of dollars, according to Professor James Bach, a close associate of William Spady and John Champlain, et cetera. He said, "I don't know of a single inner-city school in this country that hasn't used mastery learning." So there we see the deliberate dumb-down of our minority children. It worked on them, and we have the most recent evaluation of these programs, plus the infamous 1984 Spady Grant that put OBE into every classroom in the nation; we have the evaluations that show that it would be very difficult to replicate or to put these programs into the schools of America. They are not at all sure that they work academically.

The point is that they continued on because, as Gen Yvette said, they're not interested in academics. They're interested in what Skinner said. What is reinforced will be repeated. Rewards to children every time that they do something right. The computer is superb with this. They've done it with candies, and this and that. And it's totally approved by the United States Department of Education — the use of rewards.

So here we are, re-authorizing the Elementary and Secondary Education Act again, the act, that in effect, in '65, put the accountability mechanism in. If you don't reach the goal — the politically correct attitude set by the government, predetermined (and forget the academics because they're not important anymore) — your school could well be shut down and taken over. You won't get your money. Any smart school that decides not to take money from the federal government right now (and they would be smart if they did it) will find themselves in a lot of trouble. That's the accountability mechanism. You accomplish what the Federal Government, which is actually the United Nations Educational, Scientific, and Cultural Organization, has set as the goal for every child on this planet. They will all use mastery learning. Professor Allen Cohen at the University of San Francisco . . . I went through a course of his, he is a close associate of Spady and Champlain. He said that UNESCO, 20 years ago, determined that OBE mastery learning would be the learning system for the world.

Williams: That's the way you actually approach true equity. We're really not talking about equity in terms of opportunity so much as we're talking about equity in terms of outcomes. The idea is not so much to break the mold, but to remake the mold in such as way so that you have a uniform product emerging from the schools. And that's where the ESEA passed in 1965 is so critical because you couldn't achieve that without a centering of authority and accountability at the national level. And the NEA had been involved since 1918. That's when they first began to lobby and propose federal legislation and they were extremely persistent. And then the emergence of the National Defense Act in 1958 — probably spurred more by Sputnik than by the NEA — set the pace for the development of federal funding in education, and it was just a short step then to '65 and this massive program of public education funding from the federal level.

Loeffler: As early as 1947, the NEA was talking about preparing American students for global government. But if this is a national or international curriculum, whatever happened to local control, and/or what are the goals?

Sutton: It's such a deviation from what our founding fathers intended when they wrote the Constitution. Education was seen to be a prerogative of the states and of local control.

This means the local school districts and the parents who funded the system would determine what their children were taught. With the massive funding infusion in 1965, all of that changed. The parents lost control of education and most parents know this. Every parent who has had a child in the public school system in the last 30 years has had to deal with this. That's how most of us got involved; it was through our children. We began to understand and appreciate that things were changing, that our children were gradually spending more time on the couch than they were at the desk and that our beliefs from home not only were being *challenged* at school, but they were being *changed* at school. Once I realized what was happening, it was not only alarming, it was frightening.

What we have found out is that by taking the grant money they would have to do what the government told them. They would have to fall in line with that national agenda if they were to account properly for the money. That meant that the curriculum in the schools was changing. Of course, that affected the children. All of us parents had a lot of questions. We went up to school and we said, "What's going on here?" And the school teachers and principals basically lied to us.

Loeffler: Regularly.

Sutton: Regularly, over and over again.

Loeffler: There seems to be a favorite lie that every parent has heard when they try to get involved with school. What is it?

Sutton: It's "You're the only parent that has a problem."

Loeffler: Right; even if there are 100 other parents complaining about the very same thing. That's what you're told.

Iserbyt: This has been going on a long time. When I originally came back to the United States they had a new textbook that John Goodlad, the very famous educator and internationalist who is involved in changing all of our schools, had recommended. I saw it in 1972, and it was called *World of Mankind* by Follette. I looked at it and I was very upset because it showed elementary school teachers taking the little kids through the town and identifying rich and poor families.

They'd say, "Who do you think lives in that big house?" A big colonial house in Camden, Maine. "That family is a rich family." And then they'd say, "And across the street, what kind of a family lives there?" Children would say, "I guess quite poor, in a mobile home." "What do you think they eat in that house?"

I thought, *What is this?* So I went in and I said, "I don't like this. What are you doing to these little children? They get along just fine if you leave them alone. They don't care whether they're rich and poor."

The principal said to me, "Charlotte (they called us by our first names), you're the *only* parent who's ever complained."

I replied, "I don't care whether I'm the only parent who's ever complained." I went to the school board and discussed it, and of course they all said I was wrong. Finally I was so concerned about the whole thing that I took a course in how to become a change agent.

A teacher came to my house and said, "Charlotte, I really think that you should go to this in-service training." This was a retired teacher. I went but it didn't make sense to me. There were teachers and principals talking about identifying "resistors" in the community, and how to get sex education and "critical thinking" into the schools. They wanted to target people in the community like in the Rotary and other influential people to use them to fight the resistive parents using our tax dollars. I went through this course which was funded by the U.S. Department of Education — where, by the grace of God, I mysteriously ended up working. My office funded Ronald Havelock out of the University of Michigan in Ann Arbor, to produce a large detailed guide for change agents. It's been used all over the United States for 20 years for implementing these programs. It's the same program that parents have been complaining about. They've been told they're crazy.

No; you're not crazy, parents. You believe in the rights of the individual, you have your own values, you believe it's up to you to determine the values of your children. These people are purposefully changing the attitudes and destroying the values of your children. They've poured millions of dollars into changing our children's thinking so that they will be comfortable living in a controlled world government. That blew my mind. I thought this was a free society. That is when I woke up.

Loeffler: Change agents were the people who were installed — and the reason I'm saying this is that a lot of teachers who are going to hear what you just said are going to go, "Well, I work in the public school system and I don't do that." But they've been duped into this. Change agents are the people trained to mislead parents *and* teachers.

Iserbyt: I couldn't go back to the second session, it was so sickening. But what we have to remember is that we're talking about Benjamin Bloom. He is the father of mastery learning, which is based on pigeon training. He said, *"The purpose of education is to change the thoughts, actions, and feelings of students, and to get them to discuss issues."* He also defined good teaching as "challenging the student's fixed beliefs." Now if you understand what that means, you understand the training I went through to be a change agent. Because that would enable our communities to have access to all of these mind-bending, federally funded programs coming out of the NEA office. Every state has offices in them under the National Diffusion Network. That network was used basically for attitude and value change. They are funded with mammoth amounts of money.

Sutton: Before we even get into Bloom taxonomy, I think it would be good to restate what education has always been in the whole course of mankind, which is, "the disinterested pursuit of truth." That's why what the NEA is doing is such an aberration. We are totally conditioning the children to a predetermined outcome. That includes not just what they know but what they do and their behaviors.

Loeffler: While using a vocabulary that makes it appear as if all values are still in force at the same time that we're looking for the same goals. There's a double-speak. You hear presented to the public, "We're doing this; we want people to be achievers," when in reality the training is just the opposite.

Sutton: But they have always identified themselves as agents of change.

Williams: The point of the change agent, in the long term is to grease the skids, so to speak, for the implementation of Outcome-Based Education. That's the ultimate change vehicle. Under Outcome-Based Education, you begin to define the universe for student learning. We no longer have this ultimate pursuit of truth, but now we have specific outcomes, with a curriculum built down from there. Put into that curriculum are only those things that are significant for meeting that outcome. So you define the limitations of student learning to those things that you specifically want students to have.

Loeffler: Berit, we've been talking about the framework, but what are these paradigm changes?

Kjos: A paradigm is a cultural world view. It is a mental pattern or framework for thinking, for organizing information, and for explaining reality. A paradigm shift is a cultural transformation. Our education system has passed through two paradigm shifts since the sixties when prayer and Bible reading were outlawed in our schools.

Here are three examples:

1) The Judeo-Christian paradigm, which is based on biblical truth.

2) The Humanistic paradigm, which was a transitional stage, where there are no absolutes. We talked about the fact education has traditionally been a pursuit of truth. We're back to the pursuit of truth again, but a different set of truths, or absolutes. It has no foundation in reality or fact. For example, take one of the biblical absolutes like "the Bible reveals reality." Then humanism came in and said, "science explains reality."

3) The new, Global paradigm, which says feelings and experience prove reality. They come up with a new set of truths or absolutes that explain what reality is all about.

In the Christian paradigm, or mental framework, God is transcendent and personal but in the humanistic paradigm, God is an illusion. In the new global paradigm, God or

Goddess, or Gaea, or Mother Earth, whatever you call this pantheistic force that infuses all things, is universal and present in everything. Therefore, everybody is already sacred and perfect, able to accomplish anything.

The New Emphasis in Education	
Old Paradigm	**New Paradigm**
Biblical truth	Earth-centered myths
Facts	Experience and feeling
Observation	Imagination
Logic	Speculation and feelings
Science	Politicized pseudoscience
Reality	Fantasy
Factual history	Fictional or multicultural stories
Objective thinking	Subjective feelings
Individual responsibility	Group thinking

Today, if children fail, educators blame Christianity, which supposedly produced low self-esteem by teaching that children weren't born perfect. Terms such as sin and guilt have been replaced by the new global "truth" that every person is basically spiritual and good, and has no need of God.

Sutton: The importance of that is that once you take away the Judeo-Christian foundation of original sin (that things are not ever going to be perfect on this earth) and replace that with the utopian idea (things can be perfect on earth and that someone can make them perfect) then you have this whole movement that someone is going to decide what "perfect" is for us. And since we can achieve it, the social engineers will move us in that direction to this perfect utopia.

Loeffler: But force is the only way to achieve that.

Kjos: Or deception. One of the reasons for bringing in these global values that will somehow unify children around the world, is that they help justify the absence of facts and logic. Without a factual and logical foundation, people can't resist or argue back. They can't communicate the devastating consequences of paganism or communism unless they have an historical perspective.

Western thinking, globalist educators tell us, is too closed, too limited, logical, and linear. Eastern or global thinking is open ended. So they bring in all kinds of models for global spirituality from earth-centered cultures around the world. Those cultures are basically pantheistic, monistic, and polytheistic. They all fit the new paradigm.

Pantheism means that all is god because everything is infused with this common spiritual force that pervades all things. Monism just means all is one. It naturally follows pantheism, because this pantheistic spirit connects everything. That's why some of the new environmental philosophers will say things like, "If you pick a flower, it moves a star."

Children must see everything in the universe as connected. Which means that if they eat too much bread or use too much water, it will affect children in Africa. This makes sense to those who have accepted the global paradigm. Like eastern philosophies, it transcends fact and logic and takes students beyond reality in whatever direction a trained facilitator can lead them to imagine.

Benjamin Bloom's taxonomy laid the foundation for this new way of thinking. It put facts at the bottom of a set of thinking skills and called them "lower order thinking skills." Educators explain that facts and knowledge are not very important anymore, neither is comprehension. What is important is application, analysis, synthesis, and evaluation, the higher order thinking skills.

You might ask the kind of logical question that's not permitted within this system: "How can you analyze, synthesize, and evaluate, and then come to any kind of valid conclusion if you don't start with facts and comprehension? You can't, unless you're using the new global paradigm.

Williams: The point was not to draw firm conclusions. Evaluation was said to be resulting in formulating in subjective judgments with no firm right or wrong answers based on fact. That's why we see this change to an appeal through the educational process and affective mental processes. Because in order to sell this thing to the public, you have to have people no longer depending on logic, reason, and cognitive types of processes; instead you respond to the horrible pictures of the starving Ethiopians that are flashed on television. If you're going to control the actions of society through the media, you have to have people responding through feelings, attitudes, and beliefs; not through the realities of active logic.

Loeffler: In other words, they make a decision based on the feeling of the immediate moment rather than on some kind of eternal value, long-term type of value, or something arrived at through reason as to what works, what doesn't work, or what we can do.

Sutton: It's all based on feelings and emotion or what I call "emotionless reason." That's what enables them to move this agenda forward so quickly. You can only be angry if you have a solid, absolute value inside yourself that propels or motivates you to react angrily to someone denying or acting against what you believe is true. Under these ground rules, you cannot question anybody else's beliefs or values because they're all subjective; you have no right to question anybody else's beliefs or values. There is no basis there at which to really react to what anybody else is doing.

That's why with some of the methods that they use like values clarification in class, the ground rules are that you don't get angry with anybody; everybody's entitled to believe what they want and you have no foundation. And what happens then, without true emotion based on deeply held beliefs, is that we just become processors much like a computer. We have to be very careful when we reduce our children to the level of a computer where they are simply being processed. Information is coming into them that they are not reacting to because computers don't really know and they sure don't care.

Loeffler: We still hear appeals being made to people's rights, to a right or a wrong. In this floating scheme of things, how do we get to right or wrong, because obviously now, you could have a world of moral chaos?

Sutton: It has to be purely arbitrary.

Iserbyt: It also has to be a dictatorship at the top. What we're talking about basically is a deliberate dumbing down because the less people know, the less likely they are to question. The national curriculum outline says at the end,

> With the former curriculum, elementary students were expected to master 2,175 separate bits of information that included skills, concepts, and content, organized within eight discreet disciplines. The new K-5 Education 2000 curriculum requires mastery of only 6 major themes, 60 concepts, and 132 core skills organized within three curriculum strands. This revision greatly reduces the fragmented nature of the former curriculum and significantly decreases the number of specific requirements to approximately one-tenth the original number."

They are reducing to one-tenth of the whole that our children are going to learn. They have said all along that facts don't make any difference because there's so much out there. Their justification for this is that the amount of information in society is exploding so rapidly children shouldn't really have to learn anything!

Here is a report card. This is the Effective School Report, 1994, from the *Educator's Journal*. It's called "Alternative Assessment of Student Achievement: The Open Book Test." I would have loved it if when I had to take a test back 20, 25 years ago, the teacher had said, "You don't have to learn anything, go out and play. I'm going to give you the book when you take the test."

It states, *"All classroom tests should be open book tests."* We are talking about moving toward higher-level thinking and away from memorization of facts. Once we leave school, we can use references anytime we want. We are no longer required to memorize endless lists of facts. It continues, *"Open book tests will move school activities much closer to real-life activities. The human brain should be used for processing, not storage. This will cause classroom tests to be constructed to measure critical thinking, induction, deduction, analysis, synthesis. Since critical thinking is what will be measured, critical thinking is what will be taught."*

Loeffler: But critical thinking is not logic and reason, by their definition.

Iserbyt: No. Absolutely not.

Sutton: We need to remind ourselves what true education does. True education should expand all the faculties of the mind: memory, conscience, imagination, insight, intuition, and the brain. But when you just process information, you deny, cut off, those other functions of the mind.

Loeffler: The problem is that later in life, they have no way of filtering what they're hearing and they become subject to the latest government decisions.

Sutton: Columbia Teachers' College in the late 1970s had a symposium on knowing how we come to know things and how important this is. They are the ones who looked at this and said that much of what they were doing in education was denying these other functions of the mind and reducing them to the brain alone. They reminded us that it is the other functions — memory, insight, intuition, conscience, imagination — by which we know absolutes and truth. For instance, how we know God. These functions are cut off under Outcome-Based Education. The outcome is predetermined. The child has to know exactly what they say to know. They have to perform or show that they know it, and they have to be a certain way based on the attitudes that they say they have to have. So right away, the outcome is cut off and that denies insight. Insight is that light that goes off in your head that says that what they're teaching me is not what I know to be true. Memory, likewise, tells you that maybe what they're teaching you is not what you've been taught in the past.

Loeffler: We're being told that each local school district determines its own outcomes.

Kjos: That's simply not true. Many of us have been studying the education goals and frameworks adopted by various states. They're virtually the same. The sentences may differ slightly, but the wording is so similar that you know they came from a central plan.

Williams: In my own district in Kiowa, Colorado, a small district of 200+ kids in K-12 grades, there was a new superintendent change agent that came in dedicated to the establishment of a global, holistic form of education. We went through five name changes of this program. As parents complained, they changed the name of what they were doing but continued implementing the same concepts.

The first thing they developed was a human development curriculum. They had 458 individual learning exercises in a K-12 scope and sequence. Of those, we traced 232 directly, word for word, in order, including spelling and grammatical errors to Cherry Creek, Colorado, schools. And then 131 of them were shared between Cherry Creek, Littleton, and Kiowa; another 93 were common to Aurora, Cherry Creek, Littleton, and Kiowa; and the whole thing was traced to Eugene, Oregon.

Iserbyt: In the past, education was to help the individual child become competent and be able to move forward in whatever he wanted to do. It is now for the benefit of the state. The children are nothing but human resources to be used, molded, and recycled to come to predetermined attitudes and values. They're creating a new person. Some people have even called it "the new Soviet man." That's what we're looking at, a Soviet system of education. We've gone through the 1992 Russian curriculum. It's exactly the same as ours, with site-based management, community service, mastery learning, cooperative learning, and critical thinking, which is Leninistic. We're putting in the Russian education system. But we've been doing it since 1959, when Dwight Eisenhower signed the first agreement with the Soviet Union to do that.

And at the peak of the Cold War, which is the most interesting part of it, why would we do that? Then you can thank President Carter for having broken those agreements when they moved into Afghanistan, but then Ronald Reagan came along and signed them again and allowed the Soviets to come right into our classrooms to work with our teachers, our professors at Harvard, to develop higher order, critical thinking, curriculums for the computer student, what Berit's talking about in the area of social sciences, war, peace, et cetera. They're sitting down there in Cambridge right now with the Russians, developing these programs for our schools. That happened under Ronald Reagan. We never had them really developing curriculum until then.

Kjos: I'd like to just add one fact or two to what you were saying about the Russian system and the communistic education. Because it reflected an atheistic perspective, it fit into the humanistic paradigm. Now the educational establishment has added the spirituality that goes with globalism. Everybody wants spirituality.

Many humanists have realized that man by himself can't make it. They used to think that he could; that was the utopian belief that predominated in humanistic societies 20 years ago. Now they see that secular humanism alone has failed for all except super people, and they want to empower children with spiritual values and power.

So religion is back in the schools. I have a cover of a brochure which is used for teacher training saying, "Ideas and Resources for Teaching About Religions in Secondary Schools." It shows the symbols of the world's major religions. But the cross is missing!

In our local high school newspaper a couple of years ago, one of the girls who's on the editorial board had written an article about witchcraft. She called it "Common Misconceptions Haunt Students." She was a witch and she interviewed five other students who were witches about witchcraft. They all talked about how it empowered them, made them feel good about themselves, helped them take care of the earth and so on.

A Christian boy who also wrote for the student newspaper asked if he could write an article about Young Life on campus. He was told both by the editorial staff and the supervising teacher that no, he could not, because Christianity is over-exposed in our culture; paganism is not. Now they need to teach about witchcraft and Native American spiritism and all the other religions that are misunderstood because Christianity condemned them.

Sutton: I think we need to interject here that even though there is great fear from the educators about Christians invading the school systems, they need not fear. The Supreme Court specifically outlaws Christianity from being taught in the schools.

Kjos: Most are not really worried about a Christian takeover, they're just worried about how we might block their goal of quenching the last remnant of the old paradigm, the framework of thinking that's based on Christianity. They can't put the new global beliefs in place until they totally stamp out the old. This is why it's so important for the educational establishment to get the children at a very young age. Five and six is too late, because if children start school with a strong biblical world view, they will resist paganism. Those children are considered "mentally ill," as some educators have said, because they trust God and obey parents. They have a mental framework which sorts information and filters facts according to a Judeo-Christian perspective, and that no longer fits.

Loeffler: They call that "mental illness"?

Kjos: Unfortunately, yes. It's because they come to school "with certain allegiances toward our nation, their parents, and a supernatural being." That's what Dr. Chester Pierce said at an international childhood education conference in 1972. Many other leaders have said the same thing.

The paradigm shift is a worldwide cultural transformation. Those who are engineering it know they need to eliminate the old loyalties and facts. They need to produce a change in consciousness and a new way of seeing reality. So, they're putting old concepts into the context of the new paradigm. Even history must be seen from within the new system. That means that the same old words and terminology used in the Judeo-Christian context take on a new meaning. When you move them into the new global context or paradigm, their meanings change.

Iserbyt: When we're talking about all these things, the word "standards" keeps coming into my mind. When you do what they're doing, as Berit has explained, all standards of excellence, or standards of anything, are removed. That's why they've taken out the Carnegie unit. They've taken out testing. It's individualized education where the child works at his own pace. It can take him as long as he wants as long as he can master whatever it is, and the standards are not there any longer. There are *none*. In fact, the child is not being compared with any other children in his classroom or in the country. So that's why you're going to find that your children are going to learn less and less and less. The bright children are going to be teaching the less bright ones and won't be moving forward. This causes a real dumb-down — even the brighter students are affected.

There are no standards, and this new portfolio testing, which means that the child can perform things, is totally subjective. Teachers decide if the child is performing well. But based on what? They have no standard. We've hit the bottom with the Scholastic Aptitude Test. They have been highly successful since 1965, when they put their plan in for the dumbing down of America. They would have to change the Scholastic Aptitude Test to bring it down so that the standards are much lower, and they've said, "Scores on the scholastic aptitude test will rise automatically as a result of the test's first scoring realignment in half a century," college board officials announced last week. "The re-centering of scores on the SAT, the yardstick for generations of college-bound students, will begin with the high school graduating class of 1966. The plan will shift the reference group used as a statistical foundation for scores from an elite cadre of students who took the test on the eve of World War II to a far larger and more diverse group of test-takers in 1990." I think this is the greatest insult. These people say that they're multi-cultural, they're pluralistic, they love minorities. They insult them. They're racist. They're saying that Mexicans, Chinese, blacks, can't reach the same standards that kids did after World War II. This is the proof of what they've done to education.

Loeffler: It's saying we could make more touchdowns if we'd just move the goalposts a little closer together. Plus, we can't compare to previous football games because we're now dealing with two different goalposts.

Sutton: One of the things that this brings up is that OBE is a very significant part of the restructuring, but it is only one part of the restructuring of education.

Outcome-Based Education is, first of all, a philosophy. It's a philosophy that says that all children can learn exactly the same material to the same extent. It forces all children to be the same. In order to have all children achieve, you have to lower the standard to such an extent that all children *can* achieve. That's why it's called "the great leveler." It also is based on a performance system. In other words, the children don't just know the material, they have to be able to demonstrate that they have achieved the outcome. It includes their attitudes and beliefs. They have to not only know certain things that are predetermined; they have to show that they know them, and they have to be a certain type of person. That is the philosophy behind all this; it's all predetermined. It is based on the time forever system versus time reasonable, which is what the traditional education was based upon. So, it is a philosophy that is totally different from what we have had in this country up until now; in fact, totally different than the educational system that has made this country the great nation that it is today.

It is also a list of goals. Those goals are really defined for us in Goals 2000, but they are more specifically identified in the school's list of learner outcome. Again, those outcomes are predetermined. Those outcomes have to be achieved in order for the child not only to graduate, but to move up in the system. Now, we are not talking again about the Carnegie unit, which was three courses in math, for instance, or so many courses in English that they had to take and pass in order to graduate. We are talking about specific outcomes that transcend any curriculum, are interwoven throughout the curriculum, and are predetermined for every child in the system.

It must be noted that at least two-thirds of those outcomes are affective in nature. They do deal with the beliefs and the attitudes of the student rather than any specific knowledge. So it is a list of outcomes as well, a list of goals.

Perhaps more importantly, it is a process. It is what the educators call a closed-loop process: The child is given a list of expectations, or a list of outcomes of what they have to know. The instruction follows the curriculum. The testing or the assessment of the student follows, and it continues forever in a loop — the evaluation of that assessment to see if the student has indeed achieved the outcome. If the student has achieved the outcome, they are put on what is called horizontal activity so that they will not proceed at a faster pace than the other students. If the student has not achieved the outcome, then he or she goes into remediation so that the loop starts all over again. They have to go through the loop again — through the instruction, the testing, the evaluation. Over and over again, until they're thinking the way the government wants them to think.

Loeffler: What happens to the horizontal people who have already achieved while these others go back through the re-mediation loop?

Sutton: Some are just enriching what they've already been taught. Other children will be actually helping the other ones through peer tutoring. The whole bloc moves in a predetermined course to arrive at the outcome that they want. But the children must walk through this loop every day, all day, throughout their entire education. It's one method of teaching every single discipline, which we have never had before. We've always used many different methods based on the disciplines that we've used. Yet, now this one method is to be used with every single child, all day long, all over the world.

Iserbyt: I have a study from the Northwest Regional Laboratory in Portland, Oregon, on Effective School Research, and it says right in there that "mastery learning slows down the bright kids." These are their own words. I want people out there to know that, so they can take this information to the school board.

Williams: In the Slaven report they took the top 25 percent or the fastest achieving 25 percent and the slowest achieving 25 percent and studied the differential, in terms of their learning time on a particular learning assignment. Starting out, it was 2.5 times as long for the slowest learners to achieve that result as the fastest learners. Kids are grouped without regard to ability. Actually, with regard to ability, but purpose-fully spread across the spectrum of aptitude. After three years, that time differential had increased to 4.2 times as long, in spite of the fact that the fastest kids had slowed down. So the fastest kids slowed down and the slowest kids slowed more.

Loeffler: We discussed earlier that OBE is being man-dated from the United Nations through Goals 2000 down into the United States, therefore it's a global curriculum. But we're hearing that religion is back in public school again. Right?

Kjos: Right, but it's not what many Christians think. The old paradigm emphasized biblical truths. The new paradigm emphasizes pagan myths. And those pagan myths don't show the consequences of worshiping the earth and its spirits or what happens when people use pagan rituals to contact occult powers.

Multi-cultural education means experiencing idealized forms of the worlds earth-centered religions until paganism seems more normal than Christianity. Children are taught to see the new beliefs as part of a global system that teaches everybody to live in harmony with Mother Earth and with each other. In this new paradigm, private ownership doesn't fit. What does fit is the communal or collective ownership mod-eled by Indian tribes.

Since children don't learn what actually happened in pagan cultures, they don't realize that many were not environ-mentally friendly. It's a documented fact that American Indi-ans burned forests and killed herds of buffalo by stampeding them over cliffs. When their local food supply was depleted, many tribes simply moved their camp somewhere else until the land was replenished. Disease and tribal wars usually kept their numbers low.

I'm not just talking about Native Americans. Throughout history, pagan cultures have experienced all kinds of spiritual oppression and violence. Before my native Norway became a Christian nation, it was divided by tribal rivalries. I don't think any of the world's pagan cultures have shown the cruelties of untamed human nature more dramatically than the Norwegian Vikings.

But these realities are ignored in our schools today. Instead of teaching facts, they emphasize experience. Instead of observation, they push imagination. Speculation has replaced logic and pseudo-science has replaced genuine science.

Children learn selected stories instead of history. In the San Francisco Bay area, a newspaper article listed schools that have traded social studies textbooks for multi-cultural stories and historical fiction that help students feel part of a particular culture. They teach politically correct fantasy instead of reality and subjective feelings instead of objective thinking.

I think it's important to remember that a key point of OBE and the new assessments (we saw it on the CLASS tests in California) is the emphasis, not on what a story or piece of literature says, but how a student *feels* about the story. The answers must come from the inner self — the affective or feeling-centered domain rather than from an outside author or teacher.

As this new way of learning becomes a habit, students apply it to their relationship with parents, pastors and others. Their response to advice from authority figures then depends on their subjective feelings, not the objective wisdom given. This means that many Christian children will refuse to believe what the Bible really says. Instead, they're taught to base their faith on how they feel about what the Bible says. By using the new "higher order thinking skills" taught in their schools, they analyze and synthesize God's Word through the filter of the new paradigm until they find new meanings that totally distorts His character and unchanging truths.

When teachers have trained students not to listen to the old absolutes, they can freely use all kinds of strategies for changing their student's beliefs and values. The first strategy is to present palatable versions of the new belief system: the global spirituality. Since Native American models are part of American history, they bring least resistance from concerned parents.

For example, a Houghton-Mifflin social studies text talks about the Aztecs as being an harmonious people who took care of nature. But the "expansionist Spaniards" came and destroyed everything in their path. The text ignores the fact that Aztec warriors expanded their violent domain all the way into the southern United States, killing all who tried to block their violent path.

The same textbook tells students to draw a pictures of what the Aztec culture looked like before Spanish explorer Cortez came and destroyed it, while Cortez was demolishing it, and finally, after its destruction. The exercise left an impression on the minds of the student of how bad westerners were and how good the poor, persecuted Aztec people were. Their child sacrifices, ritual human sacrifices, and incredible tortures were ignored.

The second strategy for brainwashing dismantles the students' previous beliefs. That's done simply by distorting facts and describing the worst examples they can find from America's Christian history. One national textbook tells students that the Puritans beat their children if they didn't obey their parents or refused to go to church. Then it asks "critical thinking" questions like, "How do you think that kind of punishment fits into today's society? Which kind of family would you rather be in?" Which, of course, causes children to critically conclude that Christianity certainly doesn't fit our democratic society.

The third strategy is to provide mystical experiences which conflict with the old Christian paradigm. The Bible tells children to shun paganism, spiritism, magic, sorcery, witchcraft, and divination. So when schools teach students to use visualization and mental projection to alter their state of consciousness and connect with the spirits of nature, the result is moral confusion. Educators call it cognitive dissonance, and it forces students to adjust their old beliefs to fit their new experiences. When Christian students have to make Native American medicine shields to host their personal animal spirits contacted during imaginary "spirit quests," they are again forced to compromise their faith and "pool their ideas" in group discussions.

The fourth strategy immerses students in these enticing new beliefs. Pagan parties, earth-centered rituals, and multicultural celebrations make occultism fun. For example, a New Jersey school traded Christmas for Saturnalian ancient orgiastic celebration of Saturn, the Roman god of the dead.

Fifth, words are redefined to fit the new beliefs. A book titled *The Truth About the Moon* tells how the sun and the moon argued about who would shine during the day and who would shine at night. Another book, *The Truth About Dragons*, explains that Western dragons destroyed nature and people, while Eastern dragons were kind and gentle. Both books put "truth" into a pagan context, and neither told the truth.

Sixth, the new beliefs are used to meet today's needs. Children need to be empowered, say educators, therefore they must learn to connect with spiritual forces. They must learn to love and care for nature; therefore they must learn to feel their oneness with trees and experience wolves as part of themselves, having equal rights to our land and clean water.

Seventh, the target beliefs must answer the questions earlier answered by Christianity. One of the key questions that is answered by the Bible deals with salvation: What happens when we die, and how can we know that we have eternal life with God? The Scholastics book titled *If You Lived With the Sioux Indians* gives an answers that fits the global paradigm. It says, "The Sioux believe that after a man died, he would live with the spirits forever. He would go on doing the same things he had done on earth." In other words, there's no need for Jesus Christ. It suggests that all will enjoy a happy eternal life —

especially if they embrace pantheistic spirituality.

The bottom line is that the teachers are teaching our children to trust in non-Christian (satanic) forces.

Loeffler: We are constantly hearing in arguments around the country that you can't have vouchers because this violates the separation of church and state. How has it eluded people for so long that all of these other religions are rather openly being practiced in hundreds of schools around the country?

Sutton: Because parents are lied to. When the children come home and say that they've participated in some things like this, and the parents go up to the school, they're made to look like fanatics and they're out-and-out lied to, over and over again. The importance, I think, of what Berit is revealing to us is not just that they're doing it, but that it is the one thing that is being *imposed*. This is part and parcel of the new curriculum. Some parents might want this for their children. And they have every right to pursue that. But there are parents out there who don't want this and there are taxpayers out there who don't want to pay for certain things. Because of the nature of this top-down mandate, we have no choice anymore. That's the importance of this, that it is a mandate and it is being forced. Parents have no choice as to what is going to be taught to their children.

And not just what is going to be taught, but what their children are going to be tested on, and what is going to determine whether they are going to be able to move out into the world. The spiritual element is also very, very crucial to this because what is afoot here is nothing short of a mass movement. The religious element is one of the keys to a mass movement. The other characteristics of a mass movement are also very evident here. We've hit upon it over and over again — *oneness*. We have to have one curriculum. One test. One evaluation system. One set of criteria for teachers' certification. That is one of the evidences that we are involved in a mass movement. These things are inevitable, and very much a part of the religious element that we are evolving into. It is inevitable that we are going to have this new type of world to live in. So the next characteristic comes out: necessity. It is absolutely necessary, then, that we change the curriculum, that we change the world that we live in, in order to live in this inevitable New World.

The fourth characteristic is that all of this is always placed in a very positive manner. Positive slogans always accompany mass movements. This educational mass movement is literally drowning in slogans. "Every child can learn," "Success breeds success," all kinds of slogans. The importance, again, to tie into what Berit is talking about, with mass movements, is that people are really motivated, they are driven by the "oughts" in their lives. Anytime you're talking about "we ought to do this," "we ought to do that," you are in the realm of religion, and that is what drives people. Leaders in mass movements know that this is true and that the masses will not retreat into a vacuum. If they totally break down and destroy our old belief systems — whether they be Judeo-Christian or the Islamic — we will not retreat into a vacuum. They will replace it with the new "oughts": the new environmental religion, the new spiritualism. And the masses will not retreat into a vacuum. So this is an absolutely key component to the mass movement.

It seems farfetched, but mass movements always have cropped up historically at times when we've turned the century mark, or when we've been at war, or during great crises in a society. We are being propelled forward by a mass movement.

Iserbyt: You have to point out that the key vehicle which works is they create the problem (like they've done with dumbing down the children), and then, naturally, the parents and businessmen scream and yell, "What on earth is going on?" and then they impose the solution. It's become so horrible that the people will accept any solution.

Sutton: I think you have to understand what happens in mass movements all the time is a transfer of power. That is the result of every mass movement throughout history, the transfer of power from the local school district to the state. Total power. That is what results. In order to combat what the philosopher tells in order to combat mass movement, the only antidote to total power is rival power. So that if we want to combat this, we have to create rival power. The best way to do that is to understand what OBE is, which we have just explained, and all the problems that surround OBE or the restructuring. People have to become very familiar with the controversies that surround OBE. It's a good time to mention that this is by no means a settled philosophy, even in the halls of academia. My husband is the vice president of a university. They were the last to know that this change was being forced on the American public. So we might talk about some of those issues that surround OBE so that people can become equipped to deal with them in their local school districts.

Loeffler: Let's look at the demonization of those groups that don't go along so that they can be ostracized from the society.

Iserbyt: Yes. That's the identification of resistors.

Loeffler: In Colorado, the SAT scores came back and it was interesting that in Jefferson County, one traditional school didn't use OBE methods. When the SAT scores came back, all of the other schools employing OBE ranked in the 36th percentile. The one traditional school ranked at 86 percent. So hands down, you can see what's going on just by the statistics. That's why they want to change the statistics and the testing.

Williams: I'm not totally convinced that we've really told people in an understandable way what OBE is all about. I think we've talked about what OBE is doing, and what it's for, its purpose, and where it comes from, but there's more to this philosophy than just "all students can learn." The second half of that is "all students will succeed." That's where the lowering of the bar occurs. That's the one critical aspect of this thing: all students will succeed to the outcome, and they're going to stay there and stay there until they do. These lateral enrichment programs we talked about earlier mean taking a tape measure and measuring a room and writing down the results. In the most radical instance I ever heard of, a mountain community here had a lateral enrichment program that centered around sending kids off into a room to play Dungeons and Dragons. They used role-playing games, anything to occupy the top achievers long enough for the slow achievers to get over the bar.

And it's done on an individual basis. We talk about mass movements and this world movement and all of this, but the reality of it is they're changing this on an individual student basis day by day. Each student is programmed in terms of the subject matter he receives; each student is assessed individually on whether or not he's achieved the right behavior, attitude, or aptitude; and each student is then either determined to have achieved mastery or is innovatively remediated — recycled through the program. So while we talk about all these big things, parents can't lose track of the fact that it individually affects their child or their grandchild in the public schools.

As far as the money is concerned, this is a special interest dream come true. When you start talking about ambiguous, generalized outcomes, such as "a student will be an effective communicator," what does that mean? It means something entirely different to a fundamentalist Christian than it does to someone who's on the extreme liberal left because part of that effective communication is, "What are you communicating? What is your point of view? What are your attitudes? What are your opinions?" There's no way to measure, but anybody can throw anything they want to in. So you've got major industry who shares a critical interest in this by virtue of shifting something like $40 billion every year that they spend on training of employees to the public education system.

You've got the National Education Association, which obviously is interested in improving the salaries and benefits and that type of thing for teachers. You've got local school districts who want more dollars coming in by virtue of these grants from the federal level, and all this money comes from the federal level. There's nothing wrong with the worm; the danger's in the hook. That's where the power shift achieves. That's where the centralization occurs.

Loeffler: Not to mention the cost of remediating.

Williams: Absolutely. Dr. Robert Slaven from Johns Hopkins University issued a report in 1987 called "Mastery Learning Reconsidered." Bill Spady said in the December

1992/January 1993 *Education Leadership Magazine* that 42 disciples of mastery learning came together in Chicago and they agreed at that point to use a new name because mastery learning had been destroyed as a term. The new word that came out was Outcome-Based Education.

Loeffler: Is the argument over what the outcomes are, or is the argument over the whole system?

Iserbyt: Twenty years ago, I remember fighting health education in Maine where one of the outcomes on the health education for seventh graders was knowing the four different types of sexual intercourse. I became very upset about that. That's a bad outcome, right? The NEA Bicentennial was in 1976, when the cardinal principals were re-written with David Rockefeller, Benjamin Bloom, Ralph Tyler, Theodore Seizer —all people involved in OBE. The point right here is that those outcomes, as bad as they are, have been the goals of the NEA for a long time. But the people involved at the top are working with people that you would never believe. So they approve of the system, and the system is mastery learning, and it has been defined as the system for international work force training.

I have come to the conclusion now they have no concerns whatsoever about academic education except as it relates to the identification of what jobs that a child in second grade will have in the global economy. Now they're doing all sorts of shadowing, taking them into nursing homes, identifying where the child should go in the future for the good of a global economy. They will not educate that child in the traditional way. They will educate them so that they're down to one-tenth of what they learned before. So the child who's going to be a mechanic or a ballet dancer will be narrowly tracked through and only those things that pertain to the child's future in the global economy, for the global economy, will be taught. And mastery learning is the only form of education using Skinner. Skinner says what is reinforced will be repeated. That is the only way to get our children all over the world to perform according to what David Rockefeller, Theodore Seizer, and Benjamin Bloom say. It is unbelievable to see who has jumped in bed together — the top internationalists and the NEA. And it's the global economy we're looking at. It's money. It's the dollar sign or the mark or the Japanese yen. That's what they're looking for. It's always been that, so why would people say this is unusual?

Sutton: This is the process that will create that new worker to fuel that new global economy. It's the process that going through that loop over and over every day, that denies those other functions of the mind, so that the child not only doesn't learn anything else, but it causes them to take longer to learn. It does something to the children's minds.

Loeffler: What is this going to mean to teachers?

Iserbyt: At a governor's conference in Minnesota they said, "Don't bother to re-tool the defects."

Loeffler: They're calling some teachers "defective"?

Iserbyt: The teachers were referred to as defective. Their solution was to fire or retire the defective ones and hire the ones who have been educated in total quality management — which is just another name for OBE — management by objective, and mastery learning. The teachers out there, when they heard that, were furious. They said, "What does that have to do with us?"

Loeffler: A friend of mine came back from a teacher's conference recently, and they were very openly referring to teachers who did not go along with this agenda as "defective teachers." I understand we're going to track teachers' psychological profiles now.

Sutton: Teachers will be the most scrutinized segment of society because they are the key. If the teacher does not implement this, does not go along, does not teach that curriculum the way she's supposed to, then the whole thing will be exposed for what it is. So the way the databanks are set up is they link the teacher with the curriculum with the student. And they can tell immediately if those students in that classroom are not being taught that curriculum.

Loeffler: In other words, they can take the whole population, compare it to her class, and then they know whether she's defective or not.

Sutton: It's brilliantly conceived.

Iserbyt: It's so narrow, it certainly can work. Cooperative worker, in groups, cooperative learning. The whole education system really is being geared for the workplace . . . team learning, cooperative learning for the new workplace. Japanese management.

Loeffler: We already know that in Oregon and Indiana right now, we have what they're calling Certificates of Initial Mastery (CIM). If you don't have this CIM, you will not be able to get a job because an employer cannot hire you.

Kjos: And you can't go to college, and you can't go to training centers to be trained for various types of jobs. Everybody will be reshuffled back into learning centers if they finish high school and haven't earned their Certificate of Initial Mastery. And children who are home-schooled or go to Christian schools will also be moved into the learning centers in order to get their Certificates of Initial Mastery if they didn't learn the proper beliefs and attitudes at home or in their Christian schools.

Nobody will be left out. Because Goals 2000 calls for lifelong learning, this system is for everyone. All working adults will have to pass through the brainwashing session, where they are taught to blend their beliefs through facilitated dialogues or group sessions. To build the envisioned world of peace and equality, all must participate. All must accept the global values and agree not to complain, argue, or resist the coming changes. All must learn to tolerate and feel their oneness with all others — no matter what their lifestyle.

Iserbyt: Common unity. People talk about community education. They used to use that word. That's what we're looking at now. It was referred to by an Alaskan educator 15 years ago at a Washington conference as being similar to the Communist Chinese system. We have that on record. It's very interesting: If you take the word "community," break it down it is "common unity." We will be totally controlled in our communities. We're not talking about education. We're talking about the whole thing. Total control in our communities, being watched very carefully with block captains. They're going to have advisory councils. I looked it up in the dictionary the other day. Council: soviet. This is what's being said in un-elected officials, site-based management. They're doing away with school boards. They don't want anybody who's been elected. They're going to appoint the people they want. What does this sound like, folks? You can call it what you want. You name what a system that has un-elected officials running it, and five-year plans in place, and goes into the home to see if you're bringing up your children correctly.

Loeffler: What about the legality of all this? Most Americans haven't read Goals 2000. If the American public as a whole understood what's intended, they would scream. It seems to fly in the face of an awful lot of constitutional and other issues.

Sutton: That question is important because as you're presenting this to groups, many of them will say, "Well, I don't think it's so bad to track what the teachers are doing. They should have to be accountable." And the question you always have to ask is, is it legal in this country to not only test the children's attitudes and behaviors and track those and feed it into a databank, but also to remediate these children until they come around? Is it legal to have national surveillance on every citizen in the United States? It is not legal. We have privacy rights in this country. We need to demand a fair data reporting law just like we have a fair credit reporting law that says where this information can go. They'll have to tell us where our file is going, who receives it, who has access to it, and who receives that information. Our laws must catch up with technology.

Williams: The third thing I think we really need to talk about is, how do you recognize it coming into your own home district? Because the average parent gives education a "D," but gives their own individual school an "A." There's a lot of programming and training that goes on at that local school level to produce that kind of attitude. For one thing, Johnny's probably getting an A or a B, because if too many D's come down, then principals start telling teachers, "We're getting too many D's; I'm getting parent complaints." They factually don't want parents in the schools. They don't want parents seeing what's happening on a day-to-day basis. So you give an A and the parents stay home. That's one of the reasons behind grade inflation that we've seen over the past several years.

There was an article a week or so ago about Stanford University. For the last 25 years, 93 percent of the grades they've given have been either A's or B's, with no failing. They still don't have the failing grade. They now have an NP and non-pass it; it's still not a failure. You're just not quite there yet. It's something like the "in progress" grade, I think, that you'll see in your local public school K-12. But ultimately what happens is you move to these things in a very subtle fashion. It will be disguised as a response to some current legislation or in response to some grant that you've received. It's a very gradual process. The design is to keep parents as much in the dark as possible.

We had parents out here in Littleton, Colorado, who had to sue to get into those curriculum meetings. That's where the back-to-basics movement in Littleton was born, by those parents who wanted to be involved in this process, and who had to sue to get it. Again, in my own home district, all of our curriculum committee meetings were taking place at 10 a.m. and 3 p.m. We surveyed our community and 80 percent of the registered taxpayers with a local address in that school district said they would like to be involved in this process at some level, but 78 percent said they couldn't meet at these times. In response to that problem, we were told, "Well, where were you when the first meeting was held and we decided when to meet?" Our response was, "When was that meeting held?"

The design is to keep you out, absolutely, and to center this in the school building as closely as possible, and to give lip service to community involvement and input by having a few individuals who are very close to the schools, who are friendly with the school, so as to give this pretense of parental involvement. But you'll see it in your report cards. You'll see a subtle changing in the grading system. You'll see a much more complex and complete report card in terms of that individual student. It may not give you much more valuable information. One report card out here in Aurora had 70 different grading categories, but the only 55 categories a student got an "A" in were those places where the student evaluated their own progress. The rest were all "satisfactory's" and "incomplete's" when it came to academics. The A-B-C grades the student received were the ones he gave himself on his own self-evaluation on his own report card. A parent must be on the lookout for these subtle types of things to occur.

What you'll be told is, "We're not really changing anything; we're just reorganizing things. We have to have a clear flow from one grade level to the next. If we bring in a new teacher, they have to know precisely where they fit into this new structure." When you start hearing those types of things at your schools, you can depend on the fact that you're in the process of developing and moving to an Outcome-Based Education program.

Loeffler: Is OBE everywhere?

Iserbyt: Yes. Unchecked, OBE will be everywhere, including private schools *and home schoolers*. We know that because of the legislation that's being passed in various states like Minnesota and Michigan where they're passing legislation to create OBE charter schools. It's unbelievable that home schoolers and other Christians are falling for this. They're getting involved in setting up charter schools. They've been fighting OBE; they took their kids out of the public school system to get away from OBE and now they're jumping on the OBE charter school bandwagon. It's not just charter schools that are the New American School Development Corporation. This is a corporation that was set up under President Bush, and it's been planned for a good 30 years. I have an old site-based management paper from the Aspen Institute that's 20 years old on how to get rid of school boards. So don't think anything is new; it's all been planned.

The New American School Development Corporation is a private corporation, privately funded. I don't believe in partnerships with the public sector. There is no accountability whatsoever. If a corporation comes into a school or takes a child on the job, something happens to that child, he cuts his finger off — who is accountable? The school board isn't going to be there. Charter schools will have no school boards. Carefully selected people will run them; they will probably be in the private sector, but will be paid for with tax money.

Iserbyt: Yes, it is. It's totally unconstitutional. People aren't making much of it now, because they're making excuses, saying, "Oh, it's just in school. Kids should learn how to be good to one another and go out and help." But all of us are going to have to perform community service in this new society. But the schools, the New American School Development Corporation, and for those who are listening, we have all of the reports on each particular school. Fortunately, we had enough opposition and did manage to get rid of one of them. It was the Odyssey Project in North Carolina. I love to point out that it had three-year-olds doing community service. Not third-graders; three-year-olds. This is the focus. It's total socialism. They were taking three-year-olds into nursing homes to get the feeling of "my good is of no importance; I am working for the group. I am working for the collective."

With all of these New American School Development Corporations, the philosophy that runs straight through is the OBE. No Carnegie units — mastery learning. Everything we've talked about today is used in each one of them, although each one of the design teams is different. It's just going to blow Americans' minds in a couple of years when they wake up and say, "What happened to my school?" And then we're going to say, "Where were you; why didn't you listen?"

We get back to the work force and as we've said before, they've set up a Secretary's Commission on Achieving Necessary Skills. Those are skills our children will have to demonstrate they're capable of doing before they get a Certificate of Mastery and then they move on. All of us, including myself and anybody who loses their job, are going to have to go through that. Remember that Thomas Sticht, who is on the Secretary's

Commission for Achieving Necessary Skills, and William Spady, so very famous on the international Outcome-Based Education, those two put OBE into the District of Columbia in 1978. Mastery learning. Ten years later, Sticht says it's not important whether the children can read or write. He said what's important is that they're manageable and trainable and that we can change their values. This is a direct quote from the *Washington Post* of August 17, 1987.

Williams: I have that exact quote. It's incredible. "Many companies have moved operations to places with cheap, relatively poorly educated labor. What may be crucial, they say, is the dependability of a labor force and how well it can be managed and trained, not its general education level, although a small cadre of highly educated, creative people is essential to innovation and growth. Ending discrimination and changing values are probably more important than reading in moving low-income families into the middle class."

Loeffler: Meaning we have an elite group and we have the workers.

Iserbyt: They are deliberately dumbing down our kids so they can move them in the track for the global work force and the parents are going to say, "Oh, at least they can get a job." Parents, don't fall for it. They should teach the academics first and then they can help your child later on, like in the European system, which I don't particularly approve of. I have nieces and nephews from Europe who visit me and the ones who are in ninth grade are speaking two or three languages and doing higher math. If the Europeans want, in the 10th or 11th grade, to shoot the kids off into a track for specialized training, I say, "Okay." They were highly educated first. They come out in eighth grade in Europe with more education than a four-year college degree in the United States.

Sutton: Of course, we need to realize that the United States is more productive than France. There is a correlation between education and productivity and it's exactly the opposite of what we all assume. If you look at the United States, our rate of literacy has been going down; it's at an all-time low. But correspondingly, our productivity is going up. We are at an all-time high in productivity. This economic fact has certainly not been missed by major global businesses.

Williams: That's exactly right. Here's a quote from the book *Human Capital and America's Future,* which was co-edited by Lester Salamon and David Hornbeck. Hornbeck helped initiate the State of Alabama OBE program and served on the Business Roundtable. They say, "Employer beliefs about the superior capability of educated employees turned out *not* to be confirmed in fact. Educated employees have higher turnover rates, lower job satisfaction, and poorer promotion records than less sophisticated employees." Referring to employers providing training for employees, they summarize with, "One final complication arises from the fact that, unlike physical capital, human capital cannot be owned by someone else."[1]

Sutton: We have to realize in all of history, the most productive economies are the slave economies. Big business understands this.

Loeffler: Shifting gears a bit, now that parents are beginning to understand the gravity of the problem, what can they do? And are home schoolers and private schoolers going to be included with public schools?

Kjos: Everybody will be tested. The new assessments will include everybody, including private schoolers and home schoolers. As has happened in Oregon, that's the model for the country, home schoolers and children from Christian schools will be a part of the system. They will not be able to go to college, to training centers, or work unless they have a Certificate of Initial Mastery through the education system.

Iserbyt: I've home-schooled my children and I know all I've done is buy time. They believe that there can be no control groups with this system. None. There can be no children, no adults, outside the loop.

Sutton: Because of data collection they have to have all children in the system.

Williams: In Colorado we've had legislative attempts,

through the Governor's Initiative, Amendment 6, the Sales Tax Initiative, and in the Standards-Based Education Bill, to include a certified state diploma in the educational process. We've been able to beat it down twice. But as we move to this standards-based idea, the idea of statewide standards, more and more people are beginning to talk favorably about the idea of students meeting state standards. This is a half-step away from a certified diploma or Certificate of Initial Mastery. Once you get to that point, if you want to be certified, you'd better be involved in a certified program.

Sutton: The building is on fire and parents need to protect their own children. They need to get them out of the system right away. When I first started giving speeches three years ago, we encouraged people more to work within the system. I took my children out a year and a half ago, and it's not an easy decision to make. My husband has spent his entire married life in education; he's vice president of the university. The thought of relying upon me to teach the children was difficult for him to make. But it has bought my children time and it has taken them out of that fire for the moment. More and more parents are realizing that home schooling is a very viable alternative. One of the professors that I work with at Rutgers University told me that many of the professors within the education department at Rutgers are taking their children out and home schooling them.

Loeffler: But the home schoolers are being painted by the media as extremists or kooks. Or you will hear other parents say something like, "Oh, but I want my child to have a better education than that," or "My child is a social butterfly." They don't realize the stats show that home schoolers, across the board, are better educated and better adjusted socially at age 18 than 99 percent of children attending public schools.

Williams: The standards are very low in terms of the minimums for home schoolers. In Idaho there is no testing or reporting of any kind. Here in Colorado, you have to be performing at the 13th percentile on a national standardized test in order to be able to continue your home-schooling process. It doesn't mean that's where the kids are scoring, but that's the minimum cut-off and so that's the perception.

The thing that I think is important about home schooling is that, unless the progression is stopped, it's a way to run, but there's nowhere to hide. Because under the system they're trying to roll out nationwide, even the home schoolers will have to have the CIM, the certified diploma, if they want a job. We must stop this process.

Iserbyt: When I first went to work in the Department of Education, our office dealt with learning technology. A very fine career officer, the number one man in the Office of Library and Learning Technology, took me through and showed me the comprehensive computer software. And I said, "Hey, that's great! You could teach your children at home with that." And he said, "Charlotte, that's the way it will be." This was in the early 1980s. "The learning can go on at home, but you will always have the schools for socialization purposes." That's where we are right now. They're going to allow home schooling, but they will require them to meet the same goals. Their plan is to take home-schooled children for part of the day over in the school doing all the cooperative learning, all the critical thinking, all the mandated outcomes.

Williams: Through the Parent as Teachers program, they're going to ensure that the right attitudes, opinions, and points of view are taught from the home.

Iserbyt: And the computer will be connected with the school's and the child will have an individual education plan. Realize that when you talk about funding, the money will follow the child. It will not be like it is now. If a fifth grade child is very talented and they see tremendous possibility for engineering, just like in the Soviet Union and in magnet schools, they will fund him through to the top. The money will follow the child.

Kjos: But anybody who qualifies for this funding would have to go through a more intense socialization to fit the new system.

Sutton: She has brought up something that is so crucial to understanding why they are pushing OBE so hard. OBE is the only method available to them that allows them to follow the individual child with scrutinization. It's the method that allows them to put their thumb on every child in this country and lift that thumb up periodically to assess their economic value and, if they are only half-baked, put them back into the oven until they are the perfect cookie-cutter worker that they need. There is no other method that allows that except OBE.

Loeffler: During the crisis created over HR-6 (a bill requiring home school and private school parents/teachers to be approved by the government), all of the home schoolers and private schoolers rose up in mass. They were heard loud and clear and shouted, "Victory!" when the Armey Amendment passed to protect them from being under the federal government's control. Now I'm afraid they're going back to sleep.

Williams: It's like the house is on fire and you just closed a fire door thinking you stopped the problem. But the real problem is still there. That's the point, we have only temporarily closed a fire door. The real way to stop this is with a big tanker plane full of fire retardant cutting off federal funding for education. President Johnson said in 1965, referring to the passage of the original Elementary and Secondary Education Act, "We got it started, but we'll never get it stopped." I think it can be stopped — when the federal debt ceiling gets so high the federal government agrees to go out of business.

Fortunately, there is more attention lately on state's rights. There is a relatively small percentage of money flowing into the states from the federal government, on the average of 7 percent of the education budgets. We can replace that funding by getting rid of one counseling position out of every nine! That alone would save enough money to send the Feds back their money and their mandates, saying, "No, thank you." If this is going to be stopped, and I think it's absolutely critical to our republic that it be stopped, we must elect people in the states that will stand up and say, "We're going to find another way to fund education."

Loeffler: Berit, some closing thoughts about philosophical safeguards that parents can build in.

Kjos: There are many parents who can't afford to put their children in Christian schools, nor do they feel that they have time to home school their children because both mother and father are working, and they're very, very concerned. What I want to encourage them to do is to teach children the Judeo-Christian paradigm, the biblical view of the world. Build into them a mindset which will enable them to filter everything they see and hear in such a way that they know truth. We as parents are given the responsibility of teaching our children biblical principals first, the education is built on top of that foundation. But it starts at home.

It's very exciting to me that Ephesians 6:10-18, for example, gives us a perfect outline for that kind of framework — the armor of God. Children need to understand that truth is absolute, eternal, and it reveals who God is. He is the only Way, the only Truth, and the only Life. The new paradigm teaching tells them that truth is relative, subject to personal interpretations, changing myths, and whatever you want to make it.

The world will tell them that God is pantheistic, monastic, polytheistic. But children need to be taught that God is transcendant, personal, monotheistic, and their Shepherd. And more than anything, that He's a God and Father who loves them. They need this solid teaching on a consistent (daily, not just Sunday) basis to rebut lies.

Finally, they need to know that man was basically sinful, that we're born with a sin nature and the only way we can be free from that sin nature is through the Cross. The only way we can be cleansed and purified, just as if we never sinned, is through the blood of Jesus. The reason we need to know that and our children need to hold that so clear in their minds is because the world and the schools and all the myths that they will be reading will teach them the false teaching about their "sacred human nature." They will be taught that if they want to know themselves they need to develop self-awareness and self-actualization. Then they will become the perfect child of the world, one with the earth and everybody else. You can see why it is so important that we teach a solid foundation to our children. Without the spiritual armor, they can fall for Satan's lies.

The world, again, will tell them that they are evolving toward a perfect state and toward a universal, cosmic salvation through the rising human consciousness that somehow is going to bring us to this omega point or point of ultimate perfection.

The best thing that we can do whether our children are in public schools, Christian schools, or home schooling, is to have them memorize Scripture. They need to hold up those swords every day, all the time. God made a wonderful statement to us in Proverbs 22:6: "Train up a child in the way he should go and when he is old, he will not depart from it."

If we train up a child in biblical truth, they will know the Christian view of the world. This is what schools are so afraid of and why various educators are afraid of children not being put into the hands of educators until they're five years old because they will build up a Christian paradigm and then they won't be receptive to what the schools are telling them. It's imperative that *parents* build Christian views into their children's lives.

Loeffler: This has probably been some of the most information-packed time in the history of education, but we're hoping it gives parents a tool with which to understand what is happening to their children in the public school system. Thank you.

[1]Lester M. Salamon and David Hornbeck, *Human Capital and America's Future* (Baltimore, MD: Johns Hopkins University, 1991).

Steeling the Mind of America

Volume I

The Battle for the Heart and Mind of America
- *John Ankerberg*
Seven Keys to Watch in Bible Prophecy
- *Chuck Missler*
The Coming Persecution of Christians in America
- *Don McAlvany*
The Armageddon Scenario
- *Hal Lindsey*
Europe: The Stage Is Set for World Dominance
- *Chuck Missler*
America at the Crossroads: Freedom or Slavery
- *Don McAlvany*
Russia Invades Israel: The Explosion Is Near
- *Chuck Missler*
The Long War against God
- *Henry Morris*
Is America Moving toward Socialism?
- *Don McAlvany*
Dead Ahead — What to Watch, What to Do
- *Chuck Missler*
Fourteen Ways to "Steel" against the Future
- *Don McAlvany*

trade paper • $11.95 • ISBN: 0-89221-294-2 • 300 pages

Available at Christian bookstores nationwide

Behind Steeling the Mind of . . .

Steeling the Mind of America Conference began in 1993 with a mission to disseminate information on conservative Christian issues in a professional setting. Each year we invite the best and brightest Christian thinkers of our day to make presentations covering a wide range of topics. Compass International, Inc. was formed in 1994 as a non-profit ministry to continue the Steeling conferences and add other evangelism and Christian conferences.

Past speakers and topics:

Frank Peretti	Spiritual Warfare
Hal Lindsey	Bible Prophecy
Alan Keyes	Christians and Politics
David Barton	Christian History
John Ankerberg	Apologetics
Chuck Missler	Bible Prophecy
Henry Morris	Apologetics
Alan Sears	Christian Legal Issues
Tom Cloud	Christian Finances
Berit Kjos	Christian Education
Pat Matrisciana	Government Corruption
D.A. Miller	AIDS/HIV Issues
Anita Hoge	Christian Education
Dale Berryhill	Media Deception
Don McAlvany	Political Deception
Edward Krug	Environmental Issues
Jason Baker	Christians and Internet
Harley Hunter	Christian Finances

If you wish to be placed on Compass International's mailing list for future conferences, or receive a free catalog of video and audio tapes available from past conferences, contact:

Compass International, Inc.
460 Canfield Ave., Suite 1000
Coeur d'Alene, ID 83814
1-800-977-2177
(208) 762-7777
Fax (208) 762-3363
email: bill@compass.org
Web site: www.compass.org